To Professor Leech
with gratitude

Martin Schaad

St Antony's Series
General Editor: **Richard Clogg** (1999–), Fellow of St Antony's College, Oxford

Recent titles include:

Craig Brandist and Galin Tihanov (*editors*)
MATERIALIZING BAKHTIN

Mark Brzezinski
THE STRUGGLE FOR CONSTITUTIONALISM IN POLAND

Reinhard Drifte
JAPAN'S QUEST FOR A PERMANENT SECURITY COUNCIL SEAT
A Matter of Pride or Justice?

Simon Duke
THE ELUSIVE QUEST FOR EUROPEAN SECURITY

Marta Dyczok
THE GRAND ALLIANCE AND UKRAINIAN REFUGEES

Ken Endo
THE PRESIDENCY OF THE EUROPEAN COMMISSION UNDER
JACQUES DELORS

Ricardo Ffrench-Davis
REFORMING THE REFORMS IN LATIN AMERICA
Macroeconomics, Trade, Finance

M. K. Flynn
IDEOLOGY, MOBILIZATION AND THE NATION
The Rise of Irish, Basque and Carlist Nationalist Movements in the
Nineteenth and Early Twentieth Centuries

Anthony Forster
BRITAIN AND THE MAASTRICHT NEGOTIATIONS

Azar Gat
BRITISH ARMOUR THEORY AND THE RISE OF THE PANZER ARM
Revising the Revisionists

Fernando Guirao
SPAIN AND THE RECONSTRUCTION OF WESTERN EUROPE, 1945–57

Anthony Kirk-Greene
BRITAIN'S IMPERIAL ADMINISTRATORS, 1858–1966

Bernardo Kosacoff
CORPORATE STRATEGIES UNDER STRUCTURAL ADJUSTMENT IN ARGENTINA
Responses by Industrial Firms to a New Set of Uncertainties

Huck-ju Kwon
THE WELFARE STATE IN KOREA

Cécile Laborde
PLURALIST THOUGHT AND THE STATE IN BRITAIN AND FRANCE, 1900–25

Julio Crespo MacLennan
SPAIN AND THE PROCESS OF EUROPEAN INTEGRATION, 1957–85

Jennifer G. Mathers
THE RUSSIAN NUCLEAR SHIELD FROM STALIN TO YELTSIN

Eiichi Motono
CONFLICT AND COOPERATION IN SINO-BRITISH BUSINESS, 1860–1911
The Impact of the Pro-British Commercial Network in Shanghai

C. S. Nicholls
THE HISTORY OF ST ANTONY'S COLLEGE, OXFORD, 1950–2000

Shane O'Rourke
WARRIORS AND PEASANTS
The Don Cossacks in Late Imperial Russia

Laila Parsons
THE DRUZE BETWEEN PALESTINE AND ISRAEL, 1947–49

Karina Sonnenberg-Stern
EMANCIPATION AND POVERTY
The Ashkenazi Jews of Amsterdam, 1796–1850

Miguel Székely
THE ECONOMICS OF POVERTY AND WEALTH ACCUMULATION IN MEXICO

Ray Takeyh
THE ORIGINS OF THE EISENHOWER DOCTRINE
The US, Britain and Nasser's Egypt, 1953–57

Suke Wolton
LORD HAILEY, THE COLONIAL OFFICE AND THE POLITICS OF RACE AND EMPIRE IN THE SECOND WORLD WAR
The Loss of White Prestige

St Antony's Series
Series Standing Order ISBN 0–333–71109–2
(*outside North America only*)

You can receive future titles in this series as they are published by placing a standing order. Please contact your bookseller or, in case of difficulty, write to us at the address below with your name and address, the title of the series and the ISBN quoted above.

Customer Services Department, Macmillan Distribution Ltd, Houndmills, Basingstoke, Hampshire RG21 6XS, England

Bullying Bonn

Anglo-German Diplomacy on European Integration, 1955–61

Martin P. C. Schaad
Researcher
Einstein Forum
Potsdam
Germany

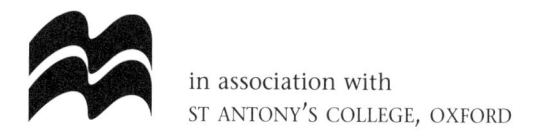

in association with
ST ANTONY'S COLLEGE, OXFORD

First published in Great Britain 2000 by
MACMILLAN PRESS LTD
Houndmills, Basingstoke, Hampshire RG21 6XS and London
Companies and representatives throughout the world

A catalogue record for this book is available from the British Library.

ISBN 0–333–69231–4

First published in the United States of America 2000 by
ST. MARTIN'S PRESS, LLC,
Scholarly and Reference Division,
175 Fifth Avenue, New York, N.Y. 10010

ISBN 0–312–23483–X

Library of Congress Cataloging-in-Publication Data
Schaad, Martin P. C., 1968–
Bullying Bonn : Anglo-German diplomacy on European integration, 1955–61 / Martin P.C. Schaad
p. cm. — (St. Antony's series)
Includes bibliographical references (p.) and index.
ISBN 0–312–23483–X
1. Germany—Foreign relations—Great Britain. 2. Great Britain—Foreign relations—Germany. 3. European Union. 4. European Economic Community—Germany. 5. European Economic Community—Great Britain. 6. Europe—Economic integration. I. Title. II. Series.

DD120.G7 G35   2000
327.43041—dc21

00–027242

© Martin P. C. Schaad 2000

All rights reserved. No reproduction, copy or transmission of this publication may be made without written permission.

No paragraph of this publication may be reproduced, copied or transmitted save with written permission or in accordance with the provisions of the Copyright, Designs and Patents Act 1988, or under the terms of any licence permitting limited copying issued by the Copyright Licensing Agency, 90 Tottenham Court Road, London W1P 0LP.

Any person who does any unauthorised act in relation to this publication may be liable to criminal prosecution and civil claims for damages.

The author has asserted his right to be identified as the author of this work in accordance with the Copyright, Designs and Patents Act 1988.

This book is printed on paper suitable for recycling and made from fully managed and sustained forest sources.

10 9 8 7 6 5 4 3 2 1
09 08 07 06 05 04 03 02 01 00

Printed and bound in Great Britain by
Antony Rowe Ltd, Chippenham, Wiltshire

Contents

Acknowledgements	vi
List of Abbreviations	vii
Introduction	1
1 From Indifference to Hostility: Britain, Germany and the Messina Project	13
2 Entering Wedge or Counterblast? Britain's Plan G	39
3 Mistaken, Misled or Misguided? British Hopes for German Mediation during the FTA Negotiations	69
4 'Bridge-Building' or: the Trade War That Never Was	115
5 'Bully the Germans – Buy the French': Towards Britain's First Application	135
Conclusion: Intersection or Periphery?	162
Notes	174
Bibliography	225
Index	236

Acknowledgements

I am very grateful to Lothar Kettenacker, Piers Ludlow, Alan Milward, Roger Morgan, George Peden and Jonathan Wright whose guidance and critical advice has been invaluable. Furthermore, I would like to thank Joachim Jens Hesse for supervising the DPhil thesis that formed the basis of this study, and St Antony's College, Oxford, for providing a setting most conducive to academic inquiry and exchange. I owe thanks also to the staff of the various archives I visited during the course of research, and to Michael von Brentano for his kind permission to view the private papers of the German Foreign Minister. I am forever indebted to the Carnegie Trust for the Universities of Scotland for funding the doctorate, and to the German Historical Institute, London, for the encouragement accorded by awarding the thesis the annual prize of the Institute. Finally, I am very thankful to John Daly, Gabriele Karl and Verena Strinz for their help in preparing the typescript.

List of Abbreviations

AA	*Auswärtiges Amt*, Foreign Ministry
BA	*Bundesarchiv*, Federal Archive
BDI	*Bund Deutscher Industrie*, Federation of German Industry
BMA	*Bundesministerium für Arbeit*, Federal Ministry for Labour
BMF	*Bundesministerium der Finanzen*, Federal Finance Ministry
BML	*Bundesministerium für Landwirtschaft und Forsten*, Federal Ministry for Agriculture and Forestry
BMWi	*Bundesministerium für Wirtschaft*, Federal Ministry for Economics
BMWZ	*Bundesministerium für wirtschaftliche Zusammenarbeit*, Federal Ministry for Economic Co-operation
BoT	Board of Trade
BStS	*Büro des Staatssekretär*, State Secretarial Office in German Foreign Ministry
BuKa	*Bundeskanzleramt*, Office of the Federal Chancellor
CAB	Cabinet
CBI	Confederation of British Industry
CDU	*Christlich Demokratische Union*
CSU	*Christlich Soziale Union*
DPA	*Deutsche Presseagentur*, German news agency
EC	European Community
ECSC	European Coal and Steel Community
EDC	European Defence Community
EEC	European Economic Community
EFTA	European Free Trade Association
EP	Economic Policy Committee
EPC	European Political Community
EPU	European Payments Union
ES	Economic Steering Committee
EU	European Union
EURATOM	European Atomic Community
FAZ	*Frankfurter Allgemeine Zeitung*
FBI	Federation of British Industry
FO	Foreign Office
FTA	Free Trade Area
GATT	General Agreement on Tariffs and Trade

List of Abbreviations

HM	Her Majesty's
HMG	Her Majesty's Government
HMSO	Her Majesty's Stationery Office
HOPS	Home and Overseas Planning Staff Division (Treasury)
HPA	*Handelspolitische Abteilung*, Foreign Ministry Department: Trade Policy
IMF	International Monetary Fund
ITV	Independent Television
LA	*Länderabteilung*, Foreign Ministry Department: Foreign Relations by Country
MAC	Mutual Aid Committee
MAD	Mutual Aid Department (Foreign Office)
MADiv	Mutual Aid Division (Treasury)
MB	*Ministerbüro*, Ministerial Office in Foreign Ministry
NATO	North Atlantic Treaty Organisation
NDR	*Norddeutscher Rundfunk*, Northern German radio broadcasting corporation
OECD	Organisation for European Co-operation and Development
OEEC	Organisation for European Economic Co-operation
PA	*Politische Abteilung*, Political Department of the Foreign Ministry
PREM	Prime Minister's Office
PRO	Public Record Office
StBKAH	*Stiftung-Bundeskanzler-Adenauer-Haus*
T	Treasury
TUC	Trade Union Congress
UK	United Kingdom
WEU	Western European Union

Introduction

A recurring theme in the history of postwar Anglo-European relations is that of numerous lost opportunities for Britain to have taken part in continental integration well before she eventually became a member of the European Economic Community (EEC) in 1973.[1] Though the precise timing as to when the euphemistic 'bus' or 'boat' was missed remains in dispute, few commentators doubt that Britain could have joined the six founding members of the EEC at some stage before they had decided on the essential features of their endeavour. A subtext to many expressions of this view is the assumption that Britain could have (and not few implicitly argue that she should have) taken the lead in the integration process.[2] Officials, politicians as well as many a commentator, appear to agree that the path of European integration could have been decisively influenced and – if the need had arisen – redirected had the British government been prepared to negotiate from within, rather than 'proffering advice over the garden wall'.[3]

And indeed, the single most important document leading to Britain's first and unsuccessful EEC application in 1961, the so-called Lee Report, based its recommendations almost exclusively on the perceived need to be inside the inner councils of the Six in order to steer the development of the Community.[4] Similarly, whenever British politicians of the 1990s have argued for greater involvement in Europe, their chosen metaphors have alluded to Britain returning to 'the heart of Europe' or, more recently, for her to 'take the driving seat'.[5]

Histories of Anglo-European relations frequently echo this view, with a most explicit expression of this kind being found in Roy Denman's account of the British entry negotiations of 1970: 'Our historic task was to repair the mistakes of the past and to restore our position at the centre of European affairs.'[6] Moreover, even those who had formulated and implemented British policy on Europe when the said 'chances were missed' later seemed to acknowledge their misjudgement. Speaking during a radio interview in 1980, Russell Bretherton, who had briefly represented Britain at the negotiations leading to the establishment of the EEC in 1955, restated a conviction he had held at the time: 'If we are prepared to take a firm line, that we want to come in and will be part of this, we can make this body into whatever we like.' In the very same radio broadcast, Peter Thorneycroft, his erstwhile superior as President of the Board of Trade, agreed: 'We threw away a great opportunity.'[7]

Evidently, the attraction of counterfactual scenarios of this kind lies in their irrefutable character and their expedience in current political debates.[8] Yet, for the historian of Anglo-European relations, such scenarios may also serve to direct the attention to the factors underlying policy failure – the inevitable judgement implied in the 'if only!' is to be translated into the more explanatory question of 'why not?' Much of the literature on Anglo-European relations therefore seeks to uncover the factors which led Britain to ignore a policy option which – with the benefit of hindsight – seemed hers for the taking as well as most promising for future development.

Most frequently, reference is being made to the distinct historical experience of Great Britain: the safety of insular geography had allowed the English nation to develop stable and successful institutions – epitomized in the concept of parliamentary sovereignty as it had evolved since the Glorious Revolution. Yet, having successfully defended the Isles against invasion not only enabled political institutions to adapt rather than be overthrown, social change to be accommodated peacefully rather than having to end in revolutionary upheaval, but also freed the productive and exploratory capacities of what consequently became the first industrial nation as well as a great empire with political, financial and trading interests extending far beyond the realm of the Old World. If these experiences for centuries had set Britain apart from the nations on the European Continent, accounts of Anglo-European relations emphasize the Second World War as reinforcing this trend – regarding mentality as well as perceptions of national interest. World-power status and the superiority of the institutional arrangement appeared reaffirmed by the victorious campaigns. Unlike the six founding members of the EEC, Britain had neither been defeated nor occupied, while her economy, though strained by the wartime effort, had re-emerged as the strongest in Europe. Unlike her neighbours, she had little to gain from economic integration, reflected in a trade pattern in which Continental Europe was the recipient of only 23 per cent of total export.[9] The political case for integration was even weaker, after the nation state had proven capable of defence and victory. Taken together, the British are thus said simply to have shared neither the economic nor the political motivation driving the integration efforts. No account of Anglo-European relations which emphasizes these historical legacies as explanatory factors would be complete without citing Winston Churchill's famous dictum of Britain being at the intersection of three circles: the Commonwealth, the Atlantic Alliance and – ranking as a poor third – Europe.[10]

Yet, merely elucidating the historical forces shaping British policy-making in the 1950s does not seem to explain the blind spot: the alleged failure to even grasp the potential of the integration venture, especially after early successes of the Six contrasted with the first signs of Britain's economic and political decline – at least by the mid-1950s. Here, different – yet at times overlapping – perspectives have had some currency. Firstly, emphasis has been laid on individual responsibility, attributing the lack of judgement to leading figures in the British political establishment. The persuasive power of this type of interpretation is derived from two sources: one is biographical, whereby the supposedly distinct historical experience of the British Isles is transferred onto individual policy-makers. The character, outlook and, perhaps most importantly, the imaginative horizons of the generation of politicians who allegedly missed the opportunity to take the lead in Europe are said to have been shaped by their wartime and immediate postwar experience. This led them to greatly overestimate Britain's position in the world whilst at the same time dismissing European integration as suitable for lesser nations only. Indicative of this double misjudgement are Hugh Gaitskill's infamous reference to a 'thousand years of history' precluding British membership and Chancellor Richard Austin 'Rab' Butler's statement about Anthony Eden being 'even more bored' about the Messina project than he himself was.[11]

The case for individual responsibility is strengthened further by the fact that it corresponds to a particular view on European integration at large. Traditional accounts have stressed not only that the driving force behind the efforts of the Six was to replace the nation state as the dominant mode of political organization, but also that the process itself was initiated and carried forward by a small number of enlightened political leaders who believed that only supranational integration in the economic and ultimately the political field would prevent the re-emergence of the antagonisms which had led to the horrors of two World Wars.[12] The argument regarding individual responsibilities for Britain's failure to take the lead in Europe thus represents an inversion of traditional integration history: the enlightened leaders on the Continent were simply faced with less enlightened counterparts in London.[13]

However, even if – as Alan Milward has so convincingly done – the European enterprise is stripped of its 'saints' and the charges against individual British politicians are thus dropped, the thrust of the argument remains the same. This is due to a second set of factors which is seen to have contributed to the British miscalculations regarding the potential of the integration venture. It refers to structural characteristics of the governmental machine. The organizational set-up of Whitehall seemed at times to favour a decision-making process which accorded higher priority to interdepartmental negotiation and compromise, while giving little consideration to the position of foreign governments, let alone to the reception of British policies abroad.[14] The resulting rigidity in Britain's negotiating position was compounded further by a personnel structure, which provided little expertise either regarding the intricate economic issues involved or concerning the motivation, negotiating tactics, mentality or policy styles predominant on the Continent. At worst, the latter is said to have taken the form of institutionalized cultural prejudice against anything 'European', the endurance of such sentiments guaranteed by a recruitment policy which almost 'hermetically sealed' the civil service system. Perhaps the most damning judgement has been passed by Alan Milward:

> recruitment was designed to perpetuate the rule of the monied upper class within an elitist structure based on access to expensive education and privileged entry into two universities notable for the irrelevance of the knowledge they imparted to the task at hand.[15]

Of course, individual responsibility and structural factors are not incompatible, and the two types of interpretation also appear in tandem. While some accounts have perhaps overemphasized the role of one or the other and nuances are manifold, the available literature suggests a combination of the above-mentioned factors to explain comprehensively the British failure to grasp the opportunity to join the early European integration efforts. This, however, may be misleading as it is only part of the story. The observation that British officials and politicians were slow in recognizing the need to join the Six does not necessarily mean that the above-mentioned factors led them to ignore the venture or to dismiss it as unimportant. Instead, the evolution of British policy on Europe may also have been empirically based. While not denying the relevance of historical legacies, of war experience, of individuals or civil service structures, the 1961 pro-membership argument that one must 'steer from within' could arguably have followed from first-hand experience of the inability to influence the course of European integration as a non-member. Thus, the focus of attention may be shifted from 'missed opportunities' to the propriety of Britain's pre-1961 policy – in other words, from the question of 'why did Britain not have a different policy on Europe?' to an examination of the reasons behind the evident failure of the policy she did have.

More recent research has underlined the active character of British policy prior to the first application for membership in the EEC. Rather than merely representing a protracted reaction to a slow process of shifting relative economic and political weight of Churchill's 'three circles', the application of 1961 can be shown to have been preceded by numerous initiatives designed to safeguard Britain's position *vis-à-vis* her Continental neighbours.[16] Following Ernest Bevin's flirtations with the idea of a customs union and of enhanced Anglo-French co-operation in the late 1940s, such policies generally aimed to guide the efforts of the Continentals to ensure that these remained harmless to Britain. Results were mixed: the successes undoubtedly included the Organisation for European Economic Co-operation (OEEC) which was shaped into a vehicle for Britain's 'one-world' approach at tariff and quota liberalization.[17] Britain also made certain that unavoidably 'regional' institutions such as the European Payments Union or the Council of Europe remained devoid of any political or supranational content.[18]

Her policy was clearly less successful with regard to the Schuman plan for a European Coal and Steel Community (ECSC). French insistence on the acceptance of the principle of supranationality as a precondition for even entering into negotiations meant that Britain for the first time had to influence the Continentals 'from without'.

This proved a difficult undertaking, as any attempt to press for the adaptation of the plan was thwarted by a combination of French obstructionism, German acquiescence and staunch US-American support for the venture.[19] At the same time, the lack of economic weight of the coal and steel sectors of the Six eased the dilemma. When the continued success of the ECSC forced Britain to reconsider her stance, she negotiated an association agreement neatly separating political and economic interests in a way which allowed her to stand aloof from any supranational ideals, without having to suffer economic damage. Clearly, this process was aided by the fact that ECSC integration was confined to two industrial sectors in which Britain's extra-European economic interests were largely unaffected.

The same could not be said about security interests which were bound to be affected by the subsequent effort at creating a European Defence Community (EDC) and a supplementary European Political Community (EPC). When tabling their plans, Continental governments vividly remembered Winston Churchill's emphatic call for a common army, with which he had surprised his audience at the University of Zurich in September 1946. Yet, once back in government, the Conservative government swiftly backtracked, clarifying that Britain would support but not participate in the venture. However, on this occasion – and in contrast to the Schuman plan – France very much favoured British participation as a counterweight to a rearmed Germany.[20] While the EDC Treaty itself was concluded swiftly by 1952, its ratification by the parliaments concerned proved a long-drawn-out process, eventually collapsing with the rejection in the *Assemblé National*.[21] In the months before this crucial vote, the then Foreign Secretary Anthony Eden had unsuccessfully sought to sway French parliamentarians by offering far-reaching concessions in the form of British support, association and even troop commitments. While some accounts of British policy towards the EDC enterprise depict Eden's desire to avoid being seen to sabotage the Community as merely a tactical measure, masking the underlying intention to let the scheme collapse to relace it with an arrangement more congenial to British interests, others have emphasized the positive contribution the British government sought to make to Continental European integration without participating therein.[22] Despite the continuing dispute about whether or not there had been a calculated effort to prevent the EDC from coming into being, one feature of this episode can be stated with a measure of confidence: that the collapse of this ambitious supranational scheme of political and military integration was indeed viewed with some satisfaction in London. Britain even managed to pose as the saviour, considering Anthony Eden's diplomatic feat of subsequently brokering German membership in the more traditional security arrangements of NATO and the WEU. As an example of 'steering Europe from without', the EDC/EPC experience surely qualified as an overwhelming success, while its outcome had the effect of cementing the belief that the Continentals would not – and could not – push further the integration project without Britain's active support.

This belief, in part, explains the initial reaction of the British government to the unexpected *relance* of the European integration project at the Messina conference in 1955. In London, the chances of the proposals for a Common Market and a joint effort at the development of atomic energy were deemed negligible at best, not least because British participation had been ruled out at an early stage. Yet the subsequent six years saw perhaps the most important shift in British policy on Europe – a process culminating in Prime Minister Harold Macmillan's announcement of 31 July 1961 in which he declared that his government was to seek membership of the Community. Again, however, this policy change cannot be seen merely as a belated reaction to the success of the Six. Instead, the intervening years undoubtedly witnessed most determined efforts to 'steer from without'. After early diplomatic attempts to prevent the Six from going ahead had created mutual suspicions in 1955, a more positive approach was chosen to defuse the situation. In the summer of 1956, the British government proposed a Free Trade Area (FTA), comprising the Six as a unit as well as eleven other European nations. This proposal represented an attempt to secure the economic benefit of the integrated market, while neither subscribing to the political goal of the EEC, nor surrendering control over external trade policy *vis-à-vis* third countries. Two years later, however, Britain's European policy suffered a severe setback when the French government broke off negotiations in November 1958. The end of the FTA, in turn, led the British government to conclude a European Free Trade Association (EFTA) with Austria, Denmark, Norway, Portugal, Sweden and Switzerland. Established in late 1959, this new organization was primarily designed to strengthen Britain's bargaining position with respect to a future trade link with the EEC. Yet, any attempt at 'bridge-building' between the two organizations failed not only because of a lack of interest in any comprehensive trade agreement on the part of the Six, and particularly of France, but also because of US opposition to a discriminatory free trade link which lacked the political appeal of the Community. It was only after the failure of 'bridge-building', as the last attempt to 'steer from without', that some officials in London confidentially re-examined Britain's policy in early 1960, a process which led to the opening of membership negotiations 16 months later. In their reappraisal of Britain's position, these officials looked back on five years of unsuccessfully seeking to influence the course of European integration as a non-member. In the end, it was this experience which convinced them of the necessity of British membership. By 1961, Prime Minister Harold Macmillan agreed, arguing before the House of Commons that 'our right place is in the vanguard of the movement ... and ... we can lead better from within than outside'.[23]

If 'leading from within' was the empirically based conclusion of the inability to 'steer from without', the notion of 'missed opportunities' is no longer an explanatory factor of importance. Instead, the period prior to the first application will have to be examined with regard to contending claims for leadership in Europe. Viewed from this angle, one cannot but diagnose a 'gap' in historical research, as any explanation of the British failure to 'steer from without' has to examine the impact of such attempts on those which were meant to be steered. The available literature on Anglo-European relations does this only to a limited degree, with studies – other than broad surveys – generally falling into three categories.

First, it is not surprising, that political commentators and historians should in the first instance be interested in the evolution of national policy-making on this question. Some do look at the impact of British policy in other national environments though, more often than not, they take the reaction of foreign governments as given, treating these merely as inputs into the policy-formulation process in London.[24]

Secondly, a number of studies have appeared which focus on the multilateral dimension of Anglo-European relations, examining the dynamics of the entry negotiations for instance. While being of enormous value to an understanding of the intricacies of multilateral diplomacy, these also tend to neglect the impact of one governments' negotiation tactics on the process of policy-formulation of other governments. Instead, a *post hoc* evaluation is offered, with the success or failure of policies manifesting themselves at the negotiating table. As in the case of those works taking a national perspective, the attempts to influence others are thus examined as to whether or not they produced the desired result, and not as to why they succeeded or failed.[25]

Finally, there are studies with a more restricted view, focussing on single multilateral issues, such as trade policy or nuclear defence. These perhaps come closest to an examination of the causes of failure of Britain's attempts to influence other governments and/or Community institutions. Yet, they often neglect longer-term developments and more importantly cross-issue deals.[26]

It is the main contention of this study that the impact of Britain's attempts to influence the path of Continental European integration deserves greater attention in accounting for the evolution of her decision to eventually apply for Community membership. To corroborate this hypothesis, the following chapters will examine the period in which such attempts arguably were at their most determined: the six years in between the Messina conference and Britain's first application.

Whilst this choice of period is a standard one, replicating that of other studies or chapters thereof, and finding its rationale in the continuing success of the European Union, further justification is needed for the second limitation on the scope of this study. For its focus will be on a particular 'target' of British attempts to 'steer' the Europeans: Germany.

The German government was viewed as the one amongst the Six which was simultaneously crucial to and divided about the Common Market plans. Correspondingly, Bonn promised to be not only a most effective but also most responsive 'target' of any attempt to further, modify or halt policy initiatives on the Continent. Indeed, many a study acknowledges that British policy was often specifically formulated so as to appeal to German (largely economic) interests in an effort to induce the Federal Government to put pressure on the rest of the Six and on France in particular.[27] Yet, a further examination of why these policies failed to have an impact is not offered. The analysis is completed with reference to the well-known divisions within the German government, summed up in a simple formula:

> The reliance placed on the German ability (and willingness) to bring the French round was one of the basic British miscalculations ... and stemmed from an overestimation of [Minister of

Economics] Dr. Erhard's power and an underestimation of the depth of [Chancellor] Dr. Adenauer's conviction that the construction of unity in Europe rested, in the first instance, on the Franco-German *rapprochement* and his readiness, in consequence, to give an overriding priority to relations with France.[28]

The simplicity and appeal of this formula has so far prevented an in-depth examination of the reasons behind the ineffectiveness of British attempts to influence the chosen 'target'.[29] This study seeks to remedy this situation, providing a detailed analysis based on the archival evidence found in both countries. In doing so, its primary aim is to test the traditional interpretation as exemplified by the 'basic miscalculation' quoted above. In the course of the discussion, numerous questions will therefore have to be addressed: firstly, whether or not the British government did have an accurate picture of Germany's European policy and of the relative strength of the various factions within the cabinet in Bonn; secondly, if such information was fed into the policy-formulating process in London; thirdly, whether this process translated into initiatives specifically designed to steer the European integration process by way of influencing the German government; fourthly, whether or not such initiatives produced the desired effect; and if not, then finally, why they failed to have impact.

To be sure, in the wider context of European integration history, the discussion cannot be limited to the bilateral relations between Bonn and London. Bilateral contacts to other governments among the Six and negotiations within the emerging Community and other fora will naturally also be featured, as will the influence of the policies pursued by third countries, in particular by the United States. It is hoped that the discussion will thus shed some new light on the overall appropriateness of British policy in this crucial formative phase of the European project. *Inter alia*, it will also further illuminate the conceptual dispute within the German cabinet.

In its chronological examination of the multitude of questions raised above, the study relies mainly on unpublished material found in the governmental archives of the two countries concerned. Where these are sketchy or unavailable, however, use is made of published sources such as newspapers and memoirs of those concerned with European integration at the time. Any conclusions drawn from the latter have to be treated with the customary caution towards autobiographical writing. None the less, the fact that some events are

Introduction 11

not recorded, or that some government files remain subject to restricted access, means that no alternative account is available and that the risk of subjectivity of sources has to be accepted.

With regard to unpublished sources, the three archives used here are the *Bundesarchiv* in Koblenz (*BA*) which holds ministerial records, the political archive of the *Auswärtiges Amt* in Bonn (*AA*) containing the files of the German Foreign Office, and the Public Record Office in London (PRO), which holds all the records of the British government. The findings from these three archives are supplemented by some of the private papers of Konrad Adenauer held by the archive of the *Stiftung-Bundeskanzler-Adenauer-Haus* (*StBKAH*) in Rhöndorf. Despite the continued restrictions on access to most of the holdings of the latter, the book can rely on a wealth of material, given that the relevant date of the 30-year rule applied by the three public archives has passed even for the later stages of the period discussed.

In the PRO, first attention is given to Prime Ministerial and ministerial correspondence. Of particular interest are also Cabinet and Cabinet Committee meetings and memoranda. The Cabinet itself largely acted on recommendations, which were formulated either in *ad hoc* working groups, or in Cabinet Committees like the Mutual Aid Committee, the Economic Policy Committee, the Economic Steering Committee, or the Economic Policy Sub-Committees on Closer Association. All these were meant to co-ordinate the views and policy recommendations of the departments most concerned with questions of European integration. Hence, the study also examines the views of the Foreign Office, and in particular of its Mutual Aid Department, as well as of the Treasury and its Home and Overseas Planning Staff Division. Some attention is furthermore being paid to the records of the Board of Trade.

Of particular interest among the records held by the *Bundesarchiv* are those of the Ministry of Economics (*Bundesministerium für Wirtschaft, BMWi*) containing the papers of Departments I (Economic Policy), V (Foreign Trade Policy) and E (Questions of European integration) as well as those of the offices of Minister Ludwig Erhard and his State Secretaries. In addition to the Ministry of Economics, it is mainly the Chancellory (*Bundeskanzleramt, BuKa*) which is of interest to the question discussed here. Some attention is also being paid to the files of the Ministry of Finance (*Bundesministerium der Finanzen, BMF*) and to those of the Ministry for Economic Cooperation (*Bundesministerium für wirtschaftliche Zusammenarbeit, BMWZ*) as well as to the private papers of Adenauer's advisor and later Ambassador to Paris, Herbert Blankenhorn. The author would particularly like to thank Michael von Brentano for his kind permission to view the private papers of Foreign Minister Heinrich von Brentano. In the political archive of the *Auswärtige Amt*, the files of the offices of the Foreign Minister and his State Secretaries are of prime importance, as well as those of Departments 2 (Political Department), 3 (Foreign Relations by Country) and 4 (Trade Policy Department). Overall, the two German archives provide ample material for an analysis of the questions raised here. However, one important limitation continues to apply. For the period after 1956, the records of German Cabinet meetings have not been disclosed since they are currently being prepared for publication. For most relevant meetings, however, it has been possible to find summary conclusions or excerpts of the minutes in the files of individual ministries.[30]

1
From Indifference to Hostility: Britain, Germany and the Messina Project

Already with regard to the very early period discussed here, the inactivity implied by the term 'missed opportunity' conceals an important shift in British policy towards Continental European integration – from accepting an invitation to join the six future EEC members in their preparatory deliberations in July 1955, to an unsuccessful attempt in November to persuade the German government to abandon the project. In this sense, British policy towards the *relance* of Europe was very much an active one, and it is the evolution of official thinking after the Messina conference which is of interest to this first chapter. Given the futility of the diplomatic initiative of November 1955, it will be asked how accurately the British government had assessed the German position. In order to answer this question, the chapter will commence with an examination of Bonn's integration policy prior to the Messina conference.

Bonn and the Messina conference

The renewal of the debate about European integration after the EDC débâcle did not start with the Benelux initiative discussed at the Messina conference in June 1955. In the spring of the same year, ideas about further economic integration had already surfaced, as, for example, an extension of the competences of the High Authority of the ECSC suggested by its outgoing President, Jean Monnet.[1] It is important to trace the post-Messina debate back to this earlier period, for the German Cabinet's conceptual divisions about the Common Market intensified in response to Monnet's proposals.[2]

He had envisaged High Authority competences to be extended to cover transport, the electricity generating industries and the development of atomic energy for peaceful purposes. It was against these proposals that the Minister of Economics, Ludwig Erhard, not only publicly but also in private correspondence with the Chancellor, Konrad Adenauer, expressed his strong opposition.[3] He argued that further extensions of sectoral supranational control made little economic sense, since they would lead to a fragmentation of national economies, to a readjustment of the rate of growth to that of the slowest member of the proposed Community, and to an economic division of the Western world. Powerful interest groups shared his dislike of the extension of the ECSC principle, in particular the electricity generating industries, which warned that increased energy costs would translate into disadvantages for German industry at large.[4] While Erhard's criticism of the proposals was therefore born out of a liberal free-market philosophy resulting in a strong dislike of regulated markets and supranational authorities, he nevertheless conceded that there was a political imperative to advance the cohesion of the Western Alliance. To this end, however, he suggested co-operation of national governments in the fields of trade liberalization and currency policy with the ultimate aim of worldwide convertibility, a theme which was recurring in his public speeches at home and abroad, in which he praised the work already done within intergovernmental organizations such as the OEEC and the General Agreement on Tariffs and Trade (GATT).[5]

The State Secretary in the *Auswärtiges Amt*, Walter Hallstein, replied on behalf of the Chancellor.[6] In his letter to Erhard, he described the differences as being merely of modalities and claimed that there was agreement in principle on the question of European integration. Rejecting sectoral integration in general, he welcomed Monnet's ideas on transport and nuclear energy, claiming that these sectors were well suited to this approach. More importantly, he was outspoken in his preference for supranational institutions as a means to foster political integration in the Community. The need for such a step lay in the international situation which he described in a much more dramatic tone than Erhard had done. The achievements of intergovernmental organizations in the field of integration were, in his view, far from praiseworthy, and it is interesting to note the undisguised opposition of Hallstein to British participation, which he regarded as an obstacle to integration in these organizations.

From Indifference to Hostility: Britain, Germany and the Messina Project 15

This exchange between Erhard and Hallstein conveniently illustrates the conceptual differences within the German government in advance of Messina, although it would be incorrect to equate it with the collective views of such complex institutions as the *Bundesministerium für Wirtschaft* and the *Auswärtiges Amt* respectively.[7] Nevertheless, these statements can be taken to represent the division in principle.

In the early summer of 1955, the Dutch Foreign Minister Johan Willem Beyen tabled a plan for tariff reductions among the six ECSC countries which, combined with Monnet's sectoral ideas, came to dominate the Messina conference. It was as a reaction to this plan contained in a joint Benelux memorandum that the conflicting views had to be moulded into a single German approach. Nine days before the conference itself, the main protagonists within the government sought to thrash out a compromise during an informal meeting in Echterscheid, at the holiday home of the Head of the Economic Policy Department of the Economics Ministry, Alfred Müller-Armack.[8] What was agreed appears to have been a genuine compromise, accepting in principle Erhard's view that further sectoral integration was not desirable. Transport, electricity and nuclear energy were, however, suitable sectors, and the feasibility of integration should be examined for these cases. Perhaps the hardest point for Erhard to accept was that overall integration, as suggested by the Benelux memorandum, might necessitate the establishment of some supranational body in order to interpret and control the application of the general rules on which the Six might agree. The *Echterscheider Beschlüsse* formed the basis for the position taken by Hallstein and the German delegation at the Messina conference. This is not to suggest that they put an end to the debate about different conceptions within the German government. Yet, Müller-Armack's summing up of the meeting is revealing as it demonstrates how early the idea of a customs union found the acceptance of all those present:

> One became aware of the fact – and Erhard agreed to that too – that the European policy of functional integration should be complemented by the creation of an institutional structure which should be given the character of an irrevocable customs union, which would at first be restricted to the Six.[9]

The resolution passed at the Messina conference itself was almost identical with the Benelux memorandum and the German contribution which had to a large extent been modelled on the latter.[10] It was agreed to set up a preparatory committee to examine the possibility of integration in the nuclear energy, electricity generation and transport sectors, as well as of the creation of a Common Market of the Six. The wording of the resolution carefully avoided the question of supranationality because the experience of the EDC had instilled some caution in most participants. It was furthermore agreed that Britain, as an associate member of the ECSC, should be invited to partake in these deliberations.[11]

The Messina conference was followed by a first meeting of the preparatory committee on 9 July, which discussed procedural questions.[12] Its purpose was to establish various expert committees to examine the problems associated with the different projects. The preparatory character of these committees was reflected in the intention neither to question the content of the Messina resolution, nor to formulate solutions to the problems encountered in the discussion.[13] It was on the question of what expert committees were to be established that the dispute within the German government re-emerged despite the *Echterscheider Beschlüsse*. In a memorandum of early July, the Ministry of Economics regarded the social dimension of the Common Market as the most problematic element in the Messina proposals.[14] The document already identified France as the main obstacle to success, and anticipated much of the later discussion about harmonization of social policies, cost structures and investment problems.[15] Given limited convertibility, the differences prevailing between the cost structure and development level of national economies were not reflected in the exchange rate differentials, and it was here that the Ministry of Economics argued that the real problem lay. It is important to note that, even internally, officials did not question the establishment of a customs union as the most appropriate solution to overall integration in the form of a Common Market. Erhard's later preference for the Free Trade Area, proposed by the British government in 1956, obscures the fact that, in these early stages, the ministry, including Erhard himself, did not regard the concept of a customs union as being in conflict with the free-market philosophy it was generally advocating. As long as the customs union conformed to the rules of GATT, and more importantly to those of the OEEC, hence having an outer tariff below the current level, the arrangement was seen as a contribution to the worldwide freeing of trade.

British reactions to Messina

Whilst not being part of the core group of European integration, the British civil service was remarkably well informed about the *rélance* of Europe even before the Messina conference. As an associate member of the ECSC, there was not only an awareness of Monnet's proposals, but the British Foreign Office was also informed about the content of the Benelux memorandum.[16] Yet, due to the caution and vagueness of the ideas prevailing among the Continentals, the reaction to the renewed drive behind European integration was mixed. Some diplomatic outposts relaying the information available displayed the well-known 'nothing would come of it' optimism which persisted in the heads of some officials for a remarkably long time thereafter.[17] This attitude was not universally shared, however, as can be seen in a memorandum by Alan Edden, responsible for Anglo-ECSC relations as the Head of the Mutual Aid Department (MAD) of the Foreign Office, who rated the chances of success somewhat higher.[18] Others based their view on the EDC failure of 1954; thus, France was widely regarded as the main obstacle to any progress.[19] Germany's lukewarm reaction to further integration was also frequently noted, both before and immediately after the conference.[20] The division in Bonn was recognized and, since little detail was known about exactly what was planned, Erhard's opposition to the sector approach served as a source of comfort to some.[21] Some voices ascribed coolness towards European integration even to Chancellor Adenauer, a view which again was not shared by Edden.[22] Despite widespread scepticism about the chances of success of further integration, the Head of the MAD was anxious for the British government not to be seen to oppose these ideas. This formed a striking contrast to Britain's delegate to the OEEC, Sir Hugh Ellis-Rees, who argued that Chancellor Richard Austin 'Rab' Butler should use the forthcoming OEEC meeting to issue a strong statement about the inappropriateness of any duplication of the work done in the latter organization. Again, Edden disagreed: 'Although overlapping should be reduced to the minimum, OEEC has no right to try to call a halt to the processes started by the six countries at Messina.'[23] However, his moderating influence failed to prevent Butler from publicly ridiculing the Messina plans as 'archeological excavations'.[24]

In advance of the conference, Treasury officials appear to have been less well informed about what was planned than their Foreign

Office counterparts.[25] Immediately thereafter, however, it was the Common Market proposals which came to be regarded as being of most concern to Britain among all the elements of the *rélance* of Europe. This can be attributed, partly, to the different evaluation of the chances of success of the scheme, which also related to the German position. While Erhard's opposition to the sector approach was specifically noted, the Head of the Overseas Finance Division, William Strath, appears to have been aware that Adenauer's political enthusiasm for integration was unbroken and was likely to overrule any opposition in the German Cabinet.[26] As Chairman of the Cabinet's Mutual Aid Committee (MAC) in which the different departments co-ordinated their views, Strath had already contemplated the wholesale transfer of the Messina talks into OEEC, so as to limit the potential damage to British economic interests and to avoid the disappearance of the latter organization.[27] While this view found support from the Chancellor, this is not to say that the Treasury followed the extreme line taken by Ellis-Rees. Instead, they shared Edden's view that the potential political damage of open opposition to the plans of the Six would be too high a price for British non-participation in the committee discussions.[28]

The month after the conference was dominated by a debate about when and in what form Britain would be represented at the committees. Although Edden's insistence on the political necessity of participation as such prevailed, the Treasury showed itself more concerned about the form the latter should take, because of its view on OEEC duplication. Foreign Secretary, Harold Macmillan, on a visit to America, insisted that no decision about participation was to be taken before his return. Thereafter, it was up to the Mutual Aid Committee to decide upon the acceptance of the invitation. Here again, the views of Edden and Strath prevailed, namely that 'refusal to attend the talks at all would be politically embarrassing' and that it was economically imperative to 'stand on the touch line' given the diversity of interests of the Six which made the outcome of the initiative difficult to predict.[29] Regarding the form of British participation, the Chancellor argued for an observer, whereas the Foreign Office preferred a representative, status.[30] This, so it was argued, would allow Britain to contribute to the discussion whilst remaining uncommitted to its results. The Foreign Office view prevailed in the deliberations of the MAC, which also agreed that the Treasury and the Foreign Office should formulate the acceptance of the invitation jointly. While it was the Foreign Office which drafted the substance of the letter, the Treasury had one important alteration to make, which read that 'there are, as you are no doubt aware, special reasons which would preclude this country from joining a European common market'. This phrase illustrates the extent to which the Treasury took the Common Market proposals seriously even before the start of the committee work in Brussels. Having accepted the invitation, the Foreign Office informed diplomatic posts abroad. This summing up of Messina is notable for its insight into not only what exactly was planned but also the character of the German and French positions. While there had indeed been some officials who expected German opposition to the principle of integration, this correspondence demonstrates that the more accurate assessment of Strath and Edden prevailed after the conference:

> A notable feature of the Messina Communique is the absence of any specific endorsement of the supranational approach. No further 'High Authorities' are in fact proposed. The wording would not necessarily exclude them. But it is clear that the French are against further experiments of this kind, or at least will not agree to any in advance of the 1956 elections; whilst the Germans, though still apparently in favour of European integration, are opposed to trying to bring this about by further isolated doses of 'supranationalism', administered to individual sectors of the economy (the so-called 'sector approach').[32]

The Hallstein statement – official German policy?

The specific character of the German Economics Ministry's opposition to the Messina project became most obvious during an interministerial meeting on 7 July which was meant to formulate instructions for the delegation in Brussels.[33] When calling the meeting, the political imperative of European integration and the need for a positive German approach had been stated unequivocally by Chancellor Adenauer himself.[34] Erhard once again declared his opposition to the sector approach in transport and conventional energy, but conceded that nuclear energy could form an exception. He was most outspoken in his criticism of the Belgian plan for an expert committee on the establishment of a social fund meant to smooth the impact of increased competition on countries with structural deficiencies. His views on this matter originated in two different convictions, which can be taken to argue that his opposition to the plans for European integration were much less fundamental than had been assumed. While agreeing to the principle of a Common Market as a customs union, Erhard's main concern was to avoid unnecessary supranational institutions for the distribution of a social fund, although he conceded that some authority would be required to control cartel and other legislation against unfair competition. The second and somewhat related conviction held by Erhard was that as little as possible should be done to interfere with the free play of market forces. This is not to suggest that he denied the existence of structural inequalities and social provisions among the participating countries, but that he felt that existing inequalities would have to be alleviated by market forces on the basis of free convertibility and 'real' exchange rates, the latter of which would also neutralize the problems resulting from different cost levels. In later stages of the negotiations, these views were to bring him into direct conflict with French demands for harmonization of social costs.

Once again the reply to Erhard's views was given by State Secretary Hallstein who expressed his satisfaction that the much quoted differences within the German government were based on a simple misunderstanding about what was meant by sectoral integration and supranationality.[35] General agreement was in fact reached on both counts, with the former being firmly rejected, while the latter was envisaged only for some specific functions to ensure fair competition regarding cartel and subsidization policies. Despite its diplomatic tone, Hallstein's intervention prompted a renewed argument with Erhard, for the latter felt it necessary to insist that supranational institutions should be limited to these functions, so that national economic and financial policies would be unaffected. Once again, it was the relation to third countries and especially the furtherance of convertibility which he did not want to see compromised by supranational interference. Yet Hallstein insisted that an official statement in favour of such supranational institutions was needed to reassure those who doubted Germany's positive attitude towards European integration.

The discussion of this interministerial meeting at some length has shown the extent to which the Hallstein statement to the Brussels meeting only two days later reflected a genuine compromise between the *Auswärtiges Amt* and the Ministry of Economics.[36] Although it can be read as an endorsement of the principle of supranationality, Hallstein's speech not only argued against further sectoral integration but also explicitly stated that the institutional arrangements necessary for the control of fair competition in the Common Market should be established after unanimity about its general principles was reached with the help of a consultative board. Furthermore, to ensure the compliance of the Ministry of Economics, the latter had also been given the right to represent Germany at the Common Market expert committee in the negotiations in Brussels, while the *Auswärtiges Amt* retained representation in the steering committee named after its chairman, the Belgian Foreign Minister Paul-Henri Spaak. The Head of the Ministry of Economics Sub-Department 'ECSC', Hans von der Groeben, and German Ambassador to Brussels, Professor Carl Friedrich Ophüls, were the officials appointed to the respective posts. Unlike previous and later episodes, the distribution of representative competencies proved uncontroversial at this stage.[37]

The statement made by Hallstein in the first meeting of the Spaak Committee provided an opportunity for outside observers, including the British Foreign Office, to examine a first-hand declaration of the German position after the Messina conference. The British Ambassador to Brussels, Sir Christopher Warner, reported that

> Hallstein's main concern was to deny rumours that Germany was no longer pursuing her former policy of solid European integration, and to come out hot and strong for that as well as a common market even with a supranational authority, this being a political necessity and the only way to make Europe strong enough to secure peace. He poured cold water on a mere sector-by-sector approach.[38]

Edden had been even more outspoken in his warning that some observers had misinterpreted the German attitude at Messina as meaning that 'the German government was no longer keen on the European idea. In fact they are as keen as ever, while objecting to schemes which would involve giving up their economic sovereignty piecemeal.'[39] Now Warner's report led him to an interesting conclusion about possible British initiatives:

> Unless we are prepared to come forward, in short order, with some positive policy of our own, e.g. that the Six should integrate within OEEC rather than outside it, it looks as though only the dragging of French feet will stop the Six from forging ahead . . .

German opposition to the sector approach was already well known. What is significant is the drive they would apparently like to put into the 'overall' approach.[40]

John Coulson, Under-Secretary at the Foreign Office, clarified the view of his department when replying to the British embassy in Brussels. Therein, he agreed that there had indeed been a misunderstanding of the German attitude:

> The Germans still favour supranational integration on a broad basis, but Erhard is firmly opposed to the 'sector' approach... The Benelux Memorandum submitted to the Messina Conference favoured, of course, precisely this 'sector' approach and the unfavourable German reaction appears to have been misinterpreted as lukewarmness towards European integration in general... I think therefore that we can regard the Brussels statement as intended to restore the balance and to show that the German government remains a firm believer in the European idea, and is opposed only to further piecemeal surrender of economic sovereignty.[41]

Whatever doubts had existed in the Foreign Office about the positive German approach to European integration, Coulson's summing up appears to have settled the debate.

The Treasury, though having filed most of the Foreign Office correspondence, was less concerned with such broad assessments than with the day-to-day experience of the expert committees.[42] Its main priority was OEEC participation in the steering committee and in those preparatory committees discussing atomic energy and the Common Market, with the aim of averting a possible duplication of the work of the organization. Among the Six, opposition to this request was most pronounced among the French and German delegation.[43] Only strong diplomatic pressure changed the position of both, a fact which to the Treasury underlined Germany's determination to succeed with the integration à Six.[44] Even on the practical side of the negotiations, therefore, the Treasury's impression corresponded to the Foreign Office's assessment of German policy as being strongly in favour of further European integration.

The Spaak Committee deliberations

If the Hallstein statement represented a temporary compromise reached in the interministerial consultations, it did not put an end to the debate about details of European integration within the German government. Though the experts seemed at an early stage to have agreed on the customs union idea preferred by the Economics Ministry and had rejected both free trade arrangements and sectoral approaches, Erhard still feared that important powers over national financial and economic policy would be subjected to supranational control.[45] In an article written for the *Bulletin des Presse- und Informationsamtes der Bundesregierung*, Erhard strongly criticized plans for the establishment of investment and adaptation funds which were meant to smooth out the transitional difficulties of those countries with structural weaknesses and to finance compensatory payments for labour displaced by increased competition.[46] French demands for harmonization of working hours and wage differentials for men and women and for a high outer tariff raised further concerns. All these points were naturally unacceptable to the Minister of Economics, who sought to protect the cost advantage of the German export economy. Implicit in his article was the fear that – for overriding political reasons – the *Auswärtiges Amt*, the Chancellor and even some of his own staff would be more willing to compromise in these matters. This concern was not dispelled by the conference of the six Foreign Ministers in September, which was largely a stock-taking meeting and did not itself arrive at any agreements or solutions.[47] Discussing the results of the conference in a Cabinet Committee meeting, the State Secretary of the Ministry of Economics, Ludger Westrick, once again expressed concern that a harmonization of the different national cost-structures would be damaging to the German economy. Instead, such differences should find their reflection in 'real' exchange rates under the conditions of free convertibility.[48]

The fears of Erhard and Westrick were not entirely unjustified, as can be seen in the progress made by the expert committees in September and October 1955. The inclusion of the investment and adaptation funds in the report of the Common Market committee was not opposed by the German delegation under the more European-minded von der Groeben.[49] As on many other points, the expert reports submitted to the Spaak Committee in November recorded differences in opinion rather than suggesting solutions.

It was decided at the aforementioned Cabinet Committee meeting that the imminent completion of the expert reports meant that the Cabinet itself needed to be informed about progress made and the German position taken. It fell to the *Auswärtiges Amt* and the Ministry of Economics to jointly formulate a Cabinet memorandum for this purpose. Yet the document completed in November and signed by both Brentano and Erhard revealed that the *Auswärtiges Amt* had had the greater input.[50] It argued most strongly for European integration to be continued as a political necessity arising from the East–West conflict and only briefly described the schemes envisaged. No account was taken of the Economic Ministry's reservations about the remaining problems, other than what was contained in the official version of von der Groeben's report from Brussels, enclosed in the Cabinet memorandum.

Soon after having signed the memorandum, Erhard declared his objection to some unspecified elements therein and claimed that the document should serve only as a basis for discussion.[51] The minister does not appear to have been isolated with his criticism. Not only did he receive support from certain industrial interest groups, but also his views were shared in the Cabinet.[52] The Minister of Finance, Fritz Schäffer, took exception to the adaptation and investment funds as well as to the degree of harmonization.[53] Erhard added his concern about the question of who was to be responsible for potential negotiations about tariff questions between the Common Market and third countries. On this point, he was reassured by von der Groeben that, even if the Council of Ministers were to conduct these negotiations, a liberal tariff policy would prevail due to the majority of low-tariff countries of Germany and the Benelux in this institution – an interesting reply considering that this power was eventually given to the Commission instead.[54]

Second-guessing German policy

Closely associated with the deliberations in Brussels, British interest in the positions taken by the various governments increased in the autumn of 1955. The Foreign Office received an in-depth assessment of German attitudes, with a four-page report by Roger Jackling, Economic Minister at Britain's embassy in Bonn.[55] He claimed that there was a common denominator to Erhard's and Adenauer's views, arguing that, while there was indeed some opposition to the Messina proposals, differences in motives needed to be distinguished:

firstly, there were those who had always regarded ECSC and NATO membership as a means to achieve German sovereignty. Secondly, now that this goal was in fact achieved, Messina was seen as an unnecessary limitation of the new-found sovereignty. Jackling contrasted this view with the type of opposition found among those who adhered to what he called the Erhard school of thought. This group merely opposed the institutional or sector approach not out of nationalistic principles but because of an internationalist, strictly economic doctrine. Thirdly and lastly, there were those, around Adenauer and Brentano, to whom further integration was a means to contain the very nationalism described above. Jackling did concede that there were still rifts between the two latter groups, but that they were united in their opposition to the nationalistic approach, for it was contrary to both their economic and political doctrines. Assuming, therefore, that both Erhard and Adenauer were pro-integration in principle, Jackling claimed that one had to reinterpret the Hallstein statement as primarily meant to counteract the impression made by those nationalistic opponents, rather than the opposition voiced by Erhard on other occasions. He went on to claim that:

> Adenauer is quite content to leave methods of co-operation to Erhard, provided that he is satisfied that developments on the economic front are not in directions disruptive of the European idea. He is not interested in pure economics, and his touch in them is much less sure.[56]

Jackling's correspondence and the various comments thereon exemplify the position of the Foreign Office in the autumn of 1955.[57] The main concern of the Foreign Office officials was the possibility of further supranational, sectoral integration among the Six. In this sense, their assessment of Erhard's position was remarkably accurate, given that the Ministry of Economics was indeed successful in averting further sectoral integration. The Messina resolution with its apparent lack of emphasis on supranationality, the interpretation of the Hallstein statement and the report by Roger Jackling, raised some confidence that the Germans were natural allies for the British. However, it is paramount to note that the Foreign Office was well aware that the Brussels discussions were heading towards the creation of a customs union with an outer tariff, and that the German delegation was in favour of this method.[58] There is no indication that the Foreign Office regarded a customs union as potentially damaging to British interests at this stage. Instead, it was content to see the integration debate develop on what Edden had viewed as intergovernmental lines, which made the institutions 'almost indistinguishable from the OEEC'.[59]

The Treasury now appeared to share much of the Foreign Office's assessment of the German position. Not only due to their awareness of the Jackling report, but also because of independent information, its officials viewed Erhard's opposition to supranational, sectoral integration with satisfaction. While the German preference for a customs union was not in doubt, the Treasury was more hopeful than Foreign Office officials that it might be possible to steer the German government away from the integration efforts of the Six. This view was based on a meeting between Erhard and Chancellor Butler in mid-September, when the two ministers had an informal exchange of views during the OEEC Council meeting in Istanbul. While not questioning the customs union as the preferred concept of integration, Erhard spoke out in favour of the OEEC approach of intergovernmental co-operation rather than that of 'romantic ideas' of supranational integration. Most noteworthy was Erhard's request for Butler's assistance:

> The OEEC approach was infinitely to be preferred and would lead naturally to political integration when the time was right. He [Erhard] took this matter very, very seriously and would greatly appreciate it if the Chancellor could take any opportunity which offered to support his views, particularly in talking to the United States government.[60]

It seems, therefore, that the German Minister of Economics had called on the British government to do exactly what it did in November, when it sought to convince the German and the US governments to disassociate themselves from the Messina plans. However, if Erhard's comments signalled his firm opposition to supranationalism, they did not envisage the abandonment of the customs union plan. The ambiguity of his remarks lay in the reference to the OEEC approach, which could be read as meaning either its institutional characteristics or membership. The former interpretation seemed supported by the course of the expert discussions in Brussels, and even Treasury officials were in no doubt that the German government was still very much in favour of a Common

From Indifference to Hostility: Britain, Germany and the Messina Project 27

Market of the Six. Combining the two facets of the German attitude, Strath summed up:

> The German delegation seems to have built up a reputation for solid sense and moderation. They mean business but are anxious to move by practical stages and to rely principally on techniques of intergovernmental consultation rather than on new institutions. They do not share the views of the Benelux group on the need for supranational bodies.[61]

Nevertheless, some officials thought that there were indeed sufficient grounds for approaching the Germans. Most notable among these was the Treasury's Assistant Secretary in the Mutual Aid Division, Peter Nichols, who argued that:

> If we do not want to see a Common Market set up, and if we want to avoid being blamed for its failure, it would suit us well to persuade the Germans to lean towards OEEC and making progress towards European integration on as wide a front as possible short of the establishment of a Common Market.[62]

For the Permanent Secretary, Sir Edward Bridges, however, 'the simple fact remained that the Germans (except, perhaps, for Dr. Erhard) want the Common Market to come into existence, and we surely do not'. Writing to Chancellor Butler, he also insisted that 'one must face the fact that the Americans are giving considerable encouragement to these renewed attempts at a European political community'.[63]

If there was disagreement among Treasury officials as to the character of the German position, Fritz Schäffer's visit to London in October 1955 soon provided a further occasion at which a more thorough assessment could be made. The visit was preceded by intense speculation, with advance information from the British embassy in Bonn suggesting that the latter held the view that:

> we should aim for closer co-operation between governments on a horizontal basis. The basis of this should, in his view, be full agreement between the United Kingdom and German governments, and it might be advisable to set up permanent machinery for consultation on important questions of this kind.[64]

In the same correspondence, it was, however, made clear that 'the present trend of thought was towards a European customs union' since 'it could not be imposed by a single act but demanded gradual bringing together of the relevant conditions in the different countries and this could best be done by a lot of little steps and not supranational authorities'.

The visit of the German Minister of Finance was widely regarded as an opportunity to sound out 'just how far the Germans would be prepared to go to meet the French'.[65] Furthermore, the official brief contained the recommendation to 'press the advantages of an OEEC approach'.[66] However, the record of the meeting itself does not suggest that either Strath or Edden pressed this point at all.[67] This was mainly due to Schäffer's own comments in which he made clear that, despite his opposition to supranationalism, 'the Messina Conference had agreed in principle to create new institutions'. With reference to the ECSC experience, Schäffer even defended the concept of a customs union against Strath's argument that the latter 'might have the effect for a time of hardening the tariff boundaries round the common market group'. It was therefore made clear to the Treasury and Foreign Office officials that even one of the strongest critics of the Messina proposals within the German Cabinet not only had come to accept the idea of a Common Market, but also advocated the concept of a customs union of the Six.

It might be helpful at this stage to draw some preliminary conclusions about the British assessment of the German position in autumn 1955. The expert discussions were about to be completed, while in Britain, an interdepartmental Mutual Aid Committee working group under the chairmanship of the Treasury's Third Secretary, Burke Trend, was preparing a report about the likely effects of the Common Market, upon which the ministerial decision about participation would be based. The Foreign Office was undoubtedly aware that the dispute within the German government was less fundamental than previously thought. Both the Erhard and Adenauer groups were seen as primarily pro-integration, and the dispute itself was seen as one about method rather than principle. Here, it was anticipated that Erhard's opposition to sectoral integration, supranationality and harmonization would moderate the Spaak report, which was universally viewed with satisfaction. At no point, however, was there any doubt about Germany's positive attitude towards a customs union à Six.

The Treasury, by contrast, appears temporarily to have entertained some hope of being able to dissuade the German government from establishing the Common Market, as a result of the exchange of views between Butler and Erhard in Istanbul. The latter even appears to have asked directly for British intervention on behalf of his views, in particular with regard to US policy. Yet, the visit of the German Finance Minister once again underlined the Foreign Office assessment of the German government, which, though apparently divided over the extent of supranationalism, was thought to be united in its support for the Messina plans in principle as well as for the concept of a customs union in particular.

It appears therefore that, with the exception of the opposition to British participation found in the *Auswärtiges Amt*, officials at Whitehall were remarkably well informed about the different views held within the German government. This makes it all the more perplexing as to how the British government could have arrived at the decision to approach the German government with the aim of preventing the Common Market.

The origins of the November telegram

The sequence of events, which has characterised the views of the departments, found their direct reflection in the Mutual Aid Committee. Early on, it was clear to all participants that the Common Market was most likely to take the form of a customs union. German preference for this scheme was also noted, and the argument within the Brussels committees was consequently interpreted as one between low- and high-tariff member states.[68] On the basis of two memoranda prepared by the Board of Trade and the Treasury, which had argued against British participation in a customs union on economic grounds, the MAC instructed the British representative in Brussels to argue for a low rather than a high tariff wall in order to limit the damage for British export industries.[69] The Board of Trade memorandum had ruled out participation, arguing that 'the United Kingdom, with her much larger proportion of non-European, and particularly Commonwealth, trade, has interests wider than those of other European countries'.[70] At the same time, however, the Treasury had argued that the creation of a customs union limited to the Six could not be ignored as unimportant:

> It is difficult to say whether on balance... we would gain or lose economically *as compared with the present situation* by the

establishment of a common market with our participation: we would certainly lose by the establishment of a common market without our participation.[71]

These two memoranda were to form the basis for Burke Trend's Mutual Aid Committee working group in preparing their report for ministers to take the decision about participation. However, before ministers received the report, British representation at the Spaak Committee had come to an end. Although there had for some time been a discussion within government about whether and when to withdraw, it remains unclear whether the British representative, Russell Bretherton, Under-Secretary at the Board of Trade, did indeed withdraw from the committee, or whether he was dismissed by Spaak.[72]

In the event, the circumstances of his departure did not matter much, because the Trend report firmly ruled out participation in a customs union on the grounds that 'the political difficulties in joining it would be very considerable'.[73] However, the report followed the Treasury's economic argument by endorsing the view that, in the long run, Britain would most certainly lose out if the Six were to form a customs union. There was still some hope that the French would eventually wreck the scheme, and it was this likelihood that the report concentrated upon in its assessment of the positions of other European countries. The only reference to Germany in this context read:

> of the other countries, it is important to note that the Germans are certainly not single-mindedly in favour of European economic integration, other than on political grounds. Their economic authorities seem in fact to have been over-ruled by Dr. Adenauer for political reasons.

Yet, as far as policy prescriptions were concerned, the Trend report was equally firmly against any direct interference of Britain with the aim of disrupting the negotiations of the Six. Instead, the Mutual Aid Committee agreed that the Six should be told that Britain could not take part in the Common Market, and that they should keep the OEEC fully informed. The committee recommended that the time before the publication of the Spaak report should be used to formulate an alternative non-discriminatory scheme, which could tempt the Six away from concluding their own plans.

From Indifference to Hostility: Britain, Germany and the Messina Project 31

In early November, the Economic Steering Committee (ES) discussed and approved the Trend report before it was due to be considered by ministers in the Cabinet's Economic Policy Committee (EP).[74] In the discussion itself, members of the former committee were even more outspoken than the Mutual Aid Committee about policy prescriptions for ministers. There was no mention of an approach to be made to either Germany or the US. On the contrary, it was agreed that only the presentation of a viable alternative would allow for the Messina discussions to be transferred to the OEEC:

(i) a plain negative would be too blunt and would cause unnecessary damage;
(ii) an attempt to persuade the six countries to pursue their scheme for a common market within the OEEC had no chance of success; and
(iii) the only other alternative, namely to encourage a closer liaison between OEEC and the independent discussions of the Six on the common market, was the only possible one but it could not be more than a holding operation until we could consider what we could offer them in exchange for abandoning the market.[75]

Hence, the Economic Steering Committee instructed the Mutual Aid Committee to formulate a policy towards this end. It appears, therefore, that neither committee suggested anything like an attempt to interfere with the efforts of the Six. On the contrary, the officials on these committees were aware that Britain had to come up with a substantial policy initiative herself, if the establishment of the Common Market was to be prevented. They were even aware that for such an alternative to have any appeal on the Continent, Britain would have to be prepared to compromise on the issue of tariff reductions within OEEC. This view was shared by Foreign Office and Treasury officials, with the new Chairman of MAC, Richard 'Otto' Clarke, observing that, 'it should be noted that the major causes of European disappointment with OEEC has been that organization's inability to deal effectively with tariffs'.[76]

Given such statements, as well as the two reports, it is difficult to understand why the Economic Policy Committee, chaired by Chancellor Butler, decided to approach the German government, arguing that:

Although Germany was taking part in the Brussels Conference, a substantial body of opinion was not in favour of joining in a common market. If we were to give them a lead, the Germans might decide not to join a common market and to concentrate on co-operation through the OEEC.[77]

Thus the decision to approach Germany was taken contrary to recommendations of the civil service. British opposition to a Common Market in the form of a customs union was thereby extended to an interpretation of the divisions within the German government, which had been noted only in passing in the reports. The Economic Policy Committee ignored that there was indeed general agreement within the German government on the creation of a customs union of the Six. A possible explanation for this mistake can be found in the composition of the committee as a purely ministerial forum. It included none of those officials who had been concerned with the assessment of the German position since Messina. The lack of information contained in the report led ministers to implicitly assume that the divisions within the German government were as fundamental as they had appeared not only at the beginning of the year 1955 but also in the comments of Erhard in Istanbul in October. In this sense, the decision may arguably have been based on Butler's recollection of his meeting with Erhard, combined with long-held assumptions about the German attitude towards European integration, rather than on a specific assessment of their negotiation performance since Messina. The fact that such assessments were available in the files of the Treasury and the Foreign Office but not in the report itself illustrates the lack of communication between officials and decision-makers.

The telegram to Bonn stressed the divisive effect of a customs union in the economic sphere and its negative effect on the political cohesion of the Western Alliance.[78] This was perhaps the least effective of possible arguments meant to lead the two factions within the German government away from the Common Market negotiations and towards the OEEC. Officials had been aware not only of Adenauer's enthusiasm for European integration as a means to strengthen Western cohesion but also of Erhard's and Schäffer's acceptance of a customs union as a means to achieve economic integration while continuing to strive for worldwide trade liberalization. On both counts, therefore, it is not surprising that the telegram had no effect on either of the two factions, with the exception of strengthening the conviction of the *Auswärtiges Amt* that Britain should indeed be left out of the negotiations so as to increase the chances of real integration. Yet, there was no alternative to the argument used in the telegram, mainly because no further OEEC initiatives had been formulated, let alone agreed upon, by British ministers, despite the fact that some officials had argued for such a policy as early as July 1955, and the Mutual Aid and Economic Steering Committees had confirmed the need for substantive counterproposals.[79] Unlike a year later, no such plans were available in 1955, which meant that there was no convincing argument to be used in the telegram.

German reactions to the British intervention

The final exchange of views of the different German ministries in 1955 came shortly before Christmas at a meeting of State Secretaries.[80] This meeting was significant not merely for the continued opposition of Westrick and Schäffer to the adaptation fund and for the reservations expressed by the State Secretary of the Ministry of Agriculture but also for the first official acknowledgement of the British diplomatic initiative. Hallstein claimed that:

> Certain diplomatic steps had even given the impression that the integration of the Six would not suit the British government. However, this was not going to change the determination of the Six countries, for England's relation to the continent was different from those among the Six not only by degree, but also qualitatively, namely politically, psychologically and sociologically.[81]

For the State Secretary in the *Auswärtiges Amt*, the diplomatic approach only served to substantiate what he had thought as early as March 1955: 'As long as integration formally presupposes equal treatment of Great Britain, England will not be prepared to make further concessions ... The English never bow to theoretical demands, but only to facts.'[82]

Another notable feature of the meeting of State Secretaries was the absence of any comment about the British diplomatic initiative by the representative of the Ministry of Economics. It seems that, even here, there had never been any expectation of British participation, but at most a confidence that Britain would eventually associate with the Common Market, as she had done with the

ECSC. In this respect, therefore, the ministry had shared Hallstein's view that the British 'lacked the imagination necessary to envisage the future development in a sufficiently concrete form'.[83]

If the British relation to the Common Market plan was no cause for dispute at the meeting, this is not to suggest that the differences about the modalities of the scheme had been resolved. Yet, as had been the case in the Cabinet meeting of November, the dissenting voices were silenced by Hallstein's reassurance that none of the expert findings were binding for national governments.[84] It appears, therefore, that the dispute about the modalities of the Common Market within the German government was only temporarily halted by the Auswärtiges Amt appeasing the opposing departments.

From indifference to hostility

The official papers of the German government show that the *rélance* of Europe was the subject of a prolonged internal conflict though not about the question of whether or not to integrate, but rather about the method of integration to be followed. Yet, the issues in this debate changed in the summer of 1955. Before the Messina conference, it had been dominated by the question of whether it was desirable for political reasons to accept an extension of the ECSC principle of sectoral integration. Thereafter, the more comprehensive integration approach chosen with the Common Market now focussed attention on the question of how much harmonization of national economies would have to be enforced by supranational authority. If the *Echterscheider Beschlüsse* and the post-Messina interministerial consultations had settled the conflict about sectoral integration, the Hallstein speech had re-opened the debate about the methods and extent of harmonization and supranationality. The positions of the two most important ministries appear to have remained largely unchanged until the end of the year, with the *Auswärtiges Amt* being on the whole more ready to compromise with French demands, whereas the Ministry of Economics consistently opposed harmonization through supranationalism, with their principle argument being that free convertibility would allow exchange rates to reflect the different cost structures of national economies. The fear underlying this opposition to harmonization envisaged not only a limit of Germany's freedom of action in her economic relation to third countries, but, more importantly, its cost-increasing effect on the economy. The latter type of opposition to harmonization was also found in the Ministry of Finance, whereas the Ministry of Agriculture's opposition to integration was one of principle rather than method.

There was, however, wide-ranging agreement on the form of integration. While ministerial policies may have differed with regard to the degree and necessity of supranationalism, even the Economics Ministry did not, at any time, object to the concept of a Common Market in the form of a customs union. It was generally believed that low external tariffs would be negotiable given the liberal German/Benelux alliance. In 1955, Erhard and Müller-Armack viewed the question of free trade itself primarily as one of convertibility, and only secondly one of tariff reduction.[85]

The personalities most prominent in the exchanges between the two ministries were the State Secretary in the *Auswärtiges Amt*, Walter Hallstein, and the Minister of Economics, Ludwig Erhard. Their respective ability to influence the outcome of the internal German deliberations was subject to important constraints. One such factor was found in the relative detachment of the Chancellor from questions about the method of integration, once he had reaffirmed the imperative of German participation. Effectively, the Chancellor thereby enhanced the position of Hallstein *vis-à-vis* that of Erhard, for the former was better placed after having represented Germany at both the Messina conference and the first meeting of the Spaak Committee. Erhard's ability to influence German decision-making was further reduced by the fact that his own ministry was not united on the issue, with Hans von der Groeben being perhaps the most important internal proponent of supranational integration. Despite the apparent difficulties faced by Erhard, the outcome of the decision-making process was by no means certain, given that his view found support from the Ministries of Finance and Agriculture. The fact that a semblance of unity of the German Cabinet could be maintained until the end of the year has to be attributed largely to Hallstein's skilful manoeuvring. Backed by the Chancellor's commitment to integration as such, he had been able to use the issue of sectoral versus overall integration apparently to compromise over the former, thereby extracting the compliance of Erhard with the latter goal. Once the dispute shifted to the issue of how much supranationalism was needed for overall integration, Hallstein appeased the Cabinet by referring to the non-binding character of the committee findings, in the full knowledge that the forthcoming work on drafting the Spaak report would significantly reduce the ability of individual ministries to make their weight felt in Brussels. The British civil service, in contrast, has been shown to have had remarkably accurate information about the German position and about the character of the divisions therein. The main sources of information available to Whitehall included the Hallstein statement and the Jackling report, while Erhard's conversation with Chancellor Butler and Finance Minister Schäffer's visit to London provided opportunities to test German opinion directly. A further direct measure of German views on European integration lay in their contribution to the work of the Spaak Committee.

Not surprisingly, there were always various interpretations of the above information, though a consensus appears to have been reached after the initial confusion surrounding the Messina conference. The reassessment following the Hallstein statement and the Jackling report produced a more balanced view, which was widely shared across Whitehall departments. The Foreign Office and the Treasury both regarded the Erhard faction as a natural ally, for the German Ministry of Economics appeared to share their dislike of supranationalism. Yet both departments were also aware not only of the unbroken political enthusiasm for further integration shown by Adenauer and the *Auswärtiges Amt*, but also of the fact that a customs union was advocated by both factions in the debate. In the Treasury, there was a short-lived hope that Germany might be tempted away from the scheme, following the meeting between Erhard and Butler, in which the former made ambiguous statements which could be read as calling for such a move. It cannot be argued, however, that the Treasury was responsible for the decision to approach the Germans directly, for the Schäffer visit had reconfirmed the view that the conflict within the German government centred on the extent of harmonization and supranationality rather than questioning a Six-power customs union.

This consensus found its reflection in the Trend report and the recommendations of both the Mutual Aid Committee and the Economic Steering Committee. The report echoed the views of the Treasury and the Board of Trade that, while there was still some hope that the Common Market plan would collapse due to French obstructionism, Britain could not afford continued indifference towards the plans pursued on the Continent. Direct intervention was regarded as counterproductive, however, not least because it was estimated that the Germans felt that the political preference for integration should override any other consideration. The committees essentially recommended that British policy move from indifference to the formulation of an alternative scheme. Withdrawal from the Spaak Committee and a demand for consultation with the OEEC were suggested as a holding operation in the belief that only constructive proposals for trade liberalization and tariff reductions would have an effect on the Six and, among them, on Germany in particular.

None the less, the Economic Policy Committee decided to approach the German government in an attempt to prevent the establishment of a Common Market with the argument that a customs union of the Six would be economically and politically divisive for the Western Alliance. This development from an accurate interpretation of the available information to the formulation of an inappropriate tactical approach was the consequence of the combination of two factors. Firstly, there was a lack of communication between civil servants and decision-makers, apparent in the Trend report itself. The main preoccupation of the committees of officials was the co-ordination of departmental views on the economic problems the Common Market was expected to pose for Britain. Having ruled out participation as well as direct interference, the report gave only very little space to an appreciation of the positions of other countries.

The sparseness of the information in the report allowed a second factor to contribute to the decision to contact the German government. The meeting was chaired and dominated by Chancellor Butler. His uninterested and dismissive attitude towards the Messina project was well known, and manifested itself in his introductory remarks in which he recommended a warning to be issued to the Six that their project was regarded as divisive by the British government. Although it is not clear from the records who introduced the idea of contacting the German government, Butler's recollection of his meeting with Erhard in Istanbul can be expected to have played a part in the final decision. Clearly, the Trend report's warnings, both against direct interference in the efforts of the Six, and about the nature of the German position, had not been strong enough to prevent ministers from basing their decision on long-held assumptions about Britain's influence in Europe, and personal recollection of a singular and ambiguous expression of the German attitude. Against the advice of Whitehall officials, therefore, British policy towards the Messina project had developed from indifference to hostility.

The significance of the Economic Policy Committee meeting went far beyond the temporary deterioration of Anglo-European relations which was to follow during the winter of 1955. It was here that a new British attitude towards European integration emerged. While British governments had previously shown benevolence towards Continental European integration, from 1955 onwards increasing use was to be made of the two negative and interrelated arguments put forward by Chancellor Butler: firstly, that Continental European integration was divisive due to the resulting economic discrimination against non-participants; secondly, that economic division would ultimately lead to political division. These two arguments came to dominate British policy towards Europe, and towards Germany in particular. They were subsequently employed in arguing for a Free Trade Area arrangement, for the necessity to 'build bridges' between the EEC and EFTA, as well as for acceptable conditions of British membership.

2
Entering Wedge or Counterblast? Britain's Plan G

The failed attempt to persuade the German government to abandon the Common Market negotiations had left British policy towards European integration in disarray. The subsequent 16 months were dominated by two interrelated developments: the drafting of the Treaty of Rome and the emergence of a British inspired OEEC plan for a Free Trade Area surrounding and including the Six. In the context of this study, the central question is, of course, whether the latter was meant to undermine the former, and, in doing so, whether it was aimed specifically at German discontent with the negotiations on the Six-power customs union. This chapter will therefore examine the policy reappraisal in Britain and the motives behind the Free Trade Area idea. As in the first chapter, however, the starting point will be an appraisal of Bonn's European integration policy in 1956, in order to determine the appropriateness of the new British policy as a means to appeal to Germany.

Division and anxiety

Given the unresolved conflicts in the German government over certain elements of the Common Market plan, the year 1956 started with an attempt by Adenauer to put an end to the debate by issuing a guideline to all ministers concerned. The political motive for integration led him to state unequivocally that 'the framework of the OEEC is not sufficient' and that the integration of the Six should be pursued further.[1] While the guideline did not put an end to the conflict, in combination with other factors it did temporarily silence the debate so that the first half of 1956 saw the German government present a more unified stance than the year before.

The first of these factors concerned the Brussels negotiations themselves. Here, the discussions had reached a stage at which further expert deliberations were deemed unnecessary. At the meeting of the Foreign Ministers of the Six in February 1956, it was decided that a small committee of three should be asked to combine the findings of the various sub-committees into a single report which was then to be considered and, if approved, used as a basis for opening negotiations on the necessary treaties. The temporary lack of direct involvement of individual German ministries in the Brussels discussions clearly reduced their ability to force a debate about specific contentious elements of the plan onto the domestic agenda.

Another factor which helped to prevent a debate about the substance of the plan was a lack of opposition from pressure groups. In the previous year, lobbying by industry had provided the opponents of sectoral integration with powerful arguments. In the first half of 1956, by contrast, German industrial associations declared themselves guardedly in favour of the Common Market with the exception of the electricity generating industry, which still feared that sectoral integration and supranationality would be applied in their particular case. However, its objections were outweighed by the support for the Common Market expressed by the most powerful of interest groups, the *Bund Deutscher Industrie*, which favoured the plan as long as the outer tariff was kept low and the French demands for social harmonization and the adaptation fund were resisted as far as possible.[2]

Adenauer's politically motivated guideline had made it impossible for Erhard to attack details of the Common Market plan openly. Nevertheless, he did not cease in his efforts to steer the negotiations in a direction more acceptable to himself. Yet, before the publication of the final Spaak report and the start of intergovernmental negotiations, such attempts took the form of general comments about the necessity of a liberal, outward-looking Common Market.[3]

If these factors thus temporarily suppressed open conflict within the German government, this is not to say that the 'Euro-enthusiasts' in the *Auswärtiges Amt* and the *Bundeskanzleramt* were now more hopeful regarding the conclusion of the Common Market project. France was seen as the weakest link in the integration efforts of the Six and her attitude at the forthcoming Venice conference was the subject of intense speculation.[4] The *Auswärtiges Amt* was therefore anxious to accommodate French demands, so as to increase the chances of the Common Market in French domestic politics.[5]

However, it was Britain, with her dominant influence on the OEEC, which was seen as the main threat to the Common Market, following the diplomatic note of November 1955 which had attempted to persuade the German government to abandon the plan. The 'Euro-enthusiasts' were now expecting further sabotage, with Chancellor Adenauer remembering his Foreign Minister to have reported from the WEU conference in December 1955 that 'one had to be aware that England would continue to make attempts to hinder the integration efforts of continental Europe'.[6] One of the tactics anticipated in this respect was for Britain to challenge the Common Market plan on legal grounds, by claiming that it conflicted with OEEC rules.[7] How seriously the *Auswärtiges Amt* took the possibility of such a challenge was illustrated by the fact that the Ministry for Economic Co-operation was given the task of studying the legal questions involved. However, the study concluded in late May 1956 that such problems would only arise if, in the final stage, a particular country would invoke escape clauses allowing the reintroduction of quotas in the case of balance of payment difficulties.[8] These results were welcomed because evidence of British hostility towards the Common Market plan had been mounting since the end of 1955, including a Chatham House study which had argued that it would be in Britain's interest to prevent the establishment of a closer European Community.[9] Even the US government voiced its concern, warning the Germans that Britain would be 'absolutely hostile' towards the Common Market.[10] Despite the conviction that the Six were not in conflict with either GATT or OEEC regulations, the *Auswärtiges Amt* was at the same time acutely aware of the influence a British intervention might have on French politics and world opinion.[11]

It was therefore deemed important to use any opportunity to reassure Britain and others that the Common Market posed no threat and that its membership should not be restricted to the Six alone. The study of the Ministry for Economic Co-operation had already referred to the Spaak report's suggestion for a free trade arrangement to reduce tension between the Six and Britain. Taking up this argument in his speech at the Venice conference of Foreign Ministers of the Six, State Secretary Hallstein declared that the German government was convinced, that forms of co-operation and association can be found which would intensify the extremely important economic relations with Great Britain and strengthen the long-established co-operation with this country through other international economic organizations.[12]

However, after the Venice conference had decided to open formal negotiations, the fear of British sabotage was pushed into the background. At the same time, the *Auswärtiges Amt* was aware of an imminent change in the position of the British government, however imprecise its knowledge of the form it might take.[13]

In all, the first half of 1956 saw a German government which, though appearing more unified, continued to be divided over the nature of European integration. As before, Erhard's free trade philosophy stood against the Foreign Ministry's political preference for European integration binding Germany to the West, and to France in particular. Hence, the *Auswärtiges Amt* was more willing to compromise over the mounting French demands. Adenauer's support for his Foreign Ministry was motivated, not by a preference for any particular form of economic integration, but by the will to see Western cohesion and prosperity strengthened in the face of mounting East–West tensions. The *Auswärtiges Amt* had been responsible for gently pushing the Chancellor to favour the Common Market over the looser OEEC-style integration favoured by the British. Now Adenauer and the Common Market enthusiasts in the German government were worried about the possibility of British attempts to wreck the scheme. This concern can be shown to have been justified, for the intention to prevent the establishment of the Common Market was indeed widespread within the British government.

Formulating Plan G

In late 1955, the United States and Germany had been the targets of British attempts to prevent the establishment of the Common Market, while the other five prospective members had also been – albeit rather bluntly – notified of the new British position during a stormy informal meeting of OEEC delegates.[14] Even supporters of British involvement now seemed upset, with Dutch Foreign Minister Johan Willem Beyen displaying 'great perturbation and indignation'.[15] By the beginning of the new year, the futility of diplomatic pressure on the Six could no longer be denied. The German government, in an unusual and unequivocal step, had replied directly to the British note, declaring that:

> The Federal Government is not of the opinion that the result of the experts' discussions are so far opposed to the aims of freer trade and freer exchange of payments pursued by the Federal Government together with the British Government, or that they justify fears of a weakening of the OEEC.[16]

It was only then that the Foreign Office realized that 'the German view is diametrically opposed to HMG'.[17] However, for both Treasury and Foreign Office, the hope of successfully preventing the Six from going ahead with their plans had not evaporated altogether. The Prime Minister's visit to the United States in February 1956 can be seen as the last attempt to prevent the Common Market without replacing it with another European integration initiative. By then, it had become obvious that the US government was not to be influenced by arguments referring to potential trade discrimination which had been used in November, for the simple reason that the prime motive for American support for the Messina Six was political and not economic.[18] Hence, the Prime Minister was now urged to switch his approach and to question the American assumption that the Common Market would help to tie Germany to the West. It was agreed in the Mutual Aid Committee:

> to put as the first general argument against the Messina plans the view that they did not provide the most effective way of imposing control on Germany, and that, far from being controlled, Germany might in fact prove to be the dominating influence.[19]

The final version of the brief went even further, suggesting that 'some circles in Germany may regard it (the Common Market) as a means of re-establishing the hegemony of Germany'.[20]

In the event, however, the Prime Minister proved unable to impress his American counterparts.[21] Reporting back to the Cabinet, Eden acknowledged that the Washington discussion had shown that 'the United States Government entertained for these projects an enthusiasm similar to that which they had shown towards the European Defence Community'.[22]

Clearly, therefore, German concerns about the possibility of a

British attempt to wreck the Common Market had not been entirely unjustified for the early part of 1956, though the means chosen by the British government did not concentrate on the OEEC, but involved a more indirect approach designed to mobilize US support against the scheme. The subsequent decision to search for a new policy following the apparent failure of this approach did not mean, however, that the Common Market was now accepted as a reality. It can be shown that the idea of wrecking the scheme featured prominently in the formulation of what was to become known as Plan G.

Though the Prime Minister's consultations in Washington had finally convinced the British administration that any further attempt to 'sabotage' the Common Market would be fruitless and indeed counterproductive, this should not obscure the fact that some had realized this at an earlier stage.[23] Here, some evidence supporting Macmillan's claim of being one of the first ardent supporters of British involvement in Europe can be found.[24] It was he who, as early as January 1956, thought that the British approach was too negative, and who repeatedly and forcefully pressed for a study to be undertaken to explore possible forms of a new initiative.[25] In his new position as Chancellor of the Exchequer, he was well placed to advance this process, given that the formal machinery for such a policy review had already been established at the end of 1955 with a working group chaired by the Treasury's Third Secretary, 'Otto' Clarke, an ex-*Financial Times* journalist who had entered the civil service with the outbreak of the Second World War, and who, according to Sir Alec Cairncross, had already demonstrated 'real flair for general economic policy'.[26] Yet, it was only after Macmillan's repeated pressure that the Clarke working group started examining concrete proposals, and it was also due to his insistence on an 'objective' study that more far-reaching projects were considered.[27] In its final report of April 1956, the working group presented six possible courses of action, which included in shorthand (for the benefit of ministers):[28]

A. active co-operation within the OEEC
B. merging the Council of Europe and the OEEC
C. a European commodities tariff scheme
D. a free trade area for steel
E. a partial free trade area with an exclusion list
F. the so-called *Strasbourg tariff scheme* linking the Commonwealth with the OEEC

While alternative A represented Britain's previous policy – albeit suggesting greater efforts to be made at tariff reductions – the other schemes were novel in their approach, though C and F had previously been suggested by other countries.[29] B was clearly more an issue of cosmetics and it was therefore considered effective only in connection with one or more of the other alternatives. C, E and F suggested an item-by-item approach, necessitating the identification of products specific to European trade in the case of C, or, alternatively, of products which were seen as essential to the continuation of Anglo-Commonwealth trade, as in the case of E and F. The report itself deemed alternative F to be too ambitious, and while it contained no explicit preference for any of the other five, Clarke made clear that alternative E provided 'the only possible form of association with the Messina Common Market' and asserted that 'Europe would almost certainly jump at it'.[30]

Ministers meeting in the Treasury at the end of May asked for further study of alternative E, its compatibility with GATT rules, ways in which it could be made more attractive to the Commonwealth and its implications for British industry.[31] Most importantly, however, it was decided that the FTA should gradually cover all manufactured goods and materials, while excluding agriculture and horticulture. Dropping the idea of an exclusion list in favour of a more comprehensive arrangement had been the suggestion of Peter Thorneycroft, the President of the Board of Trade.[32]

Clearly, the Board of Trade had already arrived at the free trade idea, largely due to the work of its Under-Secretary Russell Bretherton, the former British representative at the Spaak Committee and now a member of Clarke's working group.[33] Yet, while he later claimed to have invented Plan G – as this new initiative became known – the substance of the scheme goes back to two newspaper articles by James Meade, the former head of the Cabinet Office's Section, then Professor at the London School of Economics. The suspicion that Meade's writings of February 1956 had been officially sanctioned can indeed be substantiated. Six weeks before his article appeared in the *Manchester Guardian*, Meade had approached Bretherton with the idea of British participation in a European free trade area. Bretherton, apparently Professor Meade's neighbour, had in turn passed this information on to the Treasury's Frank Figgures, Under-Secretary to Clarke.[34]

Yet, it was not merely the economics of Anglo-European relations that occupied the minds of officials and Cabinet ministers. In the evolution of the British decision on the new initiative, attitudes towards Germany had played a major role in the formulation and elimination of alternative courses of action. For the purpose of clarification, three different views can be distinguished. The first of these envisaged the possibility of the Common Market being dominated economically by German industry, threatening British exports to the expanding European market as a consequence of discrimination. This had, of course, been the theme of British attempts to convince the USA to withdraw her support from the Messina exercise in November 1955, and it was also the principle concern of Macmillan and Thorneycroft.[35] Leading Treasury officials were less concerned early in the year 1956, because there was still a widespread conviction that nothing concrete would result from the Messina proposals.[36] Yet, in the first three months of the year, there was mounting evidence to support the view that the chances of the Common Market were increasing. In France, the general election had produced a more reliable majority for the 'Pro-European' government in the *Assemblé Nationale*, while German industry seemed at last to have woken up to the opportunities of the scheme.[37] It was not surprising, therefore, that one of the most prominent themes of the Treasury-led working group was the perceived necessity of preventing German economic dominance over Europe.[38]

A second role played by attitudes towards Germany in the formulation of Plan G concerned the potential political and security dangers arising from British non-involvement in the process of European integration. Throughout the 1950s, much of the argument in favour of integration had been the twin goal of containment of Germany and of tying her firmly to the West. Traditionally, the British view had been that intergovernmental co-operation, as practised in NATO, OEEC and the Council of Europe, was sufficient means towards these ends, while supranational integration of Continental countries was a welcome addition.[39] In early 1956, however, the Foreign Office view on the latter point was about to change, with the Messina project increasingly being seen as unsuitable to the task of containment of Germany, and that, on the contrary, it would reduce cohesion in the Western Alliance.[40] What first appeared merely a switch of tactics in the Prime Minister's attempt to undermine US political support for the Six quickly gained momentum as a British view in its own right. The argument went as follows:[41] assuming Britain would not take part in the process of European integration, there were two possible scenarios. If the Common Market were to succeed, Germany would come to dominate it with the result that, at best, there would be neutralist tendencies while, at worst, a German-led Europe might aspire to becoming a third force, or indeed a vehicle for German resurgence. The second scenario envisaged a failure of the Common Market, which was expected to lead to a disillusionment of Western-minded Germans, especially the younger generation. The result would be a post-Adenauer Germany which would gravitate eastwards in order to seek an arrangement with the Soviet-Union over unification. Both these scenarios led leading officials to declare the German problem a 'major Foreign Office interest' in the formulation of any new initiative.[42] There was only one dissenting voice with Deputy Under-Secretary, Harold Caccia, declaring that 'going European' should not be based on 'speculative reasons of foreign affairs'.[43]

Moreover, the depiction of Germany as a security problem was found not only in the Foreign Office. Although Treasury officials, and in particular Clarke himself, were initially sceptical about this motive, Chancellor Macmillan shared the Foreign Office view:[44]

> What then are we to do? Are we just to sit back and hope for the best? If we do that it may be very dangerous for us; for perhaps Messina will come off after all and that will mean Western Europe dominated in fact by Germany and used as an instrument for the revival of power through economic means. It is really giving them on a plate what we fought two wars to prevent.[45]

His view was to prevail even over Clarke's scepticism, with the latter specifically referring to the two worst-case scenarios in May 1956.[46] In fact, in the report of his working group, the case in favour of a new British initiative rested almost exclusively on the argument of preventing German hegemony, with regard to both the political and the economic dimensions.[47]

In addition to these two assessments of Germany which seemed to necessitate a change in British policy, there was a further argument which was rather operational in character, in so far as it related to the question of the negotiability of any new scheme. Germany was regarded as the weakest link among the Six – weakest in the sense that it could most easily be convinced to support any new British initiative. Though the German response to the British telegram of November 1955 had clearly demonstrated to Whitehall the futility of any attempt to influence the German government without offering an alternative to the Common Market, this communication was not interpreted as signalling the end of divisions within the German government, but led to a more in-depth appreciation of the character thereof. Instrumental in this process was a report from the British embassy in Bonn, which explained the apparent silence of critics of the Common Market as the result of the character of the scheme:

> It is interesting that Professor Erhard is so-far lying low on the whole project. The Common Market is not really consonant with his own philosophy of the widest measure of economic liberalisation; at the same time, he can hardly come out in opposition to a scheme which seems politically desirable to Dr. Adenauer and which would not put Germany in any kind of economic straight jacket.[48]

This report seemed to indicate to the Foreign Office that while the division was still there it could only be utilized with a British counterinitiative which offered concrete advances on the global-approach level.[49] An opportunity to assess the validity of this interpretation came with Ludwig Erhard's visit to London in February 1956.[50] He seemed to reaffirm that he was still very much in favour of an OEEC approach and that he would welcome a British proposal along these lines. Referring to the OEEC, he

> hoped the opportunity would be taken to 'let some fresh air' into the discussions on European integration. It would certainly be made clear that Germany was opposed to European inbreeding, and it would only take part in any European group if that group preserved free and friendly relations with countries outside and did not discriminate against them.[51]

Erhard's view certainly did not come as a surprise and, by itself, it offered no guarantee that a British initiative would be welcome in Germany, given the dominance of Adenauer and Brentano which had been apparent in the reply to the November telegram. Yet, even as far as these proponents of the Common Market were concerned, there was mounting evidence that they would welcome a British initiative. A report by Britain's Ambassador to Bonn, Frederick Hoyer-Millar illustrated the extend to which Adenauer's electoral fortune depended on success on the European level, and that, given the waning support for the Common Market scheme in the *Bundestag*, he would welcome the additional impetus of a new initiative.[52] Again, an opportunity arose to test the validity of this interpretation when Foreign Minister Brentano came to visit London in early May 1956.[53] He affirmed that the German government would welcome any ideas for a link between the OEEC and the Common Market. Going even further, he said that 'the Federal Government valued our [the British] ideas so much that they would be prepared to modify their own if it would help to make things easier'. His comments were not interpreted as mere diplomatic politeness, for he specifically referred to the newspaper article by Professor Meade, asking 'whether the views there expressed were likely to be acceptable to HMG?'[54]

However, the indications that both opponents and proponents of the Common Market in the German government would welcome a change in British policy did not point to any particular one of the schemes under consideration at the time. The impression that Germany was the weak link within the Messina group clearly allowed for two alternative courses of action. Either to exploit this weak link by preventing the establishment of the Common Market and replacing it with another, less ambitious scheme, or, alternatively, to use German support to negotiate an arrangement which would leave the Common Market intact but which was economically advantageous to Britain. Commenting on the report of his working group, Clarke elaborated on the first of these two alternatives:

> We could make up a package of courses A, B, C and perhaps D, which could certainly be presented as a very significant initiative. We should then have to push ahead as fast as we could with the 'collective approach', in the hope that this world-wide freeing of trade would divert Germany from the regional European concepts – and that this diversion of Germany plus the lassitude of France would kill the Messina project. If we cannot do E (the only possible form of association with the Messina Common Market) we must kill the Messina project stone-dead; and the real question is whether we could stupefy it by a 'European' momentum in ABC(D), and then sweep it away by really vigorous action on the world scale.[55]

The Foreign Office initially favoured this approach, and it was only due to the intervention of the President of the Board of Trade that ministers decided on further study of Plan E. Thorneycroft's argument was that Plan C entailed too many technical difficulties, and, even with regard to Plan E, he argued for the simplification of the scheme in so far as the outright exclusion of agriculture and horticulture would no longer require the difficult task of negotiating a product exclusion list.[56] The Foreign Office did not object, mainly because it saw its principle aim of containing Germany fulfilled. Hence, in late May ministers asked Clarke's working group to formulate detailed proposals for a Cabinet decision on what now became known as Plan G.[57] The group was instructed to work under the assumption that the Common Market were to come into existence.[58]

While the new British policy was therefore not designed to undermine the Common Market, the decision against a 'counterblast' had been a close one. Throughout the formulation of the new policy, Germany had featured prominently in the minds of British officials. There was a curious mixture of economic and political fears of Germany, which on the one hand necessitated a change in the British approach to European integration, but which on the other hand anticipated that Germany was the most ardent supporter of British involvement. Erhard's enthusiasm for a wider scheme was taken for granted. Perhaps, more importantly, Brentano's efforts to reassure the British government in order to safeguard the completion of the Common Market had worked to strengthen this impression. So much so that his assurances had nearly backfired, as the working group had contemplated a frontal attack on the Common Market in the belief that Germany would follow Britain's lead. In the event, it had been only due to the rather technical objections of the Board of Trade that this approach was rejected.

Testing the ground

The working group under the chairmanship of Clarke, now renamed 'Economic Steering Sub-Committee on the United Kingdom Initiative in Europe', resumed its deliberations immediately after the ministerial decision.[59] Based on the assumption that the Common Market would be established, its aim was to examine the compatibility of Plan G with GATT rules, its effects on British industry, agriculture and her balance of payments, and to anticipate its likely reception among Commonwealth governments, in Europe and in the USA.⁶⁰ Initially, the Sub-Committee concentrated on the first two of these points, since only by knowing the exact provisions of the scheme could there be any assessment of its likely reception.⁶¹ Ministers were given notice of these results in an interim report which cleared the way as far as GATT rules were concerned, and which argued that, overall, industry would stand to gain from the Free Trade Area.⁶² It also contained a preliminary assessment of the position of other countries, anticipating that the USA would welcome the plan, while predicting that some of the Commonwealth countries might fear for their trade relations with Britain. On likely European reactions to the scheme, the report echoed the degree of optimism which had characterized the first Clarke working group. The persistence of optimism was largely due to two factors. The Six had demonstrated their continued interest in British participation by extending an invitation to join the discussion on the Spaak report, following their Venice conference. With a major new policy initiative in process of formulation, the British government felt confident enough to decline this invitation.⁶³ There was, moreover, a direct opportunity to test European opinion on the FTA idea, provided by the OEEC Council meeting in July 1956. Prompted by the British government, its Chairman, René Sergeant, ensured that the Council set up a working party to examine the question of surrounding the Common Market with such a scheme – a suggestion which was contained in the Spaak report itself.⁶⁴ The result of this, very thinly disguised, exploratory initiative was promising.⁶⁵ Claiming to speak on behalf of the Six, the Dutch Foreign Minister Beyen stated that 'this is the best thing that could have happened to our endeavours'.⁶⁶ Perhaps the most promising reaction was yet again shown by the Germans. Bretherton reported that 'they have "jumped for" our ideas ... we can rely on solid support from them'.⁶⁷ The French reaction, however, he could only describe as 'cool and reserved'.

Nevertheless, the British delegate to the OEEC, Ellis-Rees, claimed that British participation in the FTA would have a positive effect on French attitudes towards European integration by providing a counterweight to German dominance – a view which had been affirmed by their State Secretary for Europe Maurice Faure in June.⁶⁸ On balance, therefore, the interim report was upbeat:

> We should expect the Plan to be enthusiastically received by some European countries, particularly the more highly industrialised.

The Plan would be a major encouragement to the 'European Movement' and to the supporters of the Messina initiative, who would see their hopes of tying Germany into Western Europe... enormously strengthened.[69]

The report called for further study of the likely reactions to Plan G, and it was indeed followed by a more in-depth examination of this question. At home, there were clear indications that industry on the whole would welcome the Plan, a view which was based mainly on a favourable response from the Federation of British Industry.[70] Abroad, the assessment took the form of questionnaires which were sent out to British representatives in August.[71] The responses to these were mixed. The Commonwealth Secretary felt confident that most governments would welcome the plan, especially if it could be stressed that a more prosperous Europe would benefit the Commonwealth.[72] Only the Canadian reply was still outstanding, and it was expected to be less than enthusiastic given that Canadian exports to Britain largely consisted of manufactured goods. The response of the British embassy in Washington provided a more balanced judgement with Washington not being expected to show great enthusiasm for the economics of the scheme but at least to give measured support to the political implications of Britain moving closer to Europe.[73] Despite some misgivings about the exclusion of agriculture, most European countries were still expected to welcome Plan G, though France emerged as a major problem not least due to the demands she had made concerning the inclusion of overseas territories and harmonization of social charges in the Common Market negotiations. However, it was thought that, provided the determination of Britain and all other countries to push ahead even without France, she could be coerced into joining. Only the British Ambassador to Paris, Sir Gladwyn Jebb, doubted whether 'the eleven, or so, other countries would be prepared to hold this collective pistol at France's head'.[74] If followed through to its conclusion, the argument indeed appears dubious in retrospect, for the technical difficulties of origin control involved in surrounding a customs union of Six with a Free Trade Area of which only five were to be members would have been difficult, if not impossible, to overcome. Logic suggests, therefore, that the argument of coercing France by the determination to push ahead without her only applied if the Common Market was abandoned.[75] There is room to speculate whether the British government would have seized the opportunity to present Plan G as an alternative in autumn 1956 had there been a thorough assessment of the logic of this argument. No such assessment was made, not least because the pessimistic tone of the French reply was balanced by that of Britain's embassy in Bonn which was, yet again, encouraging. Not only was it anticipated that the German government would welcome the scheme for the political benefit of British participation and for the economic benefit of access to a wider market but also that the exclusion of agriculture would not present a problem here.[76]

The replies to the questionnaires were incorporated into the final report which was hence a little less upbeat about the prospects of the scheme than the interim document.[77] The Cabinet considered the report in September 1956, and, now that it was asked to make a decision on whether to go public, there was some belated opposition to the scheme as a whole. Once again, however, it was possible for Macmillan and Thorneycroft to convince their colleagues of the necessity of Plan G, by once again referring to the perception of Germany as an economic and ultimately political threat to Britain's position in Europe and the world. Prime Minister Eden only reluctantly agreed that there really was no alternative to Plan G.[78] The decision went in favour of Macmillan and enabled him to present the plan to the public following a meeting of Commonwealth Finance Ministers in Washington on 3 October 1956.[79]

German reactions to Plan G

In the meantime, the Venice conference had opened the way for real negotiations on the Common Market. Nonetheless, German 'Euro-enthusiasts' in the *AA* were still uncertain and anxious for swift progress, for the summer of 1956 also saw renewed interministerial conflict. While Erhard had bowed to the political imperative set by the Chancellor in January 1956, he now sought to concentrate the decision-making powers in the *Wirtschaftskabinett*, or Economic Cabinet, which was dominated by his ministry and in which he could count on the support of the Ministries of Finance, of Labour and of Agriculture on questions of substance.[80] The *Auswärtiges Amt*, by contrast, argued that the Messina initiative was still predominantly political in character, and that responsibility for the negotiations should therefore remain with the Foreign Minister. In a personal letter to the Chancellor, Brentano expressed the view that only his ministry would ensure that 'the overriding political aspects which favour a continuation of the policy of European integration will find the necessary attention in all stages of the negotiations'.[81] In line with an earlier Cabinet resolution, he suggested that the *Auswärtiges Amt* was to co-ordinate with other ministries at State Secretarial level, while the Cabinet would be kept informed regularly. While the Foreign Minister succeeded in pressing the political imperative on the Chancellor, the debate also concerned personalities, as Spaak wished once again to enlist the help of Hans von der Groeben to head the Common Market sub-committee. Though of the Economics Ministry, von der Groeben did not meet the acceptance of Ludwig Erhard and his State Secretary Ludger Westrick, for he was known to be a keen supporter of the Common Market. Yet, after lobbying the Chancellor on von der Groeben's behalf, the *Auswärtiges Amt* retained the upper hand even here.[82]

The internal conflict within the German government intensified in reaction to the French demands for the harmonization of social costs and for the inclusion of overseas territories which were made at the Venice conference.[83] The Ministry of Economics seized the initiative by producing counterproposals, which, while not deviating too much from the Spaak report itself, set out the ministry's views on tariffs and on the issue of relations to third countries. The paper argued that the former should be reduced to below the GATT level, while responsibility for the latter should be given to the Council of Ministers acting on qualified majority. The arguments against harmonization and the inclusion of overseas territories were of a general nature, given that no detailed proposals had yet been tabled by the French. Nonetheless, the German Foreign Ministry was concerned that driving such a hard bargain would put an end to the negotiations, and consequently refused to discuss the Economics Ministry's proposals at interministerial meetings.[84]

The German government was thus as divided as ever, when Britain introduced the idea of the FTA covering the OEEC countries and including the Six as one unit. The *Auswärtiges Amt* first learned of the new initiative through a confidential report from its London embassy on 13 July 1956.[85] Given the fear of 'sabotage' during the previous months, officials clearly welcomed the change of heart of the British administration. More importantly, they regarded the plan as a means to increase the chances of the Common Market scheme in the French National Assembly – a view which continued to be held until the OEEC meeting of February 1957.[86] The benefit of hindsight after President Charles de Gaulle's rejection of the Free

Trade Area in 1958 should not obscure the fact that this view about the psychological effect of British participation was widely held in 1956, not least due to the EDC failure, which had, at least partly, been attributed to British non-involvement.[87] The most direct indication thereof was given by the French State Secretary for Europe, Maurice Faure, in a meeting with his counterparts of the other five, claiming that 'many French demand the participation of Britain in the European unification efforts'.[88] Yet, the *Auswärtiges Amt* also saw potential dangers in British participation, since this looser, less regulated and less supranational scheme might attract critics of the Common Market both at home and abroad. It was the new Head of the Sub-Department 'European political integration', Wilhelm Hartlieb, who was most outspoken in his comments to this effect: 'We must, however, take care that our concept of a Common Market of the Six shall not one day dissolve in the wider OEEC container.'[89] While Hartlieb continued to voice these suspicions about Britain throughout the ensuing FTA negotiations, it was not generally suspected that such diversion from the Common Market had been the motivation behind the British initiative. Instead, a clear connection was seen between the likely establishment of the Common Market and the British desire to avert economic damage.[90] An additional advantage of the FTA scheme lay in that it allowed the *Auswärtiges Amt* to counter the free trade argument against the Common Market in so far as the critics of the outer tariff could now be reassured with reference to a tariff-free OEEC wide-Europe.[91]

However, the tariff question had not reached centre stage in the Common Market negotiations.[92] Instead, it was the French demand for a harmonization of social costs which dominated the discussion. These were based on the concern that the social system of France would leave her producers at a cost-disadvantage, if tariffs and quotas were to be abolished. In order to prevent their exports from out-pricing French products in the Common Market, the other five were therefore asked to revise their social systems upwards. The most contentious elements of the French proposals were the equalization of pay for men and women, of overtime rates paid and of the length of the working week. For Germany, accepting these demands meant not only a worsening of the cost-structure of industry, but also an infringement upon the constitutionally guaranteed autonomy of the wage bargaining process. Consequently, all concerned ministries rejected the French proposals when they became public.[93] Within the *Auswärtiges Amt*, it was the Trade Policy Department which argued for a tough negotiation stance on these issues, and even the Political Department had reservations.[94] The problems created by the French demands were of such magnitude that after the OEEC's meeting in July, Chancellor Adenauer himself observed that the Common Market was 'politically finished', and that one now had to 'try to arrive at a Common Market indirectly, via the British Free Trade Area plan'.[95] For his meeting with Prime Minister Guy Mollet in September, the Chancellor was briefed to the effect that Germany should stand firm against the French demands with the argument that 'harmonization is the consequence of – and not a precondition for – the Common Market'.[96] Fierce opposition to the French ideas was also found in the *Bundesministerium für Arbeit* (Ministry of Labour, BMA) and the Ministry of Economics.[97] A working party of the latter produced a report on the French position in which harmonization of social costs and special escape clauses for the French were rejected outright, while less powerful institutions were suggested.[98] When the report was about to be translated into a Cabinet memorandum, which in substance recommended the abandonment of the Common Market plan in favour of an OEEC-style integration, there was growing fear in the Political Department of the *Auswärtiges Amt* that the issue of harmonization, combined with the existence of the more attractive FTA proposals, might put the negotiations in jeopardy.[99] It now began to advocate a more moderate line, arguing that equal pay for men and women had already been accepted in Germany as a long-term goal. Yet, no compromise was apparently to be found on the issue of the equalization of total costs, of over-time rates and the 40-hour working week.

With the Brussels negotiations in deadlock, it was agreed that the Foreign Ministers of the Six were to meet in Paris in late October to find a compromise. The month before the conference saw perhaps the fiercest polemics against the Common Market from within the German government. Most noteworthy in this respect are two tightly argued letters, with which Erhard and Minister of Labour, Anton Storch, respectively tried to convince Adenauer of the economic damage resulting from harmonization.[100] The *Auswärtiges Amt* appeared to lose the argument about the economics of the Common Market plan, with the Chancellor commenting that the reservations of the two letters 'appear very noteworthy to me, and I believe they have to be considered in the negotiations with State Secretary Faure'.[101] Erhard seized the opportunity provided by the British FTA plan, which allowed him to present an alternative to the Brussels negotiations. Given the high-profile launch of the British Plan G in Washington, it was in his view 'impossible to ignore (the British proposals) and to complete the Brussels [i.e. Common Market] concept without alterations'.[102] With mounting troubles in Brussels and Erhard's attempts to wreck the scheme with the help of the British proposal, the proponents of the Common Market changed their line of argument from the economic to the political. The Vice-President of the ECSC High Authority, Franz Etzel, argued not only that mounting East–West tension necessitated European integration but also that the British initiative was merely a reaction to the Common Market, and that, if the latter were abandoned, the British would quietly drop the FTA plan.[103] Foreign Minister Brentano also sought to convince his Cabinet colleagues that the 'English preparedness was an indirect consequence of the Brussels negotiations'.[104]

Though the Foreign Minister managed to convince the Chancellor of the political imperative to complete the Common Market scheme, the Paris conference still went far from smoothly. Despite opposition from Spaak, the other five delegations and the *Auswärtiges Amt*, Erhard had managed to secure his participation.[105] While his official status as an expert advisor to the German delegation barred him from speaking in open session, the influence over his ministry's negotiators prevented the German delegation from internally formulating a compromise to be offered to the French.[106] The near breakdown of the conference meant that the issues could now only be settled at the highest level. Adenauer was to use a meeting with his French counterpart, Guy Mollet, for this purpose, and it was Brentano's skilful lobbying which ensured that the political arguments were to be decisive. The Foreign Minister passed on to the Chancellor a letter he had received from the leader of the Belgian Christian Socialist Party, Theo Lefèvre, who warned that Christian Democracy in general, and the German ruling party in particular, should not be blamed for the collapse of European integration at a time when Communism was on the offensive throughout the world.[107] At the same time, the Economics Ministry discredited itself, when Rolf Gocht, the ministry's delegate to the Common Market committee in Brussels, declared that the negotiations would be stopped, and the Free Trade Area negotiated instead. Apparently acting without instructions, the delegate had thus openly deviated from the line agreed in the Cabinet.[108] The third and perhaps most important factor which facilitated the Franco-German compromise lay in public comments of the British Chancellor Macmillan, which are reported to have convinced Adenauer that if the Common Market were to fail Britain would drop the FTA plan.[109] At a time of increasing East–West tension in the world, the Free Trade Area alone was therefore not a viable option for Adenauer in his effort to further European integration. Hence, the Foreign Ministry's political arguments prevailed over the economic reservations of the Ministries of Economics and of Labour in the compromise over harmonization, which the two Heads of Governments reached in early November. The political character of this compromise was confirmed afterwards by Karl Carstens, reporting that 'the consultations in Paris have proceeded very favourably, not least because of the gloomy world situation'.[110]

Even after the November compromise, Erhard continued to argue for the necessary changes to be made in Brussels to accommodate Britain and other OEEC countries as full members.[111] Yet, his argument was progressively weakened by mounting evidence that the British would indeed drop their FTA plan if the Common Market were abandoned. Etzel, for example, reported that he had asked the President of the Board of Trade, Thorneycroft:

> whether England would associate with a Europe which merely consisted of Free Trade Areas, i.e. whether she would participate even if Europe did not create a Common Market in form of a customs union. Mister Thorneycroft answered in a strict negative.[112]

The dispute within the German government was apparently not even halted by a meeting between Adenauer, Brentano and Erhard at which the Chancellor once again underlined the necessity of integration against the background of the Suez and Hungarian crises. The aftermath of this meeting saw perhaps the most acrimonious exchanges between Erhard, on the one hand, and Etzel, on the other, to the extent of personal accusations of incompetence and untruthfulness.[113] However, given that the matter had already been settled at the highest level, these exchanges were only ineffectual reverberations of a previously contentious issue. Nevertheless, in autumn 1956, the Common Market had only narrowly escaped the fate of being abandoned in favour of a wider Free Trade Area.

British motives revisited

To speculate whether or not Erhard could have succeeded in replacing the planned Common Market with the FTA is ultimately bound up with the question of motives behind the British initiative, meant either as a complementary and defensive policy, or as a substitute and therefore aggressive new scheme. In autumn 1956, the question indeed arose of whether the FTA negotiations should be continued in the event of a collapse of the Common Market scheme of the Six. This was a variation on an argument of the first Clarke working group, which had contemplated preventing the Common Market by offering an alternative to Germany. At that time, and largely for practical reasons, the decision had gone in favour of a scheme that was complementary to the Common Market.[114] However, the idea of the FTA as a counterinitiative had never really disappeared.[115] It's re-emergence owed much to the fact that the Common Market project was itself running into difficulties.[116] There was mounting evidence that some sections of German opinion, and also to a lesser extent French opinion, now contemplated abandoning the scheme in favour of the British plan.[117] In the case of Germany, these indications were given substance when British officials learned about Erhard's role in the Paris meeting of the Six in late October 1956.[118] Alan Edden claimed that there was now a need for the British administration to contemplate its reaction to these developments: 'If . . . it was decided that a Free Trade Area with no Customs Union would be on balance the best outcome from the United Kingdom point of view we should begin to direct our policy towards this end.'[119]

His point was taken up by the Economic Steering Sub-Committee on Closer Association with Europe. Its views can be summarized in the following three propositions. First, a Common Market or customs union of the Six in the absence of a Free Trade Area was politically as well as economically undesirable. Secondly, it was thought that, as far as Britain's economic interests were concerned, the balance was slightly in favour of an FTA which did not include a customs union.[120] Thirdly, however, the advantages of greater cohesion of Western Europe, which the customs union was thought to entail, made it politically desirable to further its establishment as long as the FTA materialized.[121]

In any case, as Chairman of the Sub-Committee, Clarke had argued that 'it . . . would be most dangerous (perfide Albion once more) if it was widely believed that we were in favour of the supersession of the Messina project by a free trade area project'.[122] There was a need to reassure the 'Euro-enthusiasts' that it was not Britain's intention to sabotage the Continental project, leading the Foreign Office to instruct British representatives abroad to stress that the scheme assumed the existence of the Common Market.[123] While Clarke's comments had reaffirmed the Foreign Office view on how to present the FTA policy in public, they failed to address the problem of future British policy in the event of the Common Market collapsing on its own. The Sub-Committee speculated that the Six might run into difficulties in a few months and that 'this might in turn lead to proposals from Europe that we should go ahead and negotiate the 12-country Free Trade Area, leaving the Customs Union and superstructure of the Six to be filled in later'.[124]

The Sub-Committee hence asked for further study not only of this question but also of the likely reaction of the USA and other countries to the possibility of an FTA without a customs union.[125] There is no indication that such a study was ever undertaken, which may have been the consequence of an increased likelihood of the establishment of the Common Market, following the compromise reached by Adenauer and Mollet in November 1956.[126]

There are two noteworthy features about this episode. Even though the FTA had greater appeal without a customs union, ministers were at all times instructed to assert that the scheme assumed the existence of the Common Market.[127] This was partly a reaction to the experience of European disenchantment with Britain during the 'sabotage' attempts of the winter of 1955/6. Yet, it also represented a temporary British emphasis on the role of European integration in fostering Western cohesion originating in the experience of the Suez fiasco.[128] The second noteworthy feature is that the British government, though shying away from 'sabotage', at this stage seems to have been prepared to continue negotiating the FTA even if the Common Market had failed. This not only contradicts recent interpretations of the British initiative as just another 'sabotage' attempt, but it also lends posthumous weight to Erhard's argument in the internal debate in the German administration which has been discussed above.[129] Plan G itself was not merely a supplement to the Common Market, and there is some evidence to assume that had the Germans decided to abandon the Six the FTA could have been negotiated instead. However, the British government had not been prepared to confirm this publicly in 1956.

Finalizing the Treaty of Rome

In the meantime, new French and Belgian demands for the inclusion of overseas territories had come to dominate the Common Market negotiations after the harmonization issue had been settled. In Germany, the main source of opposition to these proposals was found in the Ministry of Finance, which feared being required to provide the bulk of the funds needed for the development of these dependencies.[130] Even the *Auswärtiges Amt* initially disliked the idea, since it was feared that Germany would be drawn into undesirable colonial disputes and that the territories in question would exploit Germany's position as paymaster.[131] Criticism of the Franco-Belgian ideas was also found in the Ministry of Economics, with the Head of its Economic Policy Department, Alfred Müller-Armack, arguing that the sums involved would threaten Germany's economic growth, while Erhard insisted that development funds should only be used to support profitable, free-market ventures with a long-term aim of self-sufficiency.[132]

In Britain, it was feared that the provisions for the custom union which were negotiated by the Six would prejudice the FTA.[133] As early as October 1956, Macmillan urged Spaak to shelve the idea for inclusion of overseas territories for the time being.[134] The French and Belgian plan clearly presented a problem for Britain. Any arrangement giving access to European markets to countries which were producing predominantly primary goods, clearly discriminated against the agricultural exporters in the Commonwealth even if there was a Free Trade Area. The simple solution of making similar arrangements in the FTA was unacceptable for Britain and her Commonwealth partners.[135] The Commonwealth countries overwhelmingly decided against joining the FTA, mainly because it meant increased competition from European manufactures in their domestic markets, and, in the case of the dominions, it entailed discrimination against the more important trading partner, the USA. For Britain, such arrangements were also unacceptable because she stood to lose the competitive advantage of cheap imports of agricultural produce and raw materials, and her manufactures would face European competition in the Commonwealth markets.

At the end of November, Chancellor Harold Macmillan approached Economic Ministers of the Six in an effort to muster support against the inclusion of overseas territories.[136] Some hope was raised by the fact that German opposition to the scheme was noted on a number of occasions.[137] And Erhard indeed used the Macmillan letter to press for a postponement of negotiations on this issue, while Müller-Armack argued for the participation of a British representative in the Brussels negotiations, so as to avoid jeopardizing the FTA.[138] Yet, the Economics Ministry did not succeed due to three separate factors. Firstly, in dealing with the British request, the Six were already acting as one unit. The official reply to Macmillan's letter was in fact drafted jointly by the Foreign Ministers of the Six. In his answer, Erhard had to follow instructions that consultations on this question between the Six and Britain would not be possible at that stage.[139] Secondly, negotiators were able to reduce the financial commitments significantly. The compromise which eventually emerged on the German contribution was, in fact, equal to the upper limit the Finance Minister Schäffer had deemed acceptable at the outset.[140] The third factor, which once again proved decisive, lay in the Foreign Ministry's argument that a compromise with France and Belgium was necessary for political reasons. The fact that the *Auswärtiges Amt* lobbied on behalf of these two countries merely because of the overall desire to see the Common Market established, and not out of any enthusiasm for the inclusion of overseas territories itself, can be seen in the reservations which were voiced internally.[141] Clearly, the *Auswärtiges Amt* was avoiding economic arguments just as it had done during the harmonization debate. While working to exclude industrial interest groups from the decision-making process, its arguments were couched once again in political terms – an approach which appeared to have been continuously successful with the Chancellor.[142] Against the background of mounting tension in the Middle East and the Soviet intervention in Hungary, Brentano referred to the inclusion of overseas territories as part of a worldwide defence against growing Soviet influence. In a letter to the Chancellor, he stated:

> There can be no doubt about the fact that there is a conflict between the Communist states and the Western Alliance over the overseas territories, and over the countries of Africa in particular. The outcome of this conflict will be of great, if not decisive importance for future global power constellations.[143]

Having obtained the approval of the Chancellor, the *Auswärtiges Amt* supported the delaying tactics of the Brussels negotiators who claimed that they first had to formulate a common position.[144] In the new year, Erhard continued to raise British hopes for German intervention when he assured Peter Thorneycroft, the Chancellor of the Exchequer in the new government under Macmillan, that it was:

> not proper that the six should put the countries which are interested in the creation of a free trade area before established facts which will constitute a priori decisions for them or unduly limit their leeway in the shaping of the free trade area.[145]

However, Erhard's comments proved to be without official backing from Brussels. In the event, British representatives had to look on when the Six themselves finally settled the question of the inclusion of overseas territories in the Common Market.[146] After last-minute reservations of the Dutch delegation had been dispelled and Adenauer had once again used a top-level meeting with his French counterpart to strike a compromise on this issue, the successful completion of the Common Market appeared assured.[147] Thereafter, the British government made no further efforts to convince the Six to shelve the plan since the Foreign Office was anxious not to be seen to be trying to divide the Six.[148]

The OEEC Ministerial Council meeting

While the Treaty of Rome was being finalized, the British government had concentrated its efforts on advancing Plan G both at home and abroad. At home, industry's support for the scheme had been reaffirmed on various occasions, and even the Trade Union Congress indicated its approval of the policy. Moreover, with the exception of the Beaverbrook press, the media clearly welcomed closer association with Europe.[149] This generally positive mood in the country provided Chancellor Macmillan with the opportunity to seek parliamentary approval for opening negotiations. There was still some scepticism among Conservatives in the Commons, based either on support for the Commonwealth or on lobbying for particular industries threatened by free trade. Both kinds of objections led Macmillan once again to use the argument of German economic and ultimately political hegemony in Europe in the absence of the scheme.[150] Yet, he was careful not only to stress this negative motivation but also attempted to present the opportunities inherent in the scheme.

Once the approval of the House was secured in late 1956, attention turned to the task of securing OEEC agreement on the start of formal negotiations. Expert discussions in working party No. 17 were proceeding smoothly with a report being awaited for January 1957. There was no doubt that the working party would come out in favour of the opening of intergovernmental negotiations on a Free Trade Area and encouraging signs of strong German support were reported by British representatives there.[151] Elsewhere, reactions were also promising. Canada, which had hitherto been the cause of some concern, had come out marginally in favour of the scheme, while perhaps most unexpected was the positive reaction of the American President Dwight D. Eisenhower who described the FTA plan as a 'challenging idea'.[152]

However, European reactions were less enthusiastic than had been hoped previously.[153] Two distinct problems were to occupy the minds of British negotiators for months to come. Firstly, it was becoming increasingly obvious that the outright exclusion of agriculture was unpopular in many European countries, yet, given that no country was actually advocating free trade in agriculture, it was felt in Britain that satisfactory compensatory agreements could be worked out at a later date.[154] Nonetheless, in order to secure the OEEC Council's agreement on the opening of inter-governmental negotiations, the scheme had to be made more attractive to those members of the organization who were concerned about agriculture. Faced with mounting criticism, there was some movement in the British position in the new year, in so far as they committed themselves to 'further trade in agriculture in Europe'.[155]

The second problem concerned the timing of the Common Market and the FTA. The British government sought the agreement of the Six that negotiations for the two schemes would now be synchronized in order not only to prevent decisions being taken with respect to the former which would prejudice the latter, but also to avoid a situation in which the Common Market would start to discriminate against other OEEC members before the FTA had come into operation.

On both counts, the OEEC Council meeting of February 1957 could only be described as a failure from a British point of view. With regard to the second task, it became clear that the new British government under Prime Minister Harold Macmillan had underestimated the suspicion amongst the 'Euro-enthusiasts' on the Continent, that the FTA plan was designed to 'sabotage' the Common Market. Foreign Ministers of the Six, and Spaak in particular, were anxious to avert too close a relation between the proposed scheme and the Common Market, for they feared that this would lead to a delay in signing and ratifying the latter which was deemed dangerous given the instability of the French government.[156] This fear of British-inspired 'sabotage' was heightened once again by internal disputes within the German delegation. In his speech to the Council of the OEEC, Erhard labelled the FTA scheme 'a significant, not to say the decisive political and economic initiative for the integration of Europe'.[157] By itself, the speech would not have threatened the Common Market, had it not been for a question by Erhard which prompted the British representative to declare that the FTA would also be established if the Common Market failed to materialize.[158] With the press also supporting this view, Erhard's arguments of autumn 1956 were given retrospective validity, in so far as it now appeared as if the Brussels initiative could be abandoned in favour of Plan G.[159] Further ambiguous comments made by Chancellor Thorneycroft about the possibility of an FTA without a customs union only strengthened the 'Euro-enthusiasts' determination to prevent a link between the two schemes.

Perhaps the most disappointing outcome of the OEEC meeting was the failure to secure agreement on the opening of negotiations. The tactical mistake here was the British memorandum which was later published as a Government White Paper.[161] Written for European, domestic and Commonwealth audiences simultaneously, the memorandum rather over-stressed the British determination to exclude agriculture and furthermore contained undisguised opposition to any harmonization or supranationality. This advance publication of the official British negotiation position alienated many a former advocate of the FTA, with even the Danish government arguing against the opening of negotiations.[162] Partly, this was because the British paper represented a step backwards from the earlier suggestion that compensatory arrangements for agriculture could be worked out. Now, it merely stated that Britain would 'continue to play a full part in the work of the Ministerial Food and Agriculture Committee', an OEEC forum which was not known for achieving spectacular results!ced[163] In the event, the OEEC Council merely decided to set up yet another three working parties to examine the possibilities of negotiating a Free Trade Area, of securing a satisfactory agreement for the agricultural sector, and for the treatment of overseas territories.

If the OEEC meeting as a whole had been disappointing, it had once again demonstrated the extent to which the German Minister of Economics was supportive of the British initiative.[164] Thereafter, Erhard persisted with his open criticism, referring to the Common Market project as 'macro-economic nonsense' and 'European incest' on the occasion of a public lecture in New York – comments which prompted Adenauer to call him to order in a private meeting.[165] Internally, however, the Ministry of Economics had resigned itself to the fact that the Treaty would be signed, with the only positive result of the Common Market negotiations being the determination to succeed in the FTA negotiations.[166] This determination found its immediate expression in the renewal of the conflict over the competences for these negotiations, which the ministry now sought to secure.[167]

Clearly aware of the renewed interministerial dispute, British efforts at enlisting support were now firmly focussed on Germany.[168] Yet nothing substantive could be done before the opening of intergovernmental negotiations, and Britain had to witness the signing of the Treaty of Rome with increasing doubts about the chances of her own initiative.[169]

Entering wedge or counterblast?

Between 1956 and spring 1957, Britain's civil servants were well informed about the German position on European integration. The negative reply to the British diplomatic note of November 1955 had led to a reappraisal of the assessment of German opinion. Quite accurately, Whitehall and in particular the Foreign Office believed that while the division continued, it could only be turned into an advantage, if a global counterinitiative could be formulated. This assessment was based mainly on information supplied by the British embassy in Bonn, and confirmed on the occasion of the visits to London of Ministers Erhard and Brentano. Both channels provided reasonably accurate information about the views of the two factions within the German government, though Brentano's wish to reassure the British government in order to prevent further 'sabotage' led to a degree of over-optimism.

This information about attitudes in Bonn was fed into the policy-formulation process of the new British initiative. The FTA plan was welcomed by all governments concerned, and it attracted the support of both factions within German opinion, for its qualities appealed to the free trade lobby around Erhard, seemingly without posing a threat to the integration efforts of the Six, championed by the *Auswärtiges Amt* and the Chancellor. In part, this new and more realistic British approach had been the result of a learning process from hostility to accommodation, in so far as the futility of the sabotage attempts of winter 1955 had at last been recognized. A further contributing factor in this change of attitude was the increased involvement of the more European-minded Ministers Thorneycroft and Macmillan in the decision-making process, culminating in January 1957 in the move of the latter to No. 10 Downing Street as Eden's successor.

However, this should not be taken to suggest a complete volte-face of British attitudes towards Europe. The dominant feature in the process of formulating Plan G was the reactive, and wholly negative, motivation behind the reappraisal of British policy. Calls for a 'counterblast' and suggestions to 'kill the Messina Common Market stone-dead' characterized the internal exchanges, and, even though there is no evidence to support the view that Plan G was designed to destroy the Common Market, the decision can only be described as a close one, both in its origin and in the subsequent debate about the complementary or alternative character of the British initiative.

Furthermore, the formulation of the FTA plan did not lead to the disappearance of the two arguments introduced by Butler in November 1955. The scenario of economic division and its political consequences for Europe reappeared in the internal debate, now used as an argument by those who favoured a policy change towards European integration. In this context, officials and ministers alike portrayed Germany as the main threat to Britain's economic well-being and security. And it was Macmillan who most forcefully referred to these dangers of British non-participation when initiating Whitehall's policy reappraisal, as well as during later Cabinet meetings and House of Commons' debates. Although the widespread anticipation of the FTA's great popularity on the Continent prevented the two arguments from being used when dealing with foreign governments, their continued and successful use at home ensured the survival of the unquestioned belief that any opponent of the scheme could be convinced otherwise simply by referring to the economic and political dangers of Britain's exclusion. The possibility that these arguments might have a different effect on 'Euro-enthusiasts' on the Continent than on reluctant members of the British Cabinet and Parliament was not examined.

If anything, the second half of 1956 saw the belief in Britain's ability to influence Continental governments gather in strength. Indications that Germany and to some extent France were contemplating the abandonment of the Messina project in favour of the FTA helped to reinforce the perception that not only Germany, but also Europe as a whole, would agree to the latter no matter how much it was biased in Britain's favour. The belief that the FTA negotiations would pose no problem, combined with the desire to avoid a repeat of the 'sabotage' accusations of winter 1955, resulted in the British government missing an opportunity to replace the Common Market with their scheme. There is some evidence to suggest that this would have been possible, given that Erhard's and Storch's economic objections to French harmonization demands had very nearly convinced Chancellor Adenauer. In the event, Brentano's skilful switch to political arguments re-established the dominance of the 'Euro-enthusiasts' in the German government. In this, he received invaluable help from the coincidence of increasing East–West tension and the absence of a firm British commitment to an FTA without a customs union.

In the spring of 1957, the assumption that British co-operation was sought by Europe at any price was only beginning to be called into doubt by the apparent failure of the OEEC meeting to formally open the FTA negotiations. This is not to say that the British government was now ready to make substantial compromises, but at least it was recognized that some mediation was required. The assessment of Germany's position towards the Free Trade Area plan in early 1957 led British officials to turn once again to the Federal Government for help.

3
Mistaken, Misled or Misguided? British Hopes for German Mediation during the FTA Negotiations

The years 1957 and 1958 saw perhaps the most forceful attempts by the British government to utilize German support for British participation in European economic integration short of seeking full membership in the Community. It was public knowledge at the time that a sizable minority within the German government shared the preference for a Free Trade Area over the customs union of the Six. Consequently, British hopes for German support in the FTA negotiations ran high. Their ultimate disappointment in late 1958 has led many a commentator to assume that the government had overestimated the influence of the proponents of the scheme in the decision-making process in Bonn. The focus of this chapter will thus lie on British and German negotiation performance, and a particular emphasis will be placed on the impact of British tactics on the internal debate within the German government.

Harold Macmillan's visit to Bonn

Following the OEEC meeting of February 1957, the prospects of the FTA were far from satisfying to those in the British and German governments who favoured the scheme. The little enthusiasm which remained on the Continent was threatened to be lost in the complicated structure and the multiplicity of forums in which the FTA was debated – a problem which was to haunt the negotiations until their breakdown in November 1958. On the multilateral level, the OEEC meeting had decided to convene a further three working parties which, in descending order of importance, were concerned with the principles of the FTA (OEEC working party No. 21), with questions relating to agriculture (working party No. 22), and finally with problems arising for underdeveloped regions of the OEEC (working party No. 23). All three working parties were to submit their respective reports in July 1957, upon which the OEEC Council was expected finally to agree on the opening of intergovernmental negotiations. In addition to the problem of conducting multilateral negotiations between 17 countries, the procedure was complicated by the nature of the group of the Six. Although they had yet to ratify the Treaty of Rome, they were already committed to consultations about a common negotiating position *vis-à-vis* the FTA.

However, the British assessment of the chances of the FTA was not altogether gloomy. The OEEC meeting of February 1957 had confirmed the support which could be expected from some amongst the Six, particularly from the German Minister of Economics.[1] Ludwig Erhard's interest in the creation of the FTA was unbroken and was conveyed to the British administration on various occasions after the February meeting.[2] Yet, the complicated nature of the negotiation procedure made it difficult for his ministry to influence the course of events, since the question of the distribution of competencies within the German administration remained unresolved. The interministerial struggle had erupted once again with the temporary appointment by the *Auswärtiges Amt* of the Head of its Trade Policy Department, Hilgar van Scherpenberg, as the German representative at the OEEC working party No. 21.[3]

While the Ministry for Economic Co-operation under Vice-Chancellor Franz Blücher aimed to preserve its responsibility for representing Germany in the OEEC, the Ministry of Economics disputed the Foreign Ministry's claim on the representation in the working party, arguing that it was responsible for Germany's external trade policy. The *Auswärtiges Amt*, in contrast, regarded the FTA as part of the wider complex of European policy, of which it had been placed in charge by the Chancellor in 1956. Once again, only Adenauer himself could arbitrate.[4] His decision of March 1957 represented a temporary compromise acceptable to all the parties concerned. It left general responsibility for German representation at the OEEC with the Ministry for Economic Co-operation, while the substance of the government's position on the FTA was to be worked out in an interministerial committee under the chairmanship of the Ministry of Economics. The acquiescence of the *Auswärtiges*

Amt was ensured by giving the ministry full responsibility for the work of the interim committee of the Six, in which it could guard the integrity of the Community.[5]

The redistribution of competences had important consequences for the early part of the FTA negotiations. Firstly, full responsibility for the interim committee provided the *Auswärtiges Amt* with control over co-ordination among the Six. Its influence was decisive for the German support of the French wish to postpone the discussions in the OEEC Council even before working parties 21–3 were due to submit their reports.[6] Given the strong preference for the Common Market, which the German Foreign Ministry had shown during the previous two years, it came as no surprise that the French desire to ratify the Treaty of Rome before starting negotiations for the FTA fell on sympathetic ears.[7] Indeed, it was thought in the *Auswärtiges Amt* that the EEC was under threat from both the British government and the Economics Ministry, with the former attempting not only to delay ratification but also to hamper the long-term development of the Community with plans for a merger of European institutions known as the 'grand design'.[8] Erhard was expected to try and use early FTA negotiations to undermine the Common Market.[9] Following the Foreign Ministry's brief, Chancellor Adenauer supported the French wish for a postponement on the occasion of the visit of Prime Minister Macmillan in Bonn on 8 May – incidentally the first official visit of a British Prime Minister to the Federal Republic.

Well aware of the ongoing struggle over competences within the German administration, the British government relied on direct contact with Erhard to find out more about the German attitude.[10] Here, some hope was placed on the minister's ability to represent his views – and consequently British thinking – 'vigorously... to the rest of the Six behind the scenes'.[11] However, Erhard's muted warning that the FTA might not be negotiable without some concessions on British imports of cheap foodstuffs from the Commonwealth was interpreted as an 'astonishing ignorance of the responsible Germans about the reasons for our inability to include foodstuffs'.[12] Hence, the image of Erhard as a staunch supporter of the British Plan was overriding any suggestions he may have had. In fact, the trust in Erhard's ability to deliver even hardened the British negotiating position. If her demands about the exclusion of overseas territories were not met, Britain would abandon the FTA, and Chancellor Peter Thorneycroft was briefed to stress that 'the

Germans should think very carefully before they assume a share... of such responsibility. The Germans have a lot of influence; let them use it wisely.'[13] With regard to the other main figures in the German government, British officials were less certain about their attitude towards the FTA. Recognizing that the Ministry of Economics might not represent the majority view, the Treasury advised British lobbying efforts to be directed at the Chancellor and the Foreign Ministry:

> Though the forces within the Government and German industry represented by Dr. Erhard are probably more enthusiastic for the Free Trade Area than for the Customs Union, it seems doubtful whether either the economic or the political significance of the Free Trade Area has been appreciated by Dr. Adenauer or Herr von Brentano.[14]

However, there were a number of difficulties associated with selling the FTA to the German Chancellor and to his Foreign Minister. The latter, in particular, was known to be suspicious of British motives behind the 'grand design' policy.[15] British officials were also aware of the fact that the FTA itself was seen by some Germans as a 'devilish trick to sabotage the Common Market itself'.[16] Combined with the planned troop reductions, there were hence 'three reasons why the Germans suspect us of Machiavellian manoeuvres to destroy closer European integration and to disengage ourselves from Europe'.[17] The British Ambassador to Bonn confirmed this impression, quoting the *Auswärtiges Amt* State Secretary as saying that 'Adenauer was not convinced of our sincerity, either in defence matters or in European Economic Co-operation'.[18]

Despite the knowledge that the Chancellor and his Foreign Minister were suspicious of British intentions, the line of argument which had been used with Erhard was not modified for the occasion of the Prime Minister's visit to Bonn in May. The British government clearly could not object directly to the French request for a pause in the negotiations if it wanted to avoid being seen to be trying once again to openly 'sabotage' the Common Market. Instead, what was sought from the Germans in the meantime was to 'find a way of giving public support for... [the Free Trade Area] ... during the ratification debates on the Treaties of Rome'.[19] In this respect, Germany was seen as the weak link among the Six, for her trading interests were such that only 25 per cent of her exports went to the other five within the Community, compared to 60 per cent going to OEEC countries. Macmillan's brief for his meeting with Adenauer, prepared jointly by the Treasury and the Foreign Office, and approved by Cabinet, advised him to make reference to 'profound effects in our relations, political, economic and military, with our European neighbours' in case of a failure of the FTA negotiations.[20] The reason for this entirely negative approach can be found in the uncertainty about the scheme prevailing in the British administration at the time. There was still confusion over whether the FTA was a defensive measure or whether it was beneficial in its own right.[21] What was agreed, though, was that if it failed to materialise, the British government should seek to break up the Common Market.[22]

Macmillan certainly intended to use strong language with Adenauer, yet, in the event, the German side volunteered all the necessary promises for early resumption of the FTA negotiations.[23] Summing up the results of the visit, the Treasury's Under-Secretary Frank Figgures stated that Erhard, Blücher, Hallstein and van Scherpenberg all attached economic importance to the scheme, and that 'they created the impression that they all assumed [the Free Trade Area] could be got'. Even Adenauer, who 'knew little or nothing about the Free Trade Area' was now said to understand the political significance.[24] Combined with similar assurances from the French, the Bonn meeting went a long way to reassure the British government about the prospects of their new policy, so much so that Clarke now proclaimed that 'on the whole it now suits us to wait until the autumn for purposeful negotiations (e.g. no point in giving anything away)'.[25]

The way in which Germany was expected to support the FTA was to influence the other members of the Six, and among them France in particular. In the first half of 1957, however, the forum used to co-ordinate the attitudes of the Six, the interim committee, was controlled by the *Auswärtiges Amt* which has been shown to have been the least enthusiastic among the German ministries. It is important to note that even at this early stage of the negotiations, however, Erhard's ministry supported the idea of a common negotiating position of the Six, hoping to moderate the French position, but the positions of the two ministries differed in their emphasis. In an interministerial meeting in June, the Head of the Sub-Department for European political integration in the *Auswärtiges Amt*, Wilhelm Hartlieb, argued that:

the premise of the Community of the Six is a specific political concept, which had to be put into reality by the Economic Community. The Six first had to arrive at real co-operation, before the creation of a Free Trade Area can be negotiated.... We have to prevent, that the political premise of the European Economic Community is being diluted in other economic organizations.[26]

While not directly questioning Hartlieb's argument of 'cohesion first – FTA later', the Head of the Economics Ministry's Economic Policy Department, Alfred Müller-Armack, warned against the idea that the EEC and FTA were to form a unit, which he feared would lead to unnecessary regulations for the latter. Instead he argued that 'the EEC-Treaty should not be copied. The Free Trade Area Treaty should follow the tradition of the OEEC.'[27]

The proximity of the position of the Ministry of Economics and that of the British administration in these early stages of the negotiations was even more strikingly displayed in the interministerial working group which was meant to formulate the German negotiating position.[28] Its report not only reiterated Müller-Armack's argument against harmonization, it also insisted on simultaneous and proportional reductions of tariffs in the EEC and the FTA, and argued for the use of escape clauses to be limited to balance of payments crises only. Regarding institutions, it favoured a mix of unanimity and qualified majority voting, insisting, however, on simultaneous decisions in the EEC and the FTA about the question of proceeding from one to the next stage of tariff reductions. All these points reflected the free-trade philosophy of the ministry which, after having failed to prevent the establishment of a customs union, now saw as its prime goal a simultaneous FTA which would greatly offset the effect of the common external tariff. While the respective positions of the Ministry of Economics and the British were almost identical, there was no sign that the ministry was driven by either an anglophile outlook or a high priority being placed on economic relations with the island alone. From the very start of the negotiations, there was agreement in the working group that 'the creation of a Free Trade Area was of decisive interest to the Federal Republic as an export-intensive economy'.[29]

Within the *Auswärtiges Amt*, this economic concern about the FTA was shared by the Trade Policy Department which warned of the danger to the German economy and her balance of payment's position in case of a failure of the negotiations.[30] However, its influence was limited by that of the Political Department, which placed the highest priority on safeguarding and promoting the European Economic Community, agreeing to an FTA scheme only if it was to be acceptable to Germany's partners within the Six. What resulted as the official *Auswärtiges Amt* position transmitted to Brentano reflected an intraministerial compromise. The Foreign Minister was advised to continue

> to emphasize the German determination to do everything towards the realization of the FTA . . to emphasize the mediating role of the Federal Government between the partners who advance extreme positions . . . to refer to the necessity for the British government to be prepared to consider certain changes to its concept, if French and Italian acceptance is to be gained.[31]

The Paymaster-General's visit to Bonn

After the British had agreed to the postponement of the July meeting of the OEEC Council to allow for ratification of the Treaties of Rome, the Free Trade Area negotiations needed a fresh impetus.[32] However, a further delay resulted from the impending federal elections which meant that the German government was in a 'lame duck period . . . incapable of any decision or action'.[33] The Chancellor of the Exchequer, Peter Thorneycroft, speculated that if 'the present German Government were re-elected, we could expect to receive substantial support from them in resisting the protectionist policies of other members of the Six'.[34] It was therefore thought that 'effective German participation [was] really essential at the first Ministerial meeting to consider the Free Trade Area'.[35] However, this second postponement increased the danger that negotiations would fail to get off the ground. Hence, Macmillan sought to instill some urgency into the proceedings with the appointment of Reginald Maudling as Paymaster-General – a post which was to carry sole responsibility for the FTA initiative.[36]

The new member of the Cabinet used the time before the next Council meeting to tour OEEC capitals. What emerged from his soundings confirmed some of the earlier fears. While proclaiming a general desire for the FTA, the French government indicated that the main problems ahead were those relating to agriculture and tariff harmonization.[37] Given that any retreat from its highly publicized negotiating position was expected to meet fierce criticism at home and in Commonwealth capitals, the British reaction was not one of seeking compromises but a hope that other members of the Six would work to moderate French opinion. In his paper 'FTA, Prospects for Beginning Negotiations', the Board of Trade Under-Secretary, Russell Bretherton, argued that 'almost everything will depend upon how far their German, Belgian and Dutch colleagues are prepared to push [the French] on this point' and insisted that 'the Chancellor is firmly committed to the FTA idea, Dr. Erhard is an enthusiastic supporter of it, and there have been growing signs ... of a widening body of public interest and approval'.[38] This assessment which was widespread in Whitehall was based on a number of very optimistic reports which had been sent throughout the summer by Sir Christopher Steel, Ambassador to Bonn.[39] It was also a view shared by the Prime Minister: 'Good. We must strike while the iron is hot.'[40]

It was left to the Foreign Office to instill a more cautionary note into the general feeling of optimism regarding German support. The UK delegation to the OEEC had reported a continuing struggle within the German government, within which Erhard's pro-FTA policy appeared to be challenged by Hallstein and Brentano who still saw the British scheme as incompatible with the enterprise of the Six.[41] While this information appears not to have reached other departments, Paymaster-General Maudling was aware of such doubts.[42] One of the tasks of his visit to Bonn therefore was to find out 'where we stand'.[43]

The Foreign Office also sought to convince other departments through the Sub-Committee on Closer Association that some concessions on agriculture were necessary and that the scheme had to be made more politically attractive to the 'Euro-enthusiasts' on the Continent.[44] With regard to the latter, the options were clearly limited by the government's continued aversion to any supranational element and by the failure of the 'grand design' policy. Yet, it was contemplated to demonstrate good intentions by a firm commitment to a long-term presence of British troops on the Continent and by increased arms sales to Germany. Other inducements under discussion illustrated how little enthusiasm for political commitment there was within the British position, for they included plans for a channel tunnel, the conversion to the metric system and decimal coinage, as well as European-style road signs, and European logos on postage stamps! However, even these – no more than cosmetic – measures failed to gain acceptance, and were hence not recommended for use during Maudling's tour.

On the German side, there were no illusions about the fact that the main British motive was to avert the danger of trade discrimination, and no respect was paid to any political element in the FTA plan.[45] The Economics Ministry's brief for the Maudling visit was pragmatic in its discussion of details of the negotiations, recording wide-ranging agreement between the two governments on the principles of the scheme, while ascribing an important role to Germany as a mediator. She was to use her influence to prevent France from insisting on a different timetable, or *décalage*, for the EEC and FTA, while urging Britain to accept not only a compromise agreement on agriculture but also minor contractual obligations regarding the co-ordination of monetary and macroeconomic policies. The ministry therefore envisaged a true mediating role for Germany in the sense of urging both sides to compromise. However, given the opposition of the German farmers' lobby, the German delegation did not press for the inclusion of agriculture. Instead, they advocated an agreement outside the scope of the FTA.[46] In his reasoning, Erhard echoed the earlier British conviction when he stated that, even in the EEC, 'one could not speak of free trade in agricultural products'.[47] More important from Maudling's point of view was the support the FTA received from the German Foreign Minister, Heinrich von Brentano, who stressed that he 'would welcome it, if it could be stated in Paris that we agree on supplementing the Common Market with the Free Trade Area'.[48]

Not surprisingly, the meeting went a long way to reassuring Maudling of continued support from the German government.[49] After having once again diagnosed wide-ranging agreement between the two positions, he therefore thanked his German colleagues for 'trying to assert their position in Brussels'.[50] The result of Maudling's visit to Bonn was not only that full confidence in German support for the FTA was restored but also that the warnings about an internal dispute in Germany were ignored. The British representative at the OEEC repeatedly tried to alert his government to these developments, but he was unsuccessful, for his reports were contradicted by those of the British embassy in Bonn, which tended to portray even former sceptics like Hallstein and Etzel as having been converted to advocates of the FTA scheme.[51] However, there had indeed been a struggle over competencies which resulted in their comprehensive redistribution following the federal elections of September 1957, and which demonstrated – if not hostility towards the FTA – then at least the persistence of suspicions of 'sabotage'. The dissolution of the *Bundesministerium für wirtschaftliche Zusammenarbeit* (Ministry for Economic Co-operation) had made it necessary to redefine the role of the Ministry of Economics and the *Auswärtiges Amt* with regard to European integration. Both these ministries staked a claim on German representation in the OEEC and the FTA negotiations.[52] Once again, it was only the Chancellor who could temporarily settle the dispute, this time transferring competencies to the Economics Minister, not least as an acknowledgement of Erhard's crucial role as a vote winner.[53] The Foreign Ministry's by now customary reference to European integration as part of foreign policy failed to convince the Chancellor on this occasion.[54] The determination of the *Auswärtiges Amt* to secure the competencies for the FTA negotiations were once again motivated not by a dislike for the scheme but by a desire to protect the development of the European Community. In a letter to Erhard, Brentano argued that although the FTA was a 'desirable end', the protection of the Common Market was to be the overriding objective. He went on to question whether the British government shared this view.[55] Internally, however, the *Auswärtiges Amt* regarded the Economics Ministry as the main threat to the development of the Common Market – an impression which appeared substantiated by Müller-Armack whose liberal interpretation of the Chancellor's decision led him to claim that his ministry was now responsible for all aspects of European integration.[56] The ambiguities of the Chancellor's decision meant that the struggle over competencies was to continue well into the year 1958.[57] For the time being, however, the Ministry of Economics was in the driving seat.

The Maudling Committee

When the postponed OEEC Council meeting finally took place in Paris on 16–17 October, the British delegation appeared to have heeded the German advice, for it agreed to study measures to increase trade in agricultural products.[58] In reality, the apparent softening of the British position had little to do with the German intervention.[59] Nonetheless, the Ministry of Economics was convinced that its mediation policy had proven successful in this respect, and it now saw a need to get the position of the Six to move towards that of the British. However, while it had been agreed by the interim committee of the Six that negotiations were to continue in principle, the French government crisis prevented the formulation of a common stance on the more detailed questions of the plan.[60] Hence, the October meeting of the OEEC made progress only on procedural questions, setting up an intergovernmental committee at ministerial level under the chairmanship of Reginald Maudling. Evidently concerned about the French delaying tactics as well as about their demand for safeguards, Erhard stated at the meeting that 'nothing would be more dangerous, than to let things drag on even further'.[61]

Contrary to Erhard's anxieties, it had not been the intention of the British negotiators to use the October meeting of OEEC to make any progress on the details of the FTA.[62] All that was required at this stage was to set the negotiations themselves into motion. In order to gain approval for the setting up of the Maudling Committee, it was thought that a hint at possible concessions over agriculture was necessary. Any discussion beyond that was to be avoided until real bargaining was to take place in the committee itself. On both counts, the Council meeting was seen as a success, especially with the statement on agriculture being so well received.[63]

With the task of setting up the Maudling Committee having been achieved, real negotiations could begin at last. Before the committee was to commence with substantive work in November, Maudling sent an annotated agenda, as well as a catalogue of questions to all governments concerned.[64] As had become standard practice, the Six met to formulate a common response in advance of the meetings. The Ministry of Economics was now rather better placed to bring its influence to bear on the proceedings, since this time they were directly represented by Müller-Armack in the relevant sub-committee of the interim committee of the Six. The new-found strength did not, however, translate into immediate negotiation results. Despite support from the delegations of the other four, Müller-Armack was unsuccessful in putting pressure on France.[65] The delegates merely agreed to divide the responsibility of answering Maudling's questions among themselves, which allowed the German delegation to stress the importance of transition periods of equal duration for the FTA and the EEC, as well as giving some general comments about the need to co-ordinate macroeconomic policy. Informing his colleagues from other ministries, Müller-Armack was not able to disguise his disappointment, and put the blame for the failure to find a common position squarely on the French.[66]

The Economics Ministry's disenchantment with the French negotiating performance was heightened by the Maudling Committee meeting itself. Far from restricting himself to answering the allocated questions, the French delegate, State Secretary Maurice Faure, used the opportunity to give a full account of the position of the new French government.[67] In doing so, he appeared to question the very character of a Free Trade Area, for he argued that there would have to be some harmonization of external tariffs or the possibility of levying compensatory charges. Otherwise some countries would gain an unfair competitive advantage. He also stressed that there would have to be a difference in the timetables of the EEC and the FTA, and insisted on unanimity – effectively giving France a veto on the question of transition from one stage to the next. Furthermore, he claimed the right to invoke escape clauses unilaterally. In all, Faure's statement amounted to a rejection of the principles of a Free Trade Area, as they were not only specified by the GATT, but also as they were agreed upon by the British and German governments. At the end of the year the German outlook on the FTA negotiations was therefore as bleak as ever, recording 'no agreement on any of the points'.[68]

Despite the French intervention at the Maudling Committee, and the problems which were now expected for the coming year, there was still a general agreement on negotiation procedure within the German government. The *Auswärtiges Amt* was adamant that it was in Germany's 'real foreign policy interest' that the Six should formulate a common position in advance of Maudling Committee meetings.[69] Given the problems caused by the deviation of the French from the common line, the Ministry of Economics could not agree more strongly to this requirement, for it saw in it a means to contain the most far-reaching demands of the French before they would pose a threat to the negotiations in the OEEC.[70]

In Erhard's ministry, the general gloom was broken by one element of optimism, in so far as officials expected to use their influence more effectively in the new year. The result of the redistribution of competencies in the autumn was the establishment of a European Department 'E', headed for the time being by Alfred Müller-Armack. His department was to represent Germany in the FTA negotiations both in the OEEC and among the Six, while the *Auswärtiges Amt* retained the competencies for the EEC's Council of Ministers.[71] The extent to which the Economics Minister had wanted control over the FTA negotiations could be seen in the circumstances surrounding the establishment of Department E. Erhard was not prepared to await the necessary financial decisions to be made in the *Bundestag*'s budgetary committee, but was ready to transfer existing resources and personnel without delay.

Though there had been some ignorance about the internal dispute within the German government in the autumn, the British administration was well aware of the outcome thereof, which was unanimously viewed with satisfaction. Erhard's new-found strength in the Cabinet was seen as a good omen for the negotiations, and the promotion of the pragmatist Müller-Armack to State Secretary with full responsibilities for the FTA was equally welcome.[72] Only the Foreign Office still harboured some doubts about the commitment to the FTA shown by Hallstein, Brentano and the Chancellor: 'Dr. Adenauer himself may well be the weakest link, certainly not because of dislike of the Free Trade Area, but he attaches prime importance to "bringing France along" in the European Economic Community.'[73]

Yet again, the tactics recommended for convincing the Chancellor to support the FTA against French stalling efforts remained entirely negative. A draft brief for Adenauer's planned visit to London in December advised the Prime Minister to argue that without the FTA, Europe would be divided economically, 'and this division would equally inevitably affect European co-operation in the political and even the military field'.[74] In the event, these arguments were not employed as the visit was cancelled due to the Chancellor's ill-health.[75]

By the end of 1957, a certain pattern can be said to have emerged in Anglo-German relations and the FTA negotiations. In the words of the Prime Minister, Britain was looking 'to the German Government to use their special position to influence the French'.[76] The hope that the Germans would do so was based on a positive assessment of their attitude towards the FTA following the visits to Bonn by the Prime Minister in May, and by Reginald Maudling in October. However, these high-level encounters had pushed two important features of the German position into the background.

Firstly, Erhard's overt enthusiasm for the FTA tended to disguise the ministry's self-styled role of a true mediator, trying to facilitate agreement by suggesting compromises between the French and British positions. The diagnosis of a complete identity of views hardened, rather than softened, the British negotiating position in the mistaken belief that the Germans would see to it that the details of the scheme agreed by the Six were to be acceptable.

Secondly, and undoubtedly more importantly, the visits masked the suspicions of British 'sabotage' which were still widespread in the *Auswärtiges Amt*, and were harboured by Brentano and Hallstein in particular. Although in favour of the FTA in principle, the German Foreign Ministry gave overriding priority to the consolidation of the Common Market. At times, the British Foreign Office was acutely aware of the political character of German enthusiasm for European integration. However, rather than turning this into an advantage for the FTA by strengthening the political appeal of the scheme, the only argument left to deal with this preference for the Common Market was the threat that the latter would lead to an economic and ultimately political rift in Europe. Clearly, the negative character of this line of argument stemmed directly from the continued British aversion to supranationalism. What was not realized, however, was that its use was bound to reinforce suspicions about British dislike of, and hence desire to 'sabotage', the Common Market, which were held by those in Germany who viewed the EEC as a unifying rather than divisive measure. In reality, the promises of support for the FTA forthcoming from the Chancellor and his Foreign Minister were motivated by the need to secure ratification of the Treaty of Rome in France, as well as in Germany itself, given that a sizable minority in government and industry favoured the British scheme. British ministers and most officials were hence quite mistaken in their belief that the arguments about a divided Europe had been responsible for producing the desired effect. This pattern – established by default – was to continue to influence the negotiations in the following year.

In the meantime, however, a new player emerged onto the negotiation scene, with the EEC finally coming into force on 1 January 1958. Later in the same month, the first meeting of the Council of Ministers of the Community produced agreement on the appointment of Walter Hallstein as the first President of the Commission.[77] It did not take the new Commissioners long to stake their claim on participation in the FTA negotiations, and it was the German Foreign Minister who proved their most ardent supporter. The Foreign Ministry's priority of safeguarding the integrity of the new Community was evident in Brentano's readiness to override any legal considerations preventing the Commission's participation.[78] Strengthening the Commission was also a means of increasing the influence of the *Auswärtiges Amt* over the FTA negotiations in so far as the new Commission President was still very much in contact with his former ministry where he had served as State Secretary. In contrast, the interest in the successful conclusion of these negotiations was increasing with the promotion of the Head of the Trade Policy Department, Hilgar van Scherpenberg, to the post of State Secretary which had been vacated by Hallstein. Van Scherpenberg's long-standing economic interest in the FTA was reaffirmed by his insistence that the Commission, while participating, should not be allowed to take over the negotiations in the name of the Six, since this would 'severely limit the role of the German delegation in mediating between the extreme British and French positions'.[79] In the end, therefore, the task of formulating a common negotiating position remained with the national delegations of the Six. To this, Erhard and Müller-Armack could not but agree, not least because of the forthcoming French proposals which they were determined to see discussed among the Six first, so as to cushion their impact on the FTA negotiations in Paris.

This exchange in the Council of Ministers was itself part of the ongoing struggle over competencies. In interministerial meetings, the *Auswärtiges Amt* continued to argue that, since the FTA was essentially a question of the external relations of the EEC, the ministry should be represented at the meetings of the permanent delegates to the EEC, who were now co-ordinating the common negotiating position of the Six.[80] The Chancellory now felt there was a need to intervene directly, and on its initiative a compromise was reached between Müller-Armack and van Scherpenberg. It gave the *Auswärtiges Amt* formal control over external relations, while the Economics Ministry was to be in charge of interministerial discussions and external representation on 'questions of economic policy in the widest sense', including relations to OEEC and the FTA.[81] The Economics Ministry's success in the internal dispute was important, since the first meetings of the Maudling Committee in 1958 were dominated by the contentious issues of agriculture and harmonization of social legislation. Within the German administration, the position *vis-à-vis* the latter was undisputed and produced almost a re-run of earlier arguments about the Common Market. During the consultations among the Six prior to the Maudling Committee meeting in mid-January, the German delegation rejected the equalization of pay for men and women, with the argument that less developed countries of the OEEC would not be able to afford this provision.[82]

On agriculture, the German delegation attempted to mediate between the British and those who were keenest to see agriculture included.[83] In meetings of the Six and during an extraordinary meeting with representatives from Denmark and Britain, the German delegates proposed that all OEEC countries should conclude a *Rahmenabkommen*, or framework agreement, within which further bilateral concessions were permitted.[84] This was to enable Britain to make some concessions to countries with grievances relating to agriculture, while at the same time stopping short of opening her market to all. However, the proposal was dismissed outright by the British side, without any internal assessment of its merits.[85] The first German attempt at mediating on the substance of the FTA scheme had therefore come to nothing.

The French memorandum and the Carli plan

The need for German mediation was highlighted by the French memorandum on the Free Trade Area whose main elements became known to the Six in late February.[86] In essence, it put forward a plan for an entirely different scheme. Not only was the organization to have a different name (Union for European Economic Co-operation) but its provisions also bore little resemblance to the basic features of the FTA. There was to be a 3-year delay (*décalage*) between the tariff reductions of the EEC and the new scheme, a longer transition period characterizing the latter, and all participating countries were to gain access to the Commonwealth preferential system. Most importantly, free trade was to be established by individual multilateral agreements to be negotiated for each industrial sector. A precondition for such agreements was a harmonization of production costs, which could only be achieved by harmonized external tariffs.

The British administration greeted the new French proposals with extreme dismay, so much so that the Cabinet's Economic Steering Committee anticipated the complete breakdown of the negotiations.[87] Given that Britain's negotiating position was 'not a strong one', and given that no support was to be expected from the Commission, the only possibility was to 'detach certain members of the Six from their support of, or acquiescence in, the French attitude'.[88] The target of such efforts was an obvious one. Not only had the Germans been the first to provide the British with a summary of the French proposals when they were still confidential, but a meeting between Maudling and Erhard had also demonstrated once again how close their attitude was on most of the problems.[89] While urging the British side to contemplate compromises with regard to Commonwealth preferences, Erhard rejected all other French proposals as unacceptable and assured the Paymaster-General that Britain 'need not fear that Germany would show any undue weakness'.[90]

This was, of course, easier said than done, for the French memorandum had put the difficult question of definition of origin firmly on the agenda. This problem concerned the circumstances under which a product could be regarded as having been produced in the FTA, and would hence enjoy freedom from tariffs if sold in another member country. Allied to the problem of definition of origin was the question of possible deflections of trade, occurring if one FTA country had a lower external tariff on certain products which would then be sold on free of tariffs in another member country, thereby undermining the latter's tariff protection. Similarly, a particular FTA member country might have low or no tariffs on raw materials, thereby enjoying the competitive advantage of lower production costs in other member countries – a scenario applicable, in particular, to Britain.

Firmly supported by the German representative from the Ministry of Economics, as well as by the British, the Group of Trade Experts of the OEEC's Steering Board of Trade had favoured a percentage rule combined with a basic material list to be used for the definition of origin.[91] The percentage rule was meant to solve the problem by defining a product as an 'area good', as long as more than 50 per cent of the value of the finished product was added in a member country of the FTA. The basic material list was to be a supplement to this rule, identifying certain raw materials to be ignored in the percentage calculation, thereby extending the scope of products which qualified for 'area good' status. Clearly, French ideas about sectoral harmonization of tariffs and production costs were diametrically opposed to these recommendations.

While the French proposals were unanimously rejected by the other five EEC members, and met perhaps the strongest opposition from the Ministry of Economics, the *Auswärtiges Amt* made an attempt to portray them as a useful starting point when informing the Chancellor.[92] Again, it was the desire to safeguard the achievements of the EEC which was decisive. Even though the Foreign Ministry agreed that harmonization was unnecessary, its Political Department argued that it should be 'demonstrated to the French that we will not leave them alone'.[93] Furthermore, Erhard was once again thought to prefer the FTA over the EEC, with Wilhelm Hartlieb expressing the fear that the Economics Ministry was prepared to 'sacrifice the EEC'.[94] However, before these differences were allowed to come to a head, the Italian Minister for Foreign Trade, Guido Carli, introduced a plan which promised to defuse the negotiation crisis. Accepting that deflection of trade could arise from the existence of external tariff differentials, the Carli plan proposed that in cases where these differentials were substantial the disadvantaged country would be allowed to levy compensatory taxes. The Maudling Committee discussed the plan on 12 March, though an agreement remained elusive.[95]

In the event, the permanent delegates to the EEC decided to sidestep the problem of the French memorandum altogether, by recommending to ministers the establishment of a special working group designed to formulate a single document on the common negotiation position the Six were to take on details of the FTA.[96] In late March, the meeting of the Council of Ministers followed this suggestion, setting up the so-called Ockrent group, named after its chairman, the Belgian permanent representative, Roger Ockrent.[97] Together with the Carli plan, the establishment of the Ockrent group led the *Auswärtiges Amt* to inform Adenauer that the threat of a negotiation crisis had now been averted.[98] This optimism was shared to some extent by the British representative who, while not accepting the Carli plan, reported to the Foreign Office that it had at least shown them that origin problems were not insoluble. He also reported with satisfaction the 'very sharp terms' in which Erhard attacked French demands.[99]

The subsequent discussions of the Carli plan were further indications of the Economics Ministry's desire to mediate between the different interests. The ministry regarded the plan not only as being contrary to Germany's original position towards the FTA, it was also thought to severely restrict the scope of free trade, since it eliminated all those sectors where there were tariff differentials.[100] Erhard's officials therefore argued that the Carli formula should only be applied in exceptional cases, and that compensatory charges should be phased out completely after a transitional period. Müller-Armack made his compromise proposals known to the French, in confidential bilateral talks in early April in which he sought to persuade them to withdraw their memorandum.[101] Here, the German desire to mediate rather than merely to pressure the French was most obvious. While promising harmonization of competition and social policy as a sweetener to the French, he argued for a mixture of percentage rules and the Carli formula as the solution for the problem of definition of origin. Unexpected though it was, the conciliatory approach of the Economics Ministry's negotiators clearly satisfied the *Auswärtiges Amt* representatives present.[102] Concessions to the French were balanced by an attempt to convince them to drop the demand for access to Commonwealth preferences. Müller-Armack pointed out that the Commonwealth problem had been misconstrued, arguing that the import of cheap raw materials to Britain was part of the wider problem of definition of origin which was to be solved accordingly. As far as the preferences given to British industrial goods in Commonwealth markets were concerned, this was a matter to be decided by Commonwealth governments rather than being a concession that could be demanded from the British. Finally, the problem of cheap imports of agricultural products to Britain could be solved by the German compromise proposal of a *Rahmenabkommen*. However, despite his elaborate plea, Müller-Armack did not manage 'to impress [the French delegation] with arguments of logic or of economic policy'.[103] A second attempt at real mediation had therefore come to nothing.

Konrad Adenauer's visit to London – a commitment to FTA?

Faced with the stalemate following the French proposals, the British government saw a need to go beyond the discussion of economic details alone, and to inject wider political questions into the proceedings. Macmillan and Maudling were agreed on the target of such an initiative:

> The key to the whole question is Germany. The German position is as follows. Erhard is as keen as ever to reach a full European agreement. Hallstein, since his new appointment is rather antagonistic. Brentano is definitely pro-French. Everything therefore depends on Adenauer. Adenauer takes no interest in economics, but if he can be assured that the British really would react if necessary by isolating themselves from Europe, together with any friends they can collect, e.g. Scandinavia, Adenauer may shrink from dividing Europe. He only thinks about the political issue.[104]

It was with Adenauer's visit to London that such an opportunity arose. In the run-up to the meeting, the British embassy in Bonn reported increasing support for the FTA among German industrialists and press.[105] Although this was greeted with satisfaction, the main purpose of the visit was to inject political momentum at the highest level. Sir Christopher Steel, Ambassador to Bonn, recommended that Adenauer 'should be made to understand the political consequences of failure and these cannot be pointed out to him too strongly'.[106] This suggestion was taken up by the Paymaster-General's office in the preparation of the main brief for the visit, and the need to pressure Adenauer was also stressed by Maudling when informing his Cabinet colleagues.[107] A further means to influence the Chancellor on his forthcoming visit was to play on the importance he attached to American friendship.[108] After having been informed about increasing support for the FTA scheme in Washington, the Foreign Office instructed the British Ambassador to the United States, Harold Caccia, to utilize these circumstances to put further pressure on the Germans.[109]

Meanwhile, in Germany, there was a continuation of the customary wrangle over representative competencies. Only after direct intervention from Erhard, was Müller-Armack allowed to accompany him, Adenauer and Brentano to London.[110] However, on the substance of the meeting there was an unusual unity, as a number of factors had temporarily caused the *Auswärtiges Amt* to look more favourably on the FTA project. Firstly, there was the apparent need to reassure the British that they could indeed count on German support. Unfavourable reports in the British press had accused the German government of speaking with two voices, and the British embassy in Bonn had also expressed its concern over the lack of German effort.[111] Secondly, the US government appears to have heeded the advice of the British Ambassador and had leaked a document which stated that the USA now openly favoured the scheme and relied on German mediation.[112] These circumstances, coupled with the mounting crisis in France over the Algerian problem made it politically necessary to reassure Britain in the name of Western cohesion. A third element in the temporary conversion of the Foreign Ministry was once again the perceived need to safeguard the EEC, this time against the threat of British retaliatory action in the economic field, a blocking of the progress of the Community in GATT, and attempts to dissuade other countries from joining the Common Market.[113] A fourth and final feature of spring 1958 was the mounting pressure of German industry, displayed not least of all in the Anglo-German talks at Königswinter immediately before the Adenauer visit to London.[114] All these concerns were reflected in the brief prepared for the visit. However, the emphasis placed on the German mediating role was once again balanced by demands for British concessions in the field of Commonwealth preferences, harmonization of tariffs and agriculture. In the absence of such compromises, 'a successful conclusion of the enterprise could not be counted on'.[115]

The series of meetings in London followed the pattern already apparent the year before, characterized by a substantial discrepancy between the high-level talks and press reports on the one hand and the expert discussions on the other.[116] In their replies to Macmillan's warnings about economic, political and military consequences of the failure of the FTA negotiations, both Erhard and Adenauer appeared to promise direct German help in persuading the French. At the expert level, however, Müller-Armack sought to promote the German compromise proposals regarding the French memorandum and agriculture. Yet, 'the British reply to the latter [was] altogether negative, counterproposals were not made. In all, the British often behaved purely passive.' His arguments had as little impact as his plea that something – if only symbolic – needed to be done with regard to Commonwealth preferences. Even the *Auswärtiges Amt* declared itself disappointed with the London meetings, though utterly unimpressed by British warnings. Hartlieb stated:

> I do not see how this issue can be advanced. The British are threatening to turn away from the continent, a weapon which has however become blunt. No substantial proposals, no readiness to associate. Simply the demand to swallow the half-baked British cake.[117]

If there was a discrepancy between the high-level talks and the official pronouncements on the one hand and the expert discussions on the other, this was not realised in Bonn. It was only the German delegate to the OEEC, Karl Werkmeister, who felt that a misleading impression of the German position had been given. In a letter to Erhard, he warned that:

> the rather high British expectations following the talks in London fill me with concern, which I feel the duty not to conceal from you. In my opinion, we should do everything we can to prevent London from getting the impression that we are speaking with two voices.[118]

Werkmeister's warning was far from misplaced. The Adenauer visit had once again reassured the British government of whole-hearted German support for the FTA.[119] As in the previous year, top-level assurances tended to harden, rather than soften, the British negotiating position concerning economic details of the plan – a feature which was to become even more pronounced during the subsequent bilateral expert discussions. Perhaps most importantly, the visit appeared to confirm that Adenauer and his Foreign Minister were susceptible to British threats regarding the division of Europe. This belief was clearly mistaken for it was the combination of industrial lobbying, US pressure, the French crisis and the general state of Anglo-German relations which had led to the assurances given by Adenauer and Brentano. Now that a solution had been found for the problem of support cost for British troops stationed in Germany, the warnings about economic, political and military divisions of Europe lacked credibility, for no-one seriously expected such a fundamental change in British foreign policy.[120]

Enter de Gaulle

During April and May 1958, the Algerian uprising began to turn from a decolonization conflict into a fully-fledged constitutional crisis in Paris. In this period, two French governments fell owing to their seeming readiness to compromise. It was not until 19 May that the wartime hero General Charles de Gaulle took office, after a revolt of the French Algerian army had destabilized the situation of the Fourth Republic beyond repair. In the meantime, the chances of reaching compromise in the FTA negotiations, of course, seemed more remote than ever.[121] The crisis meant, in Faure's words, that 'discussions about principles could not take place', and all EEC consultations other than the Ockrent group were postponed until July.[122] In May, the French delegation also asked for a postponement of further Maudling Committee meetings.[123] The only on-going multilateral discussions which included Britain were therefore those of the OEEC's Steering Board of Trade, which was now considering the Carli plan. From a German point of view, the British were taking an unduly uncompromising stance in these consultations. Bretherton described the plan as 'foolish and silly', and it was only after the German delegate argued for the discussion to concentrate on practical measures rather than principles that British experts were prepared to talk about the plan at all, though without producing agreement.[124]

With the stalemate in the negotiations continuing, Anglo-German bilateral talks aimed to preserve the impetus. The two principle problem areas discussed in these talks were Commonwealth preferences and the definition of origin. In his meetings with Coulson, Figgures and Bretherton in May, Müller-Armack attempted to moderate the British position on the former. However, he had to report his lack of success:

> The defence of Commonwealth Preferences led the otherwise very calm delegates to more lively explanations. (In any case this reaction demonstrated how cautious one has to be in discussing this issue with the English). Even the very mild proposals... of safeguard clauses against English products which can be shown to enjoy a competitive advantage due to Empire markets, was rejected... as an inconceivable solution.[125]

Müller-Armack's failure may have been surprising, given that the British objectives for these talks had been defined by the Paymaster-General's Office as, firstly, 'to reach agreement over as wide a field as possible with the Germans', and, secondly, 'to rely on the Germans to push this agreement through the other members of the Six'.[126] Evidently, though, the term 'agreement' did not imply any British concessions on the two most contentious issues. In the case of the origin problem and the suggestion of tariff harmonization through the Carli plan, this was partly due to the fact that it was seen as a matter of principle, rather than as a practicality.[127] As far as the Commonwealth was concerned, the British attitude had been almost condescending for some time, emphasizing the need to 'educate' the Germans about the 'costs' of the preference system.[128]

In mid-May, British negotiators became aware that the discussions in the Ockrent group were heading in a worrying direction with regard to both Commonwealth preferences and origin problems.[129] Combined with the postponement of negotiations and with the ascent of General de Gaulle, these developments now seemed to threaten the entire FTA project.[130] The optimism which had followed the Adenauer visit now turned into extreme pessimism and Macmillan's reaction was one of undisguised hostility towards both France and Germany:

> I feel we ought to make it quite clear to our European friends that if Little Europe is formed without a parallel development of

a Free Trade Area we shall have to reconsider the whole of our political and economic attitude towards Europe. I doubt if we could remain in NATO. We should certainly put on highly protective tariffs and quotas to counteract what Little Europe was doing to us. In other words, we should not allow ourselves to be destroyed little by little. We would fight back with every weapon in our armoury. We would take our troops out of Europe. We would withdraw from NATO. We would adopt a policy of isolationism. We would surround ourselves with rockets and we would say to the Germans, the French and all the rest of them: 'Look after yourselves with your own forces. Look after yourselves when the Russians overrun your countries.'[131]

A link between the French crisis and the fate of the FTA was also seen in the German Foreign Ministry, albeit leading to very different conclusions. Internally, the *Auswärtiges Amt* had disapproved of bilateral Anglo-German talks for some time, but had been unable to call a halt to what had been agreed at the highest level. There was the fear that the talks would give the impression that the two countries colluded at the expense of French and Community interests.[132] With the mounting constitutional crisis in France, this antipathy was now intensifying. Rather than weakening Paris–Bonn co-operation in favour of closer relations with Britain, the German embassy in Paris strongly recommended that with General de Gaulle coming to power the only option for German foreign policy to safeguard Western cohesion lay in intensifying mutual dependency with France.[133] Hartlieb even went so far as suggesting the abandonment of the FTA negotiations, which in his view threatened the co-operative spirit of the Six. In this context, he strongly criticized the Ministry of Economics for 'making promises to the British which cannot be kept'.[134]

However, these reservations were never properly aired outside the *Auswärtiges Amt*, and the Ministry of Economics was therefore allowed to continue its course. When representatives of the British and German governments met again in June, there had been little movement in the British position on the question of Commonwealth preferences, and the discussion concentrated on definition of origin.[135] A small group of experts considered a German compromise proposal, which, as a concession to the French, recommended a sector-by-sector examination of tariffs in the first four years of the FTA. If major tariff disparities were to be found, the resulting deflection of the trade problem was to be solved by one of the following four alternative measures: (A) the percentage rule, (B) process rules, (C) harmonization of tariffs or (D) compensatory taxes. The German proposal did not make any recommendation as to which of these four was to be preferred. Clearly, it was an attempt by the German negotiators to move the British position closer towards what had been the state of the consultations among the Six before the postponement of their meetings, namely a sector-by-sector examination, and a mixture of percentage rules and the Carli formula.

However, in the parallel high-level meeting between Erhard and Maudling, the warnings of Werkmeister seemed to have been forgotten.[136] Here, Erhard once again claimed full coincidence between his and Maudling's views, promising to put pressure on the Italians and the French to choose a mixture of alternatives A and B as solutions to the problem. Not surprisingly, therefore, the meeting once again led to over-optimistic reactions in the press.[137] However, Erhard's promises stood in stark contrast to the German position in the Ockrent group of the Six, in which a mixture of percentage rules and Carli-style taxes (i.e. A and D) had already been advocated.[138] The gamble of 'speaking with two voices', if it was a conscious one, was clearly dangerous, since giving reassurances to Britain seemed to have the effect of preventing the latter from accepting an interim agreement so as to avoid discrimination resulting from the imminent tariff cuts among the Six planned for 1 January 1959.[139] It also appeared to give further substance to the impression that the Germans were susceptible to British warnings about a failure of the negotiations. Maudling's brief had emphasized steadfastness on the economic details of the plan, while his tactics once again included reference to political and military consequences.[140] The apparent success of the 'bullying' approach thereby ensured the continuance of the British view, 'that, as a matter of tactics, it is right to play the Germans off against the French'.[141]

In July, there appeared to be some movement in the French position, about which the Ministry of Economics was informed by Jean Rey, the Commissioner responsible for the Community's external relations.[142] While Erhard had previously only managed to extract a vague commitment to the continuation of the FTA negotiations from the French Foreign Minister, Maurice Couve de Murville, there were now some more details about the French position.[143] The demands for *décalage* and harmonization were dropped, while new demands included access to Commonwealth preferences and unanimity rules governing the FTA institutions. With regard to definitions of origin, the French argued for the Carli plan to be the dominant means of solving the problems arising in the planned sector-by-sector examination of tariffs. While welcoming renewed French commitment to the idea of the FTA, Erhard's ministry opposed the two new demands. The new permanent Head of Department E, Ulrich Meyer-Cording, argued that the Commonwealth was based on reciprocity, and that unanimity would give one country the means to block any further integration.[144] Undoubtedly the most difficult issue from a German point of view was the question of definition of origin, now that the new French position had made the dilemma complete. On the one hand, the French were arguing for a near wholesale application of the Carli plan, while, on the other, British negotiators advocated the exclusive use of percentage and process rules. The Germans, caught in between, had promised support to both sides, arguing in Brussels that compensatory taxes were useful in some cases, while giving Maudling a firm commitment to resist their introduction.

In Britain, there was an air of optimism about the FTA negotiations following the new French mood. A first sign of renewed French commitment to the FTA came on the occasion of Macmillan's visit to Paris in late June.[145] In his subsequent report to Cabinet, the Prime Minister summed up the Foreign Secretary's and his own impressions of the attitude of the new French leader:

> He [de Gaulle] was not well-informed about the projected European Free Trade Area; but they had impressed on him the dangers of continued French intransigence in this context and there was some hope that he might exert his personal authority to secure the resumption of practical negotiations in the near future.[146]

De Gaulle's reply to a follow-up letter by the British Prime Minister did indeed promise his personal intervention.[147] He pledged to work towards 'the enlargement of economic co-operation in Europe, in which Great Britain was naturally included', as long as it satisfied two conditions: neither the economic and financial equilibrium of France nor the existing agreements between the Six should be endangered. After the meeting, the experts of the Economic Steering Sub-Committee produced new proposals for the Paymaster-General to use with Erhard in bilateral talks and in the Maudling Committee which was to reconvene thereafter.[148] In all, these represented a modest advance on the previous British position, for while they still firmly rejected the Carli plan and advocated percentage and process rules, they now accepted the need for a sector-by-sector examination of the effects of tariff differentials. In a letter to de Gaulle, Macmillan claimed that these proposals did indeed satisfy the two conditions set out by the French.[149]

Erhard's gamble was in danger of becoming exposed, now that both the Steering Board of Trade and the British themselves had accepted the French demand for a sector-by-sector examination.[150] While the report of the trade experts left the question of safeguards open, Maudling's new proposals clearly followed the apparent agreement reached with the Germans. The Economics Ministry's dilemma was aptly summed up in its brief for the Maudling Committee meeting:

> In the Ockrent Committee, the Federal Government has agreed to reject the percentage rule, and to accept process-lists complemented by procedures of the Carli-plan (compensatory taxes). On the other hand, the German side has promised in the Bonn consultations with Mister Maudling, to argue in favour of percentage-rules and process-lists.[151]

The only credible course of action open to the Economics Ministry – incidentally one which was supported by the *Auswärtiges Amt* – was now to accept the proposals of the Steering Board of Trade, which advocated the sector-by-sector approach but which left the question of rules open. Although it meant essentially postponing a discussion about the problem, it undoubtedly saved the face of the German delegation, when the Maudling Committee followed this line in early August.[152] With movement in both French and British positions, and with the additional benefit of having escaped the German negotiation dilemma, Erhard was decidedly upbeat, closing his speech to the OEEC Council meeting in August with the conviction that 'all members [of the Council] are driven by the wish and possess the will, to reach the goal [of the FTA]'.[153]

Erhard's practical optimism, though apparently shared by Maudling, by no means reflected the state of the negotiations.[154] The Six had yet to agree on a final negotiation position, while the deadline of 1 January was approaching without an interim agreement in sight. However, after more than a year of shadow-boxing, the French seemed at last ready to negotiate. The *Auswärtiges Amt* undoubtedly welcomed this development, not for the sake of free trade, but for the calming effect it promised for European affairs. In thanking the French Finance Minister Antoine Pinay for the concessions, van Scherpenberg spelled out the position of his ministry:

> Though the Federal Government does not tend to take too seriously the English threats in case of a failure of the negotiations, since our position vis-à-vis England is rather strong, a failure of the negotiations would nevertheless cause a period of irritation and insecurity and also trade political complications, whose avoidance must lie in the general interest. However, the precondition of success of the Free Trade Area is the uncompromising maintenance of the Community of the Six, this being and remaining the central plank of our European policy, and we would do everything to ensure its functioning.[155]

Pinay himself stressed France's commitment to the EEC, which was later confirmed on the occasion of the first meeting between Adenauer and General de Gaulle in the latter's country house in Colombey-les-deux-Églises in September. The British Foreign Office feared that on this occasion de Gaulle might try to obtain Adenauer's wholesale agreement to the French position and that the latter might well agree 'for the sake of his general policy of seeking closer understanding with France'.[156] The *Auswärtiges Amt*, however, assured their British counterparts that the FTA would only come up as one minor part of a *tour d'horizon*.[157] In the event, his first encounter with the new French President went a long way to calm Adenauer's fears that his policy of European integration in the form of Franco-German *rapprochement* within the Six-power Community was in jeopardy.[158] At the same time, it also appeared to confirm the earlier impression that the new French government was less than enthusiastic about the FTA and only prepared to accept a scheme modelled on French demands.

It was now up to the meeting of the EEC's Council of Ministers in Venice in October to reach agreement among the Six. The basis for such an agreement was to be the report produced by the Ockrent group. The main sticking points were the voting procedures characterizing the FTA institutions and the problem of deflection of trade. With regard to the latter, the German delegate, and current acting President of the Council, Alfred Müller-Armack, was content to see a real discussion postponed once again, by following the

Mistaken, Misled or Misguided? 97

French suggestion of a parallel sector examination of experts of the Six. On the question of institutions, Müller-Armack was prepared to make a concession to the French in as much as unanimity could be accepted for the first phase only. Yet again, no final solution was reached on this problem, with the consequence that the Six were to meet again in Brussels a month later.[159]

There, the French Foreign Minister, Couve de Murville, once again raised the question of deflections of trade, arguing the EEC's memorandum to the OEEC's should insist on Carli-style taxes as the dominant solution. A compromise formula suggested by Müller-Armack, which merely stated that the EEC envisaged compensatory taxes only 'along with conventional rules for the definition of origin', was rejected in favour of the French proposal.[160] On the question of institutions, there was now agreement that at least with regard to the transition from first to second phase unanimity should apply.

The Venice and Brussels meetings were controversial in so far as they led some within the Six, as well as British observers, to criticize the Germans for having given in to French demands.[161] The suspicion was voiced that German negotiators were not free in their bargaining, but under strict instructions to support the French position following the meeting between Adenauer and de Gaulle.[162] How far exactly this meeting led the German negotiators to compromise over the FTA is unclear, but there is some evidence for a different motive. Van Scherpenberg claimed that he had indeed sent clear instructions to compromise with regard to the outstanding problems. Yet, his main interest appeared to have been that 'a Six-power document, however inadequate, must be approved at the Brussels meeting. Otherwise the French would merely have had an excuse for further postponement of the Maudling Committee.'[163] Müller-Armack also defended the Venice and Brussels compromise as necessary to get real negotiations started.[164] He apparently failed to convince the Paymaster-General, however, and it was only the Foreign Office which recognized that the Germans 'see themselves as in the role of the honest broker between the French and ourselves'; and that 'they had reluctantly made concessions to the French which they hoped could be modified by continuing pressure from the Eleven'.[165]

Macmillan's visit to Bonn and the breakdown of the FTA negotiations

In its brief for Macmillan's visit to Bonn in early October, the Foreign Office thus avoided any suggestion that German negotiation performance had caused disappointment in Britain. It also contained no suggestion that Macmillan should use the – by now customary – warnings about the consequences of failure in the FTA negotiations.[166] However, Macmillan had evidently been determined to do just that, not least because a useful opportunity had arisen which allowed him to disrupt Franco-German relations. A skilful scheduling of the topics placed the FTA directly after a discussion of NATO matters. The Prime Minister gave Adenauer a summary of the tripartite proposals for NATO, which de Gaulle had communicated to the US and British administrations without informing the Germans.[167] Adenauer now felt that whatever trust had been established at Colombey had evaporated.[168] Having dealt a blow to the Chancellor's confidence, the Prime Minister proceeded by threatening the Germans quite openly:

> it would be very bad if the United Kingdom found herself economically isolated. No British Government could continue to take part in the military defence of a continent which had declared economic war upon her. The United Kingdom would become isolationist. We could not have a Europe which was militarily united and economically divided.[169]

Clearly disturbed by the unexpected development in NATO which seemed to signify deteriorating Franco-German relations, and at the same time once again threatened with economic, political and military consequences of the FTA failure, Adenauer, Brentano and van Scherpenberg assured their British counterparts that the Federal Government was to use its influence to bring about the successful completion of the negotiations.[170]

On the level of officials, the Macmillan visit indeed produced German pressure on the French government, most notably at a meeting between van Scherpenberg and the French Ambassador François Seydoux.[171] However, once again, this meeting demonstrated that the *Auswärtiges Amt* was interested in the FTA not for its own sake but as a means to protect, or if possible advance, the achievements of the Common Market. A failure of the FTA negotiation was not so much feared for the possibility of a subsequent trade war, since, according to van Scherpenberg, the Germans were under 'no illusion about the economic balance between the Anglo-Saxon countries and the EEC' with the latter in the long run being 'undoubtedly the biggest consumer of sterling-area products'. Hence, while expected to cause some 'disturbances in trade policy', a trade war, if it materialized, could not be lost. Instead, the main problem as perceived by the *Auswärtiges Amt* in autumn 1958 was that a failure of the FTA negotiations might lead to increased tension among the Six.[172]

Whatever their shortcomings, the Venice and Brussels decisions had opened the way for the Ockrent report to be forwarded to the Maudling Committee which was to meet in late October. Yet, before this meeting was to take place, officials in the Ministry of Economics were shocked to learn that in bilateral talks with the British negotiators the French had introduced new demands, now insisting that an agreement on the origin problem could only be permanent if followed by a 'standstill' in tariffs.[173] Müller-Armack was enraged that, after substantial concessions had been made at the Brussels meeting, the French had thereby shown complete disregard for the principle of co-ordination among the Six.[174]

The British negotiating position was hardening in the face of the new French demands. No further compromises were contemplated after the Treasury and the Foreign Office had jointly produced a paper listing UK concessions made already.[175] Müller-Armack's attempts to move the British to consider new arrangements for agriculture and Commonwealth preferences were politely ignored.[176] In the case of the Prime Minister, the widely shared anticipation of an imminent breakdown of negotiations turned into undisguised hostility towards the Continentals. Whereas, for others, the warnings issued over the past 18 months had been a tactical device, Macmillan was now beginning to see them as the actual consequences for Britain's foreign policy. In a memo to his Foreign Secretary, he stated:

> I hardly think we could justify remaining in NATO and keeping four divisions of our troops at considerable expense to defend militarily a group of countries who were carrying on an economic war against us. Finally, I would like to consider how far this should be made clear to the French and Germany. I have already said something pretty stiff to de Gaulle but then he will

have forgotten it by now. I said the same to Adenauer the other day. He was shocked but impressed. We may be accused of the usual perfidy if we do not make it clear while there is still time how serious we would consider a breakdown and how it would cause us to review all our commitments. Fortress Britain might be our right reply.[177]

Both Treasury and Foreign Office were shocked by the realization that tactical threats had assumed their own momentum in the mind of the Prime Minister.[178] In agreement with his officials, Foreign Secretary Selwyn Lloyd politely but firmly stated that 'in terms of modern warfare our own defence as well as that of continental Europe is at stake. If our troops began to leave Europe the American troops would soon follow them.'[179] Furthermore, the two departments agreed that the implementation of the Treaty of Rome by itself did not represent a declaration of economic war on Britain, and that Macmillan's ideas would have serious consequences for Anglo-American relations.[180] In the Foreign Office there were serious doubts as to the usefulness of such warnings as a mere tactical device. Not only was there mounting evidence that the US was becoming ever more suspicious about British motives, but even in Europe itself it appeared necessary to reduce tension rather than increasing it.[181] Rather poetically, Deputy Under-Secretary, Paul Gore-Booth, asked, 'to threaten or not to threaten: that is the question'.[182]

The need for calm became all the more obvious in the negotiations themselves. When the Six met immediately before the Maudling Committee meeting on 23 October, Müller-Armack declined to comment on the new French demands, while urging their delegate Olivier Wormser – of the Quai d'Orsay's economics department – not to introduce the idea of a 'tariff standstill' in the Maudling Committee. Yet, Wormser did just that, and the tone he chose in his address was one of extreme confrontation.[183] The negotiations were now in danger of collapsing altogether, and the German negotiators were frantically searching for solutions. In a meeting of the Six, in between the Maudling sessions, Müller-Armack introduced a compromise formula which suggested a consultation procedure and, if necessary, safety clauses in case of harmful unilateral changes in the external tariffs of any one country. As so often in the past, the Six failed to agree to this proposal due exclusively to French opposition.[184] It was up to Müller-Armack to try to improve the negotiation climate in bilateral talks with Maudling and Couve de Murville –

without success in both cases.[185] The Maudling Committee could therefore only agree upon further procedural questions, in so far as a permanent sub-committee was to examine the question of the definition of origin, while the full Maudling Committee was to meet again in November. Hence, the only success which Müller-Armack was able to report to Erhard and the Chancellor was that the negotiations had not been abandoned.[186] Against the express wishes of Brentano, Erhard now decided to attend the Maudling Committee meeting in November himself, so as to use his influence to break the deadlock.[187] Yet, with the severe strain on European relations as a result of the acrimonious FTA negotiations, the Chancellor intervened and Erhard was sent on a prolonged tour of South-East Asia instead!

The October meeting of the Maudling Committee and the decreasing influence of Erhard finally convinced the British Foreign Office that it was illusionary to hope for German pressure to bring the French round, and that threats would be counterproductive.[188] However, Macmillan had by now chosen to ignore the ministry's advice and to follow his own agenda instead. Further letters to de Gaulle and Adenauer about the possible collapse of NATO were followed by a ministerial meeting called by the Prime Minister himself, which was to consider retaliatory measures.[189] Here, his confrontational approach was supported by two important allies, who prevented the moderating influence of the Foreign Office from coming into play. Maudling introduced the idea of retaliatory quotas and tariffs for the beginning of the following year, while David Eccles, the President of the Board of Trade, argued that the UK should continue 'to use the argument about dividing Europe and about the dangers of retaliation. The more they hurt the more must be in them.'[190] They all agreed that negotiations should be abandoned if the French had not modified their position by late November.[191]

Soon after, their ideas were overtaken by events. At the November meeting of the Maudling Committee, the FTA negotiations finally broke down, following a statement by the French Information Minister, Jacques Soustelle, that it was impossible to form a Free Trade Area 'as wished by the British'.[192] From a British point of view, this announcement did not come as a surprise, after de Gaulle's answer to Macmillan's latest letter had characterized French objections to the FTA as being of principle, and after the French Foreign Minister had 'torpedoed the Free Trade Area' in a meeting with Selwyn Lloyd.[193]

To the German negotiators, by contrast, Soustelle's announcement came as a shock. According to Müller-Armack, the meeting had been conducted in a 'relaxed atmosphere', and, only the day before, Couve de Murville had confirmed that his government was still actively searching for solutions.[194] German negotiators suspected that Soustelle's comments had not been officially sanctioned, and that he had merely tried to score party-political points in France.[195] Following the announcement, Maudling was said to have 'lost his nerve' over what was merely a 'philological problem' by prematurely declaring an indefinite postponement of further committee meetings.[196] The German embassy in London, however, expected the British government 'to make every effort to come back to the negotiation table as soon as it becomes clear where a real basis for such negotiations lies'.[197] At the same time, it also became obvious that Maudling's postponement of committee meetings was an unexpected but welcome development for the French Cabinet.[198]

The aftermath – searching for an interim solution

The initial reaction of the British government to the breakdown of the Maudling Committee was much more conciliatory than might have been expected after the confrontational approach chosen by the Prime Minister during the preceding months. Having themselves previously contemplated the temporary suspension of committee work, ministers now regarded as the main objective the avoidance of discrimination arising from the EEC tariff cuts due on 1 January 1959.[199] Recognizing the futility of previous attempts to influence the Germans, there was also a remarkable insight into the political priorities of Chancellor Adenauer:

> The Federal German Government had not given us the assistance which we had hoped for: it seemed that the Federal German Chancellor would be extremely reluctant to prejudice in any way his overriding objective of securing a lasting political reconciliation between France and Germany.[200]

The Foreign Office and Treasury recommended that no approach to Adenauer should be made by the Prime Minister, while officials of all departments, assembled in the Economic Steering Committee, agreed that the main task was to secure a *modus vivendi*, to wait for proposals of the Six in this matter, and to organize in the meantime a common negotiating position with Switzerland and Scandinavian countries.[201] They warned, however, that there were only shaky legal grounds for Britain to revert to retaliatory introduction of quotas, in the case of the Six failing to propose an adequate interim solution.[202] In the meantime, the Treasury recommended to 'sit back for six months, let passions cool and the Common Market get under way'.[203]

It was in this frame of mind that the British government sought to influence the outcome of the forthcoming meeting between Adenauer and de Gaulle at Bad Kreuznach, hence such pressure was not directed at an immediate restart of the Maudling Committee negotiations.[204] Summoning the German Ambassador, Hans Heinrich von Herwarth, Foreign Secretary Selwyn Lloyd explained that there was a pressing need for an interim solution so as to avoid discrimination on 1 January, and to allow a breathing space for future negotiations.[205] Maudling confirmed this to be the British position in his talks with Kurt Birrenbach, the chairman of the *Bundestag*'s parliamentary committee on foreign affairs.[206]

However, the press was building up the Kreuznach meeting as a 'make or break' for the FTA, and there was also increasing pressure from industrialists on Adenauer and Erhard to use this opportunity to facilitate an agreement.[207] Even the Federation of British Industry lobbied the German government to use the meeting to restart negotiations.[208] Within the *Auswärtiges Amt*, however, first priority remained the success of the Community of the Six. In this view, a continuation of the Maudling Committee discussions was now deemed undesirable, because of the strain it placed on relations among the Six by dividing the Community into protectionists, such as Italy and France, and free traders, such as Germany and Benelux.[209] De Gaulle himself had threatened that, if pressure on France were to mount, his government's opposition to the FTA might spill over into opposition to the Common Market itself.[210] The concern for the cohesion of the Six was not only a negative motivation to postpone further FTA negotiations, the positive element being the idea of transferring the responsibility for formulating new proposals to the Commission – an enhancement of its role which had been demanded by Hallstein for some time.[211] A second motive for not pressuring the French into an early resumption of negotiations can be found in the fact that the US government had shown increasing concern about friction between France and Germany, following the unsuccessful Maudling Committee meetings in October and November.[212] The US embassy confirmed that its government placed greater emphasis on the success of the Common Market than on the FTA. While the *Auswärtiges Amt* therefore had a number of reasons for postponing negotiations, this did not mean that they now wanted to abandon Britain altogether. In a long letter to Herbert Blankenhorn, Germany's new Ambassador to Paris, the pragmatic approach of the *Auswärtiges Amt* was summarized by the Head of Department 'West I', Karl Carstens.[213] The FTA in its purest form was simply not going to find acceptance in France, and the alternative consisted in either a maximal solution (adopting all elements of the Treaty of Rome) or a 'much less ambitious solution which would give up the idea of a regulated complete tariff elimination within a fixed timetable', with the German Foreign Ministry clearly in favour of the latter.

Measured against these priorities, the Bad Kreuznach meeting proved a complete success. Most importantly, de Gaulle confirmed that France was to fulfil its obligations arising from the Treaty of Rome for 1 January 1959, and stated his long-term interest in political and economic integration of the Six.[214] Moreover, the French President combined these assurances with the promise of staunch support in view of the mounting Berlin crisis. On 10 November, the Soviet leader Nikita Krushchev had delivered a most alarming speech in which he had threatened to hand over control of allied traffic to and from Berlin to the Government of East Germany, if there was no negotiated end to the city's four-power status within six months.[215] Yet it would be misleading to assume that Adenauer had simply abandoned the FTA in return for French promises to remain steadfast in their rejection of Krushchev's ultimatum. On the issue of the FTA, the communiqué merely suggested that the Community's tariff cuts should be extended to all OEEC members. The FTA problem was thereby postponed, but the two Heads of Governments reaffirmed their desire to 'continue the efforts towards the creation of a multilateral association between the EEC and the remaining OEEC countries' and they recommended that the EEC Commission 'be asked to examine the problems and possible solutions'.[216]

The identity between the Foreign Ministry's pre-Bad Kreuznach position and the official communiqué of the meeting was not coincidental. In secret consultations a week before the meeting itself, van Scherpenberg and Couve de Murville had worked out the common position on the question of the EEC and the FTA.[217] Nevertheless, to hear de Gaulle himself confirm these drafts in the most unequivocal manner was a success in itself.[218]

De Gaulle had even managed to charm Erhard and to impress Müller-Armack with his technical knowledge of the FTA problem. Nonetheless, the Economics Ministry could not count the outcome of the meeting as a success.[219] Firstly, the communiqué had not mentioned the FTA as such, but had merely referred to a multilateral association, which suggested a moving away from the more liberal scheme favoured by the ministry. Secondly, and more importantly, the focus had been shifted away from the OEEC and the EEC Council of Ministers, where the Ministry of Economics enjoyed representative competencies, to the Commission whose personnel were closer to the *Auswärtiges Amt*. Yet, it would be wrong to assume – as contemporary observers did – that Erhard had wished but failed to use the Bad Kreuznach meeting to restart the Maudling Committee. His ministry's 'Concept for the Continuation of the Free Trade Area Negotiations' – produced by Department E before the meeting – clearly documents that any such press speculation had been groundless.[220] It flatly stated that 'following the breaking off of the negotiations at ministerial level, [co-operation with the eleven] cannot be continued at the moment'. Instead, the aim was to facilitate an interim agreement and to secure 'a statement by all six governments, and by the French government in particular, that they still adhered to the Ockrent memorandum'. The summary protocol of the meeting – as compiled by the French authorities – indeed shows that Erhard made no attempt to restart the Maudling Committee, but unsuccessfully sought to coax the French President into a commitment to the Ockrent memorandum by declaring his 'delight that the Six had reached a common position'.[221]

The failure to extract the desired commitment on this occasion was neither surprising nor particularly discouraging, as the upcoming meeting of the EEC Council of Ministers in any case provided a more promising occasion than Bad Kreuznach. Ludwig Erhard himself was due to take the chair, and strong Benelux support for his position was expected to be forthcoming.[222] The purpose of the meeting was for the Six to endorse the Bad Kreuznach proposals for an interim solution. Erhard attempted to convince other delegations to complement notification about the former with a long-term commitment to continue the Maudling negotiations, only to fail on a technicality about the form of Council directives.[223] In conjunction with the Kreuznach resolution, the EEC Council meeting was a defeat for Erhard. In his view, the interim solution proposed by the EEC did not go far enough, mainly because it constituted a unilateral offer which could be used to justify a delay in the negotiations until the

March report of the Commission, rather than containing a multilateral agreement which could serve as a stepping stone to a restart of the negotiations. None the less, it was he who had to defend the Council's resolution when notifying Maudling in London.[224] Here, he argued against an early OEEC Council meeting, which in his view would only raise the temperature further, after the Bad Kreuznach resolution and the subsequent EEC proposals had led to very angry British reactions both officially and in the press. Despite the fact that both van Scherpenberg and Erhard appealed for calm, British ministerial reaction had turned from reconciliation to hostility.[225] In addition to unfavourable press reports, this was the result mainly of the Board of Trade's evaluation of the French and Belgian proposals for a *modus vivendi* which portrayed both as discriminatory and wholly unacceptable.[226] The main objection against the proposals was that while most tariff cuts and quota extensions were to be globalized and thereby made accessible to all OEEC members, some cases of nil and negligible quotas up to 3 per cent of national production were extended only among the Six themselves.[227] Earlier warnings were forgotten when ministers agreed that if the proposals were not adapted, Britain 'should make it plain to the Six that we should be compelled to adjust our commercial policies'.[228] It was furthermore agreed to stay in close contact with other members of the OEEC, so as to co-ordinate defensive measures. For the longer-term, the idea of a limited free trade arrangement between the United Kingdom, Switzerland and Scandinavia was also envisaged. While most departments supported this line, the Foreign Office warned that talk of retaliation should be avoided and argued against making these plans public on the grounds that it could 'destroy all hope of a Free Trade Area negotiation, amount to a declaration of economic war, and completely disrupt the OEEC'.[229]

In the event, other ministers and officials were not to be deterred amidst mounting criticism of the Continent's 'rejection' of British participation, and in particular of the German 'sell-out' at Bad Kreuznach.[230] Yet, the grounds for arguing that Great Britain was substantially discriminated against were rather shaky. British criticism could only focus on the failure to globalize 3 per cent quotas, and attempt to separate France from the other five with the argument that a country which had not fulfilled the obligations arising from the OEEC code of liberalization was not allowed to discriminate at all.[231] Britain's counterproposals had been submitted and were due to be discussed at the extra-ordinary OEEC Council meeting. In the meantime, however, Foreign Office warnings were not enough to prevent British politicians and diplomats from openly threatening retaliatory action in the economic and military fields, in particular for Germany.[232] With the mounting crisis over Berlin, and under increasing parliamentary pressure, Adenauer could not afford to ignore these developments, leading him to send a letter to Macmillan in which he appealed for calm and reaffirmed his determination to find a solution for a 'multilateral association'.[233] The draft of Adenauer's letter found acceptance both in the *Auswärtiges Amt* and the Ministry of Economics, though the latter would have preferred a substitution of the term 'multilateral association' with 'Free Trade Area'.[234] The German Foreign Ministry was also interested in a general easing of tensions, though it was unimpressed by British threats. Unlike the British, they were aware of the imminent decision by France to fulfil her OEEC obligation, thereby removing any legal threat to the EEC and its *modus vivendi* proposals. It was realized that the economic interests of Germany lay with a liberal trade regime, but the little discrimination that remained was seen as a necessary component of a customs union if membership in it was to have any meaning at all – an argument against which Britain could only mount a feeble defence, given that the Commonwealth discriminated against OEEC members for the very same reasons.[235]

With the discussion within the OEEC threatening to heat up still more, Erhard again sought to appeal for calm. In his speech to the OEEC Council meeting of December 1958, he stressed that the interim proposals were 'not based on the idea that we should consider these decisions as a possible solution to a multilateral association', and that the Commission's examination should 'not prejudice the negotiation which will take place within the OEEC over the same problems'.[236] His intervention did not, however, prevent a disastrous outcome of the meeting. David Eccles, the President of the Board of Trade, introduced his more far-reaching proposals for an interim solution with the remark that failure to agree would lead to a reconsideration of UK commercial policy and to countermeasures being taken by non-EEC members of the OEEC. The French delegation responded by refusing to negotiate under threat and were not even convinced by a joint mediation attempt of Erhard and the British Chancellor of the Exchequer, Derick Heathcoat Amory.[237] The Treasury's post-mortem of what had gone so disastrously wrong at the OEEC meeting later revealed that Eccles had indeed acted on his own initiative when threatening retaliation.[238] He had been supplied with drafts of three possible speeches to be made at the meeting, and had been advised to use the most threatening one of these only in case of a blank refusal of French delegates to consider the British counterproposals. Even though no such refusal had been voiced, Eccles chose to use his prepared threats. That this was not merely a mix-up of briefs can be seen in the fact that he stuck to the recommended speech only to take the passage about retaliation from the other draft speech. The result of the December meeting was an abrupt ending to all consultations within the OEEC.

In the aftermath of the meeting, Erhard – undeterred – made a renewed attempt to restart negotiations. In a letter to Chancellor Adenauer, he expressed his concern that the planned countermeasures would create an extremely critical situation 'particularly for us Germans with our high export performance'.[239] By now, however, his suggestion for the immediate establishment of a conference bringing together himself, Eccles, Couve de Murville, Rey and delegates from Denmark and Switzerland was met by the combined resistance of the Chancellor's Office, the *Auswärtiges Amt* and Commission President Hallstein, all of whom aimed to preserve the rapport which had been reached with de Gaulle at Bad Kreuznach, to avoid alienating Community members not represented, and to see the strengthened role of the Commission put into practice.[240]

The adherence to the Bad Kreuznach rapport also shaped the internal discussions about the British proposals, which, over and above the 10 per cent reduction in tariffs, envisaged a multilateral raising of all quotas. An interministerial meeting at the end of December was hence dominated by the line taken in the *Auswärtiges Amt* and the Chancellor's Office, that, after fulfilling her EEC and surprisingly also her OEEC obligations, France should not be pressured into accepting the British proposal.[241] Keeping with the more restricted EEC proposal furthermore satisfied the Foreign Ministry's desire to establish some objective, if not too discriminatory, difference between EEC and OEEC membership. Müller-Armack's lack of opposition at the meeting was largely due to two separate factors. First, Germany was given the right to negotiate bilateral agreements over and above the interim solution.[242] Second, and more important, was the fact that, along with other currencies, the French franc had moved to full convertibility, thereby fulfilling Ludwig Erhard's overriding goal of removing financial barriers to trade. In a radio broadcast, the minister emphatically stated that 'of all possible forms of integration of the free world, currency convertibility is the most rewarding and it may even relieve us of the unfortunate quarrel about Common Market or Free Trade Area'.[243] This is not to say that the ministry had lost interest in a multilateral FTA, but any renewed initiative had to await the Commission's report in March 1959.

In Britain, in the meantime, there was unbroken gloom about the prospects of the FTA. The Maudling Committee had been abolished, the OEEC had been severely disrupted, discrimination had finally started, and FTA matters were left in the hands of the less than sympathetic European Commission. Additionally, the French decision to liberalize trade had 'severely weakened the legal argument' against the interim proposals of the Six, so that in January it was clear that, in order to continue to work towards a compromise, Britain had to 'accept that since the Six had fulfilled their obligations as members of OEEC... they could... discriminate in favour of each other without acting contrary to the OEEC code'.[244]

Mistaken, misled or misguided?

Throughout the Free Trade Area negotiations, the German position at the heart of the co-ordination among the Six made her a preferred partner for Britain in the attempt to put pressure on France. However, German willingness to react accordingly was limited by a complex set of competing motives.

Of all the German ministries involved, it was undoubtedly the Ministry of Economics which was most concerned about a successful conclusion of the FTA. The overriding aim was economic, reflected in the effect the FTA would have on more than half of Germany's external trade. Given this motive, and not any political desire for British association, negotiators of the Economics Ministry consistently searched for practical solutions in an attempt to mediate between the diverse interests of France and Britain. There was no attachment to the concept of a 'British FTA' as such, but a tendency to work towards a European-wide scheme of the most liberal kind achievable in the face of French opposition. In doing so, the Economics Minister can indeed be charged with having created a misleading impression in Britain, in so far as Erhard's repeated reference to the complete agreement between the two sides disguised the role of practical mediator played by Müller-Armack in Brussels, Paris and London. The latter aimed to move the positions of both

Britain and France, but Erhard's assurances hardened the British negotiation position. In the event, the British position hardly moved and the French government proved not nearly as committed to the idea of the co-ordination of views as the Germans. Following Soustelle's announcement of November 1958, an attempt to resuscitate the Maudling Committee as such was never envisaged by the Economics Ministry, which gave first priority to the avoidance of discrimination so as to protect German interests. Erhard did try to restart negotiations later, but by then the French agreement to fulfil all OEEC obligations, the new rapport following Bad Kreuznach and the removal of any immediate threat of discrimination had weakened his case. The *Auswärtiges Amt*, by contrast, placed the highest priority on the achievement and, later, the success of the Community of the Six as a vehicle of political integration, which in effect meant the maintenance and furtherance of Franco-German relations. This is not to say that they were opposed to the FTA. On the contrary, a scheme which would link the European Community with the rest of Europe was welcomed on economic grounds by the Trade Policy Department while the Political Department (now renamed Department 'West I') saw in it a further strengthening of the Western world.[245] However, whenever the FTA negotiations seemed to threaten the success of the EEC, priority was given to the latter. A third motive behind the European policy of the *Auswärtiges Amt* lay in Germany's relation to the United States. This, somewhat invisible, power behind the negotiations could be decisive in so far as the US government first welcomed the FTA proposals while, towards the end of the negotiations, placed ever greater emphasis on their preference for the European Community.

The policy of the *Auswärtiges Amt* was a consistent result of this order of priorities. The FTA promises of 1957 originated in the fear that something might still prevent the ratification and implementation of the Treaty of Rome, be it Erhard's attempts at 'sabotage', German public opinion or a veto by the French National Assembly. In 1958, by contrast, the European Community had come into being, allowing for a more positive approach, while leaked US views and pressures from within the Six suggested that Germany could play a valuable role as a mediator. However, whenever the German Foreign Minister assured his British colleagues of continued German efforts at mediation, there was some confusion as to what this mediation sought to achieve. Particularly after the French memorandum, such mediation was directed towards the establishment not of a 'British FTA' but of a multilateral association, so as to avoid asking too much of their French partners. A similar scenario can be found in the case of the breakdown of the FTA negotiations and its aftermath. As far as the *Auswärtiges Amt* was concerned, there was no 'sell-out' at the Bad Kreuznach meeting, the result of which had been formulated jointly by van Scherpenberg and Couve de Murville. The idea of strengthening the role of the Commission was consistent with its preference for the Community and with the additional benefits of reducing the influence of the Economics Minister and ending the multilateral negotiations in the OEEC which threatened to divide the Six themselves – something for which they had been criticized by the US. However, the positive result of Bad Kreuznach in the form of French commitment to the European Community was not paid for by abandoning the idea of a multilateral association. With a pause in the negotiations and an interim agreement secured, the *Auswärtiges Amt* not only thought that it had answered immediate British pressure but also continued to hope for the successful conclusion of a European-wide scheme.

Adenauer's foreign policy interests were first and foremost the maintenance of good relations with France, and secondly the related issue of cohesion in the Western Alliance. Uninterested in economic matters, the Chancellor himself – and not his Economics Minister – can perhaps be charged with having contributed most to British misconceptions about German willingness to put pressure on the French government to accept the FTA. In 1957, he had been advised by the *Auswärtiges Amt* to lobby in London for a delay in the negotiations in order to safeguard Franco-German *rapprochement* in the form of the EEC. Here, the initial promise was made to use German influence towards a successful conclusion of the FTA negotiations. Adenauer repeated his promise on two other occasions, when he met with the British Prime Minister in spring and autumn 1958. This had much to do with the timing of these visits. On both occasions, Adenauer felt that the tenets of his foreign policy were threatened. In April 1958, the constitutional crisis in France appeared to undermine the EEC as the institutionalized expression of Franco-German *rapprochement*. Six months later, it was de Gaulle's tripartite idea, which not only undermined his trust in the General but also seemed to threaten Germany's position in the Western Alliance. Both occasions demanded the maintenance of good Anglo-German relations to balance a weakening Franco-German relationship. Alienating the British was hence far from Adenauer's mind, though he unwillingly raised expectations of German support, which his government could not fulfil.

Elsewhere, it has been argued that the Bad Kreuznach meeting was a turning point in Adenauer's relations with Britain, in so far as he agreed to the abandonment of the FTA in return for de Gaulle's support in the mounting Berlin crisis. Since no such assurances of support were forthcoming from Britain, his concern about security matters is said to have led him to go back on his earlier promises regarding the FTA. While not doubting either Adenauer's preoccupation with Germany's security or the strength of the personal rapport which had developed between the two statesmen, some doubt has been cast on this interpretation. The degree of personal involvement of the German Chancellor in the formulation of those elements in the Bad Kreuznach communiqué which related to the issue of European integration was negligible. Furthermore, it is questionable whether Adenauer understood the terminological subtlety in choosing between 'multilateral association' and 'Free Trade Area'. Instead, it had been the *Auswärtiges Amt* and its French counterpart which had formulated the Bad Kreuznach resolution. Rather than a concern about the Berlin issue, the overriding motive was once again to safeguard the EEC by putting an end to the acrimonious Maudling negotiations and by securing French implementation of the first tariff cuts of the Common Market. Significantly, there was no linkage between the issues of the FTA and Berlin during the drafting meeting of the communiqué.

The various motives behind the European policy of the Ministry of Economics, the *Auswärtiges Amt* and the Chancellor appear to suggest that false information about the German position had been the main cause for British hopes and their ultimate disappointment. Leading representatives of the two ministries, as well as Adenauer himself, can be said to have misled the British government about the extent of German preparedness to bring pressure to bear on France. British ministers consequently relied on Erhard to secure French consent to the economic details, though, more importantly, they trusted that British pressure had convinced Adenauer and his Foreign Minister of the political imperative of the scheme. This trust in Adenauer has been shown to have been a misinterpretation of his motives. It is in this context that the tactical approach with which the British government sought to put pressure on the German government deserves some consideration. There were mainly two arguments used, both entirely negative in character. Rather than

Mistaken, Misled or Misguided? 113

emphasizing the potential of their contribution to European integration, from a very early date the British side stressed the dangers of discrimination in Europe, threatening economic, political and military consequences in the case of a failure of the FTA. With the exception of the two meetings with Chancellor Adenauer in 1958, these arguments have been shown to have had little effect. On the one hand, Erhard needed no reminding of economic consequences, while, on the other hand, the suggestion of British troop withdrawal from the Continent was not taken seriously in the German Foreign Ministry. The continued support for the EEC shown by the US as the most powerful military power in the Western Alliance clearly reduced the credibility of the military argument. Hence, the *Auswärtiges Amt* saw in its use a reaffirmation of British insincerity and hostility to the efforts of the Six, thereby leading to the abandonment of the FTA in favour of a policy of multilateral association. After the breakdown itself, the argument of discrimination became even less convincing. The interim agreement combined with the surprising French move towards 90 per cent trade liberalization under the OEEC code removed the possibility of serious discrimination and legal British retaliation. What the British interim proposal was in fact asking the Six to do was to treat all OEEC countries as they were treating each other. The idea that the customs union was meant to facilitate greater mutual dependency and ultimately political integration would have indeed been absurd had the Six accepted the British proposals.

However, in addition to misinformation, there was another – if subordinate – cause of exaggerated British hopes for German support. Again, a lack of communication between officials and ministers contributed to the misinterpretation of the German position. The Foreign Office, in particular, has been shown to have been aware that Adenauer's promises had to be treated with caution and that they only reflected temporary insecurities. There were even some, if only few, officials who had come to doubt the effectiveness of the tactical arguments concerning economic discrimination and political division. Yet, on both counts, officials proved unable to counter the conviction of the Prime Minister and others that political pressure would ensure German compliance with British wishes – a conviction which resulted from the fact that he himself had begun to believe that the European Common Market would have the said economic and political consequences, and that it should be stopped even if Britain herself had to start the process of disintegration. Although Selwyn Lloyd and others successfully averted the most serious consequences of Macmillan's disappointment with the failure of political pressure, this did not mean that the British government ceased to hope for German support after 1958. And indeed, even after 1958, the German government was still working towards the inclusion of Britain in European economic integration. Their dilemma remained the same, aptly summed up by the *Auswärtiges Amt*: 'We are standing in between the British and the French; our sympathies lie largely with the former, but we are contractually bound to the latter in a framework which in the long term is a political concept.'[246]

4
'Bridge-Building' or: the Trade War That Never Was

The failure of the FTA negotiations was to bring some realization in London that the Six were not seeking Britain's participation at any price. Still, no serious policy reappraisal was set in motion, and the goal of a purely economic arrangement with the European Economic Community remained virtually unchallenged. Hence, the period between December 1958 and January 1960 merely saw a shift from political to economic pressure to achieve this end – the latter to be applied by the formation of a second European trade grouping, the European Free Trade Association (EFTA). What was advocated during 1959 was essentially a free trade arrangement between the two organizations – a policy which became known as 'bridge-building'. This chapter will examine the effect of the new British approach both on the development of Community policy and on the Federal Republic as one of the main targets of the said economic pressure, given her trading interests in the EFTA markets. It will also highlight the unintended consequences of the 'bridge-building' efforts because it weakened Britain's negotiating position overall and narrowed the room for maneuver for subsequent policy initiatives.

The European Commission's first memorandum

Hopes for Continental acceptance of the British *modus vivendi* proposals faded quickly within the first two months of the new year. Talks with the French revealed that they were not susceptible to threats, either political or economic, and that the only option to reduce the impact of discrimination lay in bilateral negotiations, which were indeed brought to a satisfactory conclusion later in the year.[1] However, from a British point of view, bilateral agreements did nothing to solve – or even further a solution of – the problem of a multilateral European-wide agreement. By reducing discrimination between the Six and other members of the OEEC, bilateralism instead appeared to endanger this main goal of British commercial policy in so far as it reduced the economic necessity for others to compromise.[2] Since the government did not contemplate making any changes to the substance of the FTA policy, there was no alternative to the tactics employed during the Maudling Committee negotiations. In the vacuum created by the ongoing deliberations of the European Commission, British negotiators attempted once again to put pressure on the German government directly as well as indirectly, the latter by urging the US government to do so.[3] However, it became increasingly obvious both that the Americans were unwilling to put their weight behind the British initiative and that the German government was determined to support the French on the issue of the 3 per cent quota discrimination.

The renewed experience of French intransigence, US opposition and German loyalty to the agreement reached at Bad Kreuznach led to a more in-depth analysis of the options open to Britain. In early March 1959, officials submitted a report to ministers on the question 'Free Trade Area: Is a new approach practicable?'[4] Therein, French obstructionism with regard to the FTA was described not as arbitrary but as part of a wider policy of protectionism, and it was also noted that political or military pressure would be lost on France, given that she was 'a recalcitrant member of NATO and such action by us would tend to make her own actions more respectable'.[5] As far as the 'Euro-enthusiasts' on the Continent were concerned, the report argued not only that they were strongly supported by the US but also that they harboured suspicions of the FTA scheme and foresaw the danger of the EEC being dissolved in the wider grouping. It was only with regard to the German government that the threat of disengagement was described as effective, though not recommended due to its wider implications:

> Probably such a threat would have greater effect upon the German Government. Certainly, if the withdrawal of British troops from the Continent were to be followed by a withdrawal of American troops, this would be most disturbing to the German government. It would be – and they would see it to be – a most powerful reinforcement of the 'neutralists' inside Germany. But

it would be most damaging for the UK even to appear to be contemplating such a policy. The withdrawal of US forces from Europe and the retreat of Germany into a 'neutral' camp would gravely weaken our own international position, and even if none of this happened confidence in the UK would be gravely shaken.[6]

Hence, the report concluded that a new approach to the FTA was impracticable in the near future, but reaffirmed that the scheme was to remain the goal of British commercial policy. However, in contrast to the realism which now characterized the British assessment of the positions of France and the US, the belief that 'bullying' tactics would have an effect on the German government survived the report, given that this approach was only rejected due to its wider policy implications. Significantly, no connection was drawn between the issues of confidence in the UK following such warnings and that of suspicions harboured by the 'Euro-enthusiasts' in Germany. Meanwhile, the continuing deliberations of the Commission masked the fact that the German government remained committed to the idea of a multilateral association of OEEC countries with the Common Market.[7] However, the ability of the Ministry of Economics as the most interested party to exert pressure to restart the negotiations was subject to institutional constraints. During the FTA negotiations, the ministry had fought hard to obtain, and later to retain, the competencies for representing the Federal Government in the relevant committees of the Six and in the OEEC forum. Now, the abandonment of the Maudling Committee and the Bad Kreuznach meeting had virtually removed this institutional basis. Responsibility had been transferred to the Commission, discontinuing the direct input of national governments. Faced with the sudden loss of representation in the proceedings, the Economics Ministry's main task lay in restoring an institutional framework in which it could once again use its influence. However, such an initiative had to await the Commission's report.

In the meantime, the thinking of the ministry evolved considerably with regard to the substance of the scheme of multilateral association, after having accepted that France would not agree to the British *modus vivendi* proposals.[8] It was now thought that the issue of tariff disparities had been grossly exaggerated during the FTA negotiations.[9] The solution which was advocated in the early part of 1959 once again demonstrates the pragmatism with which trade questions were approached by the ministry. State Secretary

Alfred Müller-Armack suggested an FTA covering products for which external tariff disparities were negligible and which could therefore be harmonized.[10] All other products could then be treated according to the Carli formula of compensatory taxes. The Economics Ministry's view was confirmed by a study of the *Economist Intelligence Unit* which showed that for about half of all tariffs harmonization would be possible without major changes.[11] Underlying the new proposals of the Ministry of Economics was the conclusion that the British insistence on tariff autonomy had been and continued to be the main obstacle to an agreement.[12] Again, therefore, the ministry's motive was to improve Germany's trading position through a multilateral association, rather than to support a 'British FTA'. Indeed, not only were British threats blamed in part for the breakdown of the negotiations, but it was also thought that the United Kingdom should be moved to more far-reaching compromises.[13] Yet, officials were well aware of the weakness of their negotiating position. Although the new plan was put to the Commissioners working on the March report, there was little expectation that it would be taken up.[14] Such was the pragmatism of the proposals that even the *Auswärtiges Amt* supported its submission to the European Commission.[15]

In the event, German efforts did little to change the Commission's attitude towards the problem. Neither German nor any other proposals were incorporated into the report. The document, which became known as the Commission's first memorandum, did not envisage further negotiations in Europe; instead, it merely advocated a liberal EEC trade policy towards third countries worldwide.[16] The worst expectations about the Commission's memorandum had thus been confirmed, and it was necessary for the Ministry of Economics to seek to re-establish a multilateral forum in which to discuss the problem purely as a trade issue. Given the support shown by the *Auswärtiges Amt* for the ministry's recent proposals, there was little concern about the domestic distribution of competences, but all the more the need to exclude the less than enthusiastic Commission. At the EEC Council meeting following the completion of the memorandum, Erhard therefore not only sought to secure yet another collective commitment to a multilateral association but also went on to suggest the establishment of a Comité Spécial to examine further steps towards this goal – a forum in which his own ministry was to be responsible for representing Germany.[17] Aware of continued French opposition to a reopening of OEEC-wide negotiations, the German resolution had been phrased so as to generate maximum support from the other four. The commitments contained in the Bad Kreuznach communiqué ensured that the French representatives could not dismiss it outright.[18] The resolution was noteworthy not only for the success in achieving the more limited aims of putting the multilateral association back onto the agenda of the Six and of securing Economics Ministry representation. It also represented a continuation of the temporary truce between Foreign and Economics Ministries, in so far as it was essentially based on a draft by the latter.[19] The apparent interest of the *Auswärtiges Amt* in a multilateral association was not only due to the fact that the first tariff reductions had consolidated the Community itself, but also to the fact that the spring of 1959 was characterized by increased – if temporary – interest of the US government in such a scheme as a reaction to the perceived threat of Soviet expansionism.[20]

Crisis in Anglo-German relations

Given the establishment of the Comité Spécial, the EEC Ministerial Council meeting was a success for Ludwig Erhard. Although he had failed to marginalize the Commission, considering that Commissioner Jean Rey was to chair the new committee, his ministry had obtained full competences for representing the Federal Government thereon. Furthermore, the Commission's memorandum had been rejected and the concept of a limited FTA with harmonized tariffs, which had been agreed between Müller-Armack and van Scherpenberg, had now become official German policy. The next problem was to sell the German proposals to the other parties concerned, but Müller-Armack's attempt to persuade his French counterpart in April – predictably – proved unsuccessful.[21]

Surprisingly, and despite the new-found strength of Erhard's ministry, no attempt was made to restore bilateral contact with the British government.[22] This partly resulted from the fact that Anglo-German relations had reached crisis point. In the early months of 1959, Macmillan and Maudling had formed the impression that Adenauer had been personally responsible for the breakdown of the FTA negotiations, and that he had let down the United Kingdom contrary to repeated assurances of support.[23] Macmillan was convinced not only that Germany was to blame but also that Adenauer himself accepted this, with Reginald Maudling agreeing that the

Chancellor now had a 'guilt complex'. This assessment was based mainly on reports by the British Ambassador to Bonn, who claimed that 'it is clear that the old boy knows he is in our debt'.[24] This impression led the British Prime Minister, his Paymaster-General and Ambassador Steel to ignore the advice of officials and to continue the tactics of threatening political divisions.[25] The warning of the German Ambassador to London, that Adenauer might think of British policy as anti-German, was ignored.[26]

Hans Heinrich von Herwarth was in fact closer to the truth. In addition to the ill-feeling arising from a British press campaign focussing on anti-Semitism, re-nazification and arms production in Germany, some in Bonn feared that the British government might link issues like disengagement, East–West relations and the FTA.[27] Brentano and van Scherpenberg, as well as the Chairman of the *Bundestag*'s foreign affairs committee, Kurt Birrenbach, clearly responded to this development and worked hard to find a compromise for a multilateral association in order to improve Anglo-German relations.[28] Others, like the Head of the *Auswärtiges Amt* Sub-Department 'European Political Integration', Wilhelm Hartlieb, envisaged a German nightmare scenario in which disengagement would ultimately lead Britain to support Nikita Krushchev's idea of a confederate and neutral Germany in order to stop the development of European integration.[29] Macmillan's Moscow visit at the height of the Berlin crisis seemed to give substance to the suspicion that the British Prime Minister was indeed playing the Russians off against Germany. Hartlieb's report 'The EEC and the Trip to Moscow' even depicted the British desire to break up the Six as the sole motive behind the Prime Minister's visit.[30]

While perhaps not subscribing to this extreme view, Adenauer was certainly closer to Hartlieb's than to van Scherpenberg's reaction to British policy. Rather than responding to such warnings by putting pressure on the French, he came to think of the British government and the Prime Minister as unreliable and essentially anti-German.[31] When, on the occasion of Adenauer's visit to London in March, Macmillan reiterated the customary warnings about political division of Europe in conjunction with a plan to freeze military capabilities in East and West, Hartlieb's view again appeared substantiated.[32] Unlike previous encounters, this time Adenauer felt assured of Franco-German friendship and trust, so that Macmillan's threats were counterproductive in so far as they confirmed his impression rather than stimulating interest in a solution to the problem of a multilateral association. In the aftermath of the meeting, he did not hesitate to convey his suspicions to the French government, and internally described the British as his 'enemies'.[33]

The European Free Trade Association[34]

In addition to the crisis in Anglo-German relations there was a further, and perhaps more important, reason why the British government did not wish to discuss the new proposals. The reluctance to enter into any negotiations at this stage was the result of the imminent adoption of a new policy aiming at an industrial European Free Trade Association bringing together Austria, Denmark, Norway, Portugal, Sweden, Switzerland and the UK.[35] This new policy was expected to achieve the goal of a European-wide multilateral association without the need to modify the British negotiating position.[36] This latter belief was based on two ideas: first, that negotiations between two established groups would prove easier than the clumsy 6 + 11 format of the OEEC; and secondly, that the competitive disadvantage resulting from positive discrimination between the members of the new group would lead the Six to seek a European-wide solution with more urgency.[37] Additionally, the new policy was meant to prevent other prospective members from seeking to join the European Community, which would have isolated Britain.[38] In this sense, it represented not a different policy but a new form of joint economic pressure to achieve the original FTA without concessions on tariff harmonization. The intended target was Germany, since she stood to lose out most to British competition in the important Scandinavian markets: 'The Germans are in effect fined for doing nothing.'[39] That such pressure was lost on France – the main opponent to a European-wide FTA with little interest in EFTA markets – was ignored in London. Faced with growing enthusiasm of the Scandinavians for the scheme, ministers decided on exploratory talks about the EFTA idea in March 1959.[40] The negotiations were unproblematic and swift, ultimately leading to the signing of the Stockholm Convention in December, which established EFTA as an organization aimed at the progressive achievement of an industrial free trade zone.[41]

Of course, the concept of a separate economic bloc was not new. The idea of a free trade arrangement with Scandinavian countries had been suggested by Treasury officials as early as March 1958, following doubts about the FTA negotiations raised by the French memorandum.[42] In these early stages, this alternative free trade arrangement was presented primarily as a compensatory policy, securing Britain's economic well-being in the absence of a European-wide arrangement, rather than as a step towards the latter. As such, it was far from being undisputed within the British government, with one Treasury official sarcastically commenting that one could:

> imagine only too easily the kind of cartoon which could be drawn to show John Bull, having made an unsuccessful pass at a French girl, being subsequently rebuffed by a series of progressively less glamorous substitutes of other and dowdier nationalities.[43]

Only once the negotiations had finally broken down did the idea of bringing together the OEEC members outside the Six begin to be given some credibility.[44] Now, it was not the economic value which was deemed important, but the fear of British isolation, and this became the dominant theme convincing both Macmillan and Maudling.[45] The advantage of the scheme as a means to increase economic pressure for a European-wide solution tipped the balance in favour of adopting EFTA as British policy in March 1959.[46]

None the less, some officials remained doubtful about the value of the EFTA idea. The Foreign Office, in particular, recognized the contradiction between the new policy and other pronouncements of the British government.[47] Given that the main argument used by British negotiators had consistently referred to the dangers of economic division and its political consequences, the formation of a rival bloc betrayed the government's sincerity. The Treasury official who had invoked the cartoon of John Bull also seemed to disagree with the EFTA policy, arguing that the Six were:

> not really dividing OEEC. What they have done is to start a process of fusing six member countries together. They profess to be anxious to maintain the authority of OEEC. But we shall be dividing OEEC if we make a permanent practice of holding meetings of the non-Six.[48]

Finally, there were British diplomats in France and Germany who doubted that the economic pressure of EFTA alone would lead the governments there to accept a European-wide solution.[49] While these warnings were not taken seriously, most officials recognized that there was a problem of presentation and that there was a need to point out that EFTA was to be a step towards a wider solution.[50] In practice, however, EFTA inhibited discussions about an all-European solution from the very start, by increasing British, and in particular the Treasury's confidence in a solution without concessions, once economic pressure was beginning to work on Germany and other European countries.[51] Hence, the British government politely ignored the German initiative, which had followed Erhard's successful rejection of the Commission report and which envisaged British concessions on tariff harmonization.[52] This was due to the belief that:

> the situation would be quite different in a comparatively short time if we achieved [the alternative] Free Trade Area, and this should strengthen our hands. In the meanwhile we should not allow the desire of the Six for some fresh initiative to divert us from our next objective.[53]

British hopes that the economic pressure arising from EFTA might further an all-European solution were not entirely misplaced. After some initial misgivings about the new scheme, Erhard and his ministry did indeed use the formation of EFTA to advocate a wider solution with renewed vigour.[54] As anticipated in Britain, the principle argument used in these internal exchanges referred to Germany's potential losses in Scandinavian markets. The official reaction of the Economics Ministry transmitted to the Chancellor, pointed out that more than 27 per cent of Germany's external trade would be affected, and urged an early opening of negotiations between the Six and the Seven.[55] For the year 1958, German exports to the prospective member states of the Seven were said to have exceeded even those to EEC partners.

The *Auswärtiges Amt* was also concerned about the new development. Its Trade Policy Department supported the conclusions of the Economics Ministry's memorandum and strongly argued in favour of early negotiations.[56] There were, however, dissenting voices within the Department 'West I'. Wilhelm Hartlieb saw the new British initiative as a 'throwing down of the gauntlet' in a final attempt to divide France and Germany and to destroy the achievements of the European Community, a feeling shared to some extent by his superior, the Head of the Department, Karl Carstens.[57] The former advocated an increased effort towards the political integration of the Six, while both advised their colleagues to try to prevent the establishment of EFTA by offering Denmark a deal on agricultural trade with the Community. However, with the support of State Secretary Hilgar van Scherpenberg, the moderates within the *Auswärtiges Amt* prevailed and a compromise was reached with the Ministry of Economics, in that proposals for 6 + 7 negotiations were to be worked out within the forthcoming Comité Spécial.[58] Exploiting the apparent division within the Foreign Ministry, Müller-Armack's skilful handling also ensured that his ministry retained overall responsibility for representing the German government in this forum.[59]

While the internal consequences of the EFTA proposals in the German government represented some progress for the Ministry of Economics, the scheme also made an impression – though undesired – on other forces within Europe. Surprisingly, Commission President Walter Hallstein strongly welcomed the EFTA plan.[60] When speculating on Hallstein's motives, the new Head of the Economics Ministry's Sub-Department E A 3 'Free Trade Area', Carl Hünke, warned that the Commission's negotiating position would harden. The schism created by the establishment of a second economic bloc within Europe would allow the proponents of political integration to argue that any deal on a European-wide economic solution would have to be negotiated between the two organizations, leaving the EEC's political enterprise intact. The perceived advantage lay in the fact that if such a deal was partial or incremental, rather than comprehensive, the Community itself could not be blamed for an economic or political division of Europe.

In Britain, more attention was paid to the efforts of the German Economics Ministry than to the suspicious welcome given by Hallstein, while there was no knowledge of the minority views held within the *Auswärtiges Amt*.[61] The optimism surrounding the possible effect of EFTA on the German negotiation performance was further enhanced by the possibility of Adenauer taking up the German presidency, apparently leaving Erhard to succeed him as Chancellor.[62] Even after it had emerged that Adenauer was to remain Chancellor, this optimism was unbroken, and it was not totally unjustified, for the EFTA proposals had indeed increased German unease about the absence of a European-wide solution. The creation of EFTA had already inhibited discussions about a compromise solution, however, and had threatened to render the argument about the economic division of Europe ineffective. The initial success of such economic threats masked the fact that EFTA was to continue to complicate the British negotiation position for the following two years and beyond.

The Comité Spécial and the European Commission's second memorandum

With crucial representative competencies restored, Erhard and Müller-Armack sought to achieve two interrelated goals: first, to put the issue of a multilateral association back onto the agenda of the Six; and secondly, to re-establish contact between the European Community and other members of the OEEC. These two goals were pursued by the Ministry of Economics both within the Comité Spécial and through bilateral contacts with France, Britain and other members of the OEEC.[63] In doing so, however, Müller-Armack encountered four problems, the combined effect of which led to the realization in autumn 1959 that a reopening of negotiations was unlikely to be acceptable to the parties concerned.

The first of these problems related to the obstructionist attitude adopted by the French, in the Comité as well as during bilateral contacts.[64] Discussions consistently evaded specific issues or possible remedies and instead concentrated on issues of principles which the previous two years had shown to be unsurmountable.[65] The disagreements characterizing these bilateral exchanges led to a second problem facing the negotiators of the Ministry of Economics, in so far as they alarmed those within the *Auswärtiges Amt* who feared for the integrity of the EEC. It was the 'European Political Integration' Sub-Department under Hartlieb, which continuously voiced its suspicion that Erhard and his officials were colluding with the British to 'liquidate' the EEC – a claim which, though applicable at other times, was completely unfounded at this time.[66] As a possible defence, Hartlieb and Carstens recommended that priority be given to the realization of French plans for further political integration among the Six – a point which was strongly supported by Foreign Minister Heinrich von Brentano who stressed the 'anti-integrationist' attitude of the British government in his correspondence with Chancellor Adenauer.[67] Over the course of the year 1959, it became increasingly clear that the US administration had grown to dislike the idea of any deal being struck between the Six and the rest of the OEEC – circumstances which represented the third problem encountered by the Ministry of Economics in its effort to restart negotiations.[68] Facing increasing balance of payments problems, the US would only accept schemes in which the damage resulting from preferential trade was outweighed by the perceived political gain to be derived from a united Europe. Clearly, only the EEC itself fulfilled these requirements; any scheme acceptable to the British did not. The fourth, and perhaps most unexpected, obstacle to restarting negotiations about a multilateral association lay in the reluctance of the British administration to contemplate such a step.[69] As mentioned, the British government preferred a delay in order for EFTA to start exerting the anticipated economic pressure on the Continentals, thereby encouraging them to enter into an agreement which was more favourable to British economic interests than all the schemes contemplated at the time.[70] As a result of these four obstacles to a reopening of negotiations, Müller-Armack's efforts had met with no success when the European Commission published its second memorandum in September.[71] The document attempted to clarify the external relations of the Community now that it had become clear that the Comité Spécial had been unsuccessful in finding compromise among the Six. In substance, the recommendations of the Commission echoed the March memorandum, emphasizing the importance of a worldwide liberal trade policy by extending the impending tariff cuts to GATT. Again, it failed to mention the goal of a multilateral association, but acknowledged the existence of EFTA in so far as it suggested the establishment of a 'Contact Committee' to examine problems arising from the existence of two trade organizations in Europe.

Given that the Commission's proposals had immediately followed yet another unsuccessful attempt to move the positions of France and Britain, Müller-Armack saw the need to reassess his policy.[72] The goal of an immediate reopening of negotiations was evidently unattainable, while even the secondary goal of establishing contact between the two groupings had proved elusive. While not amounting to the former, the Commission's proposals seemed to promise a solution to the latter. Müller-Armack now adopted a distinctly pragmatic position, advocating the acceptance of the Commission's memorandum on the condition that the Contact Committee was to be organized within the OEEC, rather than as a forum dominated by the Commission.[73] Aligning overtly with the Commission was expected to silence doubts about his ministry's 'European' credentials, and Müller-Armack hoped that the examination of practical problems arising from the existence of the European trade blocs would eventually result in some formal link between the two organizations. Discussions about principles could thereby be avoided, while acceptance of the document would also help to reassure the American government.[74]

Müller-Armack's policy reversal provoked strong internal criticism, leading to an open split within the Ministry of Economics.[75] Some argued that acceptance of the Commission's proposals amounted to the abandonment of the multilateral association as an official policy goal of the German government.[76] Furthermore, it was argued that the initiative would once again lie with the Commission which could not be expected to further 'bridge-building' between the two organizations. Opposition to Müller-Armack's position was not confined to the Economics Ministry. The Trade Policy Department of the *Auswärtiges Amt* agreed with the analysis that such a step would spell the end for any plan of association – a position supported by the *Bundesbank*.[77] In the event, however, the support of Department 'West I' and of the *Bundeskanzleramt* ensured that the Cabinet decided to follow Müller-Armack's approach, though its decision failed to put an end to a heated internal debate.[78] And indeed, later events were to confirm that the discussions surrounding the Commission's second memorandum, rather than the Bad Kreuznach meeting, put an end to the multilateral association as a policy goal of the German government.

The 'Special Economic Conference' – the last attempt at 'bridge-building'?

The combination of increased American dislike of an arrangement between the Six and the Seven and the new proposals of the Commission threw British policy into confusion by rendering the success of the 'bridge-building' policy increasingly unlikely. In his assessment of the second memorandum, the new President of the Board of Trade, Reginald Maudling, observed that the emphasis on worldwide trade liberalization was astute not only in its attraction to the Americans but also because it 'preserves the position of the Commission by maintaining discrimination in Europe'. He went on to argue that:

> In the second place it achieves the major objective of the French which is to exclude us from Europe and so to maintain their position of power in the little Europe of the Six. Thirdly, and

most ingeniously of all, it enables the Commission and the French to pose as the leaders of liberal thought, outward-looking, progressive, anti-restrictionist.[79]

It was thus amidst the general confusion about future British policy, that Adenauer came to visit London in November 1959. The Foreign Office had received ample information that the German Chancellor and his colleagues were unlikely to give up their support for the French position or to agree to any deal unpalatable to the US government.[80] Erhard's protestations that his government would now work towards a Six plus Seven arrangement were dismissed as unreliable, with Paul Gore-Booth, Under Secretary at the Foreign Office, commenting on German efforts to the effect that Whitehall would 'believe it when they see it'.[81] Accordingly, the Foreign Office recommended that the forthcoming visit of Chancellor Adenauer be used to improve the general political atmosphere when discussing 'bridge-building'. Adenauer was said to require reassurances about British motives, and no suggestion of political threats was made.[82] However, the Prime Minister's office followed its own agenda in the unquestioned – and by now habitual – belief that Germany was susceptible to warnings of political and military consequences. His Private Secretary Philip de Zulueta advised Macmillan to take the offensive with Adenauer. He argued that while the French should be 'coaxed' into an agreement, the Germans should be 'bullied' by hinting at the possibility of an Anglo-Soviet agreement on an armaments limitation zone in Europe![83] He also provided the Prime Minister with a list of Adenauer's 'acts of bad faith' for this purpose.[84]

Not surprisingly, the meeting did little to improve the personal relations between the two Heads of Governments, let alone improve the chances of a deal between the two economic organizations.[85] A subsequent ministerial meeting at Chequers, rather than producing clarity, only served to highlight the confusion prevailing within the British government.[86] Ministers reaffirmed 'bridge-building' as the long-term objective, while now identifying the US as an immediate target of political pressure – again, the very same tactics which in the past had proved ineffective and at times counterproductive.

However, Foreign Office officials were also well aware of the views of the US government.[87] Perhaps most outspoken was Harold Caccia, the British Ambassador to Washington, warning that 'the thought of a bridge merely joining the two European blocs and thereby

'Bridge-Building' or: the Trade War That Never Was 129

creating growing discrimination in quotas and tariffs against the United States is, not surprisingly, most disturbing to the United States'.[88] Hence, here too, the Foreign Office saw little chance of success, yet a positive campaign was agreed within the Official Steering Group on European Economic Questions, which attempted to sell to the Americans a possible Six plus Seven agreement on its political merit.[89] However, the London visit of the US Under-Secretary for Economic Affairs, Douglas Dillon, put an end to any speculation about the American attitude.[90] Macmillan himself observed that:

> the result of the talks with Mr. Dillon represents a considerable setback to our policy. They have ended in a clear statement in responsible newspapers here that the United States would back the Six rather than the Seven, that the United States do not favour a link between the Six and the Seven unless it is a political one; and that the United States do not favour negotiations between the Six and the Seven as groups. Although we knew what the American attitude was likely to be, this is the first time (I believe) that their position has been made public in such explicit and unfavourable terms.[91]

Nevertheless, it was a measure of Macmillan's inability to contemplate different tactics that his convictions survived the meetings despite the lack of impact of the Anglo-German and Anglo-American talks. He still argued that 'sooner or later, we shall have to make it quite clear (to the US and the Six) that the economic and political arguments are inseparable.[92]

To others, it was obvious that the tactics agreed by ministers had failed to produce any results and that British policy towards European integration was once again in disarray. Within the Foreign Office, there had, for some time now, been an internal debate about the dangers of British isolation. While not disputing the potential economic damage, the Mutual Aid Department, renamed the European Economic Organisation Department, argued that given the moves towards political integration within the EEC, the main danger now was that 'by failing to achieve some closer institutional link with the Six – particularly with France and Germany – our influence in Western Europe will inevitably diminish'.[93] The USA would then look to the EEC as their main partner, relegating Britain and the Commonwealth to a poor third.

However, while the Foreign Secretary was impressed by the political argument there was confusion over what could be done to achieve this closer institutional link.[94] While some demanded new concessions with regard to tariff harmonization, others doubted whether this would overcome the essentially political opposition shown by France. No credible suggestions to counter this opposition were made, though far-fetched ideas included giving the French the nuclear bomb and a delivery system – an early appearance of an idea which was to recur at regular intervals over the following decade. An alternative strategy contemplated was to persuade the Americans to reduce their troops in Europe so as to increase Continental dependency on Britain.[95] There was only one official who openly contemplated a workable solution ignored by others. Horace Rumbold argued that joining the Six was in fact the only solution 'which is going to cure the economic problem and the only one which offers a satisfactory answer to the political problem'. Reminding his colleagues that 'we have made great mistakes about Europe in the past and indeed have adopted a thoroughly hypocritical attitude about our desire for European unity', Rumbold went on to urge them not to 'perpetuate our mistakes out of a false sense of pride or from a plain dislike of admitting that we have been wrong'.[96] However, as Superintending Under-Secretary for the Western Department, Rumbold was not well placed to affect the Foreign Office position dominated by Paul Gore-Booth's European Economic Organization Department, which had discouraged early negotiations and essentially recommended a 'wait and see' approach in the hope of an improved political atmosphere in the following year.[97]

In an effort to redefine the goal of British policy, other government departments also produced memoranda to be considered by the European Economic Questions (Official) Committee and its Steering Group.[98] However, Treasury officials were as helpless as their Foreign Office colleagues. Here, the continuing danger of British economic isolation was the dominant theme though few were prepared to contemplate further concessions on tariff autonomy, while British membership was firmly ruled out.[99] The inability to move beyond the original FTA concept persisted despite the fact that the 'woodenness' of the UK position had been partly responsible for the failure of British efforts over the preceding three years, according to two 'post-mortem' memoranda produced by Frank Figgures and 'Otto' Clarke.[100] Figgures also cited the lack of appreciation of the political motive behind the efforts of the Six as a reason for the failure of the FTA policy, and claimed that French and American opposition ruled out any negotiation initiative for the near future. Some Treasury officials still harboured some hope that the Six, and Germany in particular, would feel the economic sting of EFTA in 1960, while others advocated worldwide reductions of tariffs through GATT so as to secure British trade and American goodwill. The official Treasury position submitted to the Cabinet represented a compromise between these views. Ruling out negotiations between the Six and the Seven, Chancellor Derick Heathcoat Amory recommended the consolidation of EFTA and a constructive approach to the GATT round in 1960/1.[101]

While the Cabinet supported the Chancellor's recommendations, their implementation was doubtful from the very start, given that Britain was no longer fully autonomous in its dealings with the Six. Already, EFTA had become a negotiating burden in so far as its other members strongly favoured an early offer being made to the EEC.[102] Hence, the very moment when the British government decided that the chances of a deal were so slight that a pause in the negotiations was necessary, pressure was mounting from its partners. In contrast, success of the Chancellor's ideas relied heavily on the assumption that EFTA remained united so as to exert economic pressure on the Six. With more of their trade at stake, some EFTA members, such as Denmark and Switzerland, were expected to work out bilateral arrangements with the EEC, if no progress was made towards a solution of the Six plus Seven issue.[103]

In their dilemma, the British received help – if unintended – from an unlikely quarter. Following the end of the FTA negotiations and the achievement of 90 per cent trade liberalization, the OEEC had lost its *raison d'être*, and an American initiative sought to establish a successor organization as a forum for discussing problems affecting world trade and for co-ordinating economic aid to developing countries. The Heads of Governments of four powers, the US, France, Germany and Britain, decided to set up a committee to formulate the remit of the new organization, and to report its conclusions to a 'Special Economic Conference' to be held in Paris in January 1960, bringing together representatives of 20 nations: the 17 OEEC members, the United States, Canada and Japan.[104]

The 'Special Economic Conference' provided an opportunity to escape the dilemma which Britain faced. A resolution calling for the subsequent discussions to examine with priority the problems arising from the existence of two economic organizations in Europe was formulated by the Treasury. Ministers approved this approach without much consultation, for its attractions were obvious.[105] First, it was designed to reassure EFTA partners that something was being done to further a Six plus Seven agreement, thereby preventing defections. Secondly, the participation of the US government in the new organization promised to alleviate American fears that any such deal would be detrimental to their economic interests. Furthermore, overt British interest in the new organization was expected to improve the political atmosphere – a prerequisite for the success of any real negotiations. With the establishment of the so-called Trade Committee, it also provided a new forum which, unlike the Contact Committee, was not dominated by the less than sympathetic European Commission. Above all, however, further discussions postponed real bargaining, for which Britain had yet to work out its position. Hence, when the British resolution was adopted by the 'Special Economic Conference' in January 1960, it represented a holding operation rather than an earnest attempt to restart the Six plus Seven scheme.

'Bridge-Building'

With the creation of EFTA, Britain's policy towards European integration appears to have successfully stimulated support from large sections within the German government. The reaction of the Ministry of Economics, and indeed of part of the *Auswärtiges Amt*, to the failure of the FTA negotiations and to the Commission's first memorandum had been correctly interpreted as a sign of continued German interest in a wider economic arrangement in Europe. The application of economic pressure through the formation of EFTA therefore appeared to be a suitable instrument to strengthen the arguments of former 'FTA-enthusiasts', while it was hoped that the existence of two separate organizations would reassure 'Euro-enthusiasts' of the integrity of continued economic and political integration of the Six.

However, the effectiveness of the subsequent 'bridge-building' policy has been shown to have been undermined by two other developments, both of which resulted directly from continued misjudgments about the extent to which British participation was sought on the Continent. First, the EFTA policy proved an obstacle to substantial negotiations from its origins in spring 1959. The belief in the future success of economic pressure led the British government to ignore all mediation attempts with which the Ministry of Economics sought to restart European-wide negotiations. Although such attempts were welcomed as signs of growing anxiety on the part of the Germans, the British government saw no need to contemplate concessions exceeding those offered during the FTA negotiations. Hence, they gave no consideration to even the most pragmatic German proposals for free trade treatment for products for which tariffs could be harmonized. The continuous disregard shown by the French and British governments to their mediation efforts undoubtedly contributed to the unexpected acceptance of the Commission's second memorandum by the German Economics Ministry. After the memorandum, in combination with increasing US opposition, had spelled the end of 'bridge-building', British policy towards European integration was once again in disarray, so much so that EFTA became a problem as soon as its convention was signed. Any remaining hope in the long-term success of economic pressure was conditional upon the cohesion of the organization which was threatened by defections of its more vulnerable members. While the 'Special Economic Conference' created a welcome breathing-space, a variation of this problem was to continue to affect British policy throughout the year 1960: interim tariff arrangements threatened to reduce the economic pressure on Continentals, which – for Britain – had been the *raison d'être* of EFTA in the first place.

A second factor undermining 'bridge-building' efforts lay in the lack of any political appeal to the Six and the Americans. The economic pressure inherent in EFTA was put on those who already supported wider European free trade, while having little impact on those most responsible for the failure of the FTA negotiations of 1958. In national terms, the creation of EFTA was most worrying to Belgium, the Netherlands and Germany – Britain's allies during the FTA negotiations – while doing little to pressure France, Italy, the US and the Commission – those who had done least to help the FTA project. A similar effect can be observed with regard to EFTA's reception within Germany. Here, EFTA had some impact on Erhard, the Economics Ministry and the Trade Policy Department of the *Auswärtiges Amt*, while leaving indifferent its political authorities as well as the Chancellor himself. However, the British government not only preached to the converted, but its leading representatives did so in a manner which further alienated those most in need of conversion. This was of particular importance in Anglo-German relations, for the creation of EFTA obviously invalidated the earlier

British claims that it was the EEC which divided Europe. Although British diplomats continuously stressed that the scheme was not a rival trading bloc but a step towards a wider European arrangement, their efforts were undermined by the continued employment of 'bullying tactics' during top-level encounters. If it had ever existed, Adenauer's reported repentance about the Bad Kreuznach 'sell-out' quickly turned into extreme suspicion about the reliability of Macmillan in security matters. The warnings about the economic and political consequences of a failure to agree on acceptable terms for British participation sounded increasingly hypocritical once their author had not only created a second trading bloc but had also visited Moscow during the Berlin crisis. This time, confident of French and US support, Adenauer saw no need to volunteer any promises, and Macmillan's tactics proved counterproductive in so far as they appeared to support the *Auswärtiges Amt* in its argument for increased political integration among the Six.

With regard to the accuracy of the assessment of German opinion, it was the Foreign Office which once again appeared to have been aware of the two factors outlined above. Not only was it the first department to realize the futility of an uncompromising attitude towards harmonization of tariffs and the need for additional political inducements, but it also advised against the continued use of threats. Again, however, its officials proved unable to affect the approach taken by Macmillan and his advisers who appeared increasingly out of touch with the feeling on the Continent. Yet, the disarray in which British policy towards the EEC ended the year also had positive consequences in so far as it caused a more realistic approach to be taken towards the problem. The prospect of economic discrimination and increased political integration of the Six, combined with the failure of British political pressure in 1958 and economic pressure in 1959, led to a complete reappraisal of policy options in 1960.

5
'Bully the Germans – Buy the French': Towards Britain's First Application

This chapter will examine the political and economic factors which led to a reappraisal of British policy in the summer of 1960. By then, both the Foreign Office and the Treasury officials appear to have convinced Prime Minister Macmillan of the need to apply for membership of the Community. However, it will emerge that this early effort at redirecting European policy failed due to forceful opposition within the British Cabinet. During the 12 months thereafter, Prime Minister Macmillan and officials of the Foreign Office and the Treasury worked hard to overcome internal opposition to membership, assisted not least by the German government which initiated bilateral Anglo-German expert talks to discuss European trade issues. This latter forum will be shown to have been crucial in keeping the issue of membership on the British political agenda, before political factors finally tipped the balance in favour of membership in the first half of 1961. The chapter will thus also emphasize the continuity of the widespread belief in London that staunch German support for British membership could be counted on in the subsequent negotiations.

'We are drifting'

Though the 'Special Economic Conference' of January 1960 had allowed for some breathing space, British policy towards European integration was marked by confusion and disagreement. While some officials in all departments still hoped for the economic pressure resulting from EFTA to have a long-term effect on the negotiating position of the Six, others argued for a reappraisal of Britain's policy options.[1] The British embassy in Bonn unsuccessfully advocated an acceptance of tariff harmonization, while President of the Board of Trade, Reginald Maudling, still argued for the removal of tariffs between the two organizations.[2] Though he admitted that this was basically the original FTA concept, he argued that by leaving the EEC intact the proposal would allow the Community to take further steps towards political integration, a feature with which he hoped to persuade the Six. Macmillan agreed with Maudling, but warned that some discrimination would remain, if only for the sake of preserving the identity of the EEC.[3] Despite the confusion, all but the Bonn embassy agreed on the undesirability of early negotiations or even minor compromises between the two organizations. It was argued that any short-term arrangement emerging from such discussions would only serve to reduce the urgency of a lasting agreement between the two organizations.[4] A positive contribution to the EEC/EFTA Contact Committee was ruled out by officials with the argument that it 'could divert attention from our main purpose of reaching a long-term agreement' and that 'it might be made to look like acceptance by the Seven of the impossibility... of achieving a wider agreement'.[5] Nonetheless, it was realized that these circumstances could not be allowed to persist for too long. As early as February 1960, the new joint Permanent Secretary of the Treasury, Sir Frank Lee, noted the contradiction:

> Ministers were repeatedly saying that the present trade division in Europe was bad, and we could not at the same time take comfort from the fact that the discriminatory pressures which would develop might help to bring about a free trade area.[6]

However, a further complication of the British position lay in that EFTA had become a 'noose around Britain's neck' by creating a dilemma in which the effectiveness of the organization in applying economic pressure was undermined by some of its members who advocated early resumption of talks as well as short-term compromises.[7] As a consequence, the need for a wider arrangement was emphasized in public, while negotiations were resisted in practice. In March, Maudling was able to water down the most ambitious Swiss proposals to no more than an offer of mutual extensions of tariff cuts between the two organizations.[8] Nonetheless, the Prime Minister warned 'we are drifting'[9]

Continuing uncertainty over the way in which Britain could move closer to the Continent did not, however, lead to the abandonment, or even temporary cessation, of the familiar tactics of threatening the Six with the economic and political consequences of their European integration efforts. In public speeches in early 1960, Maudling and Selwyn Lloyd insisted that, in the absence of British participation, the ensuing trade war would undermine political co-operation and ultimately the security arrangements in Europe.[10] This constant reiteration of the same theme since 1955 did not help to change the image of Britain in the eyes of the 'Euro-enthusiasts' in Bonn, despite the efforts of the German embassy in London to portray its host government as more conciliatory.[11]

The acceleration debate

In the early part of the year, the exchanges within the German government were characterized by a complete misjudgement of British intentions, with both *Auswärtiges Amt* and Economics Ministry assuming that the 'Special Economic Conference' had been a purposeful and sincere attempt to restart negotiations between the two European trade blocs. As far as the *Auswärtiges Amt* was concerned, the policy of a multilateral association in the form of a 'bridge' between EEC and EFTA had been buried with the European Commission's second memorandum of September 1959.[12] Further discussions were still regarded as potentially dangerous for the cohesion of the EEC, and the decision to accept the memorandum was eased by two factors which made a Six plus Seven link both undesirable and unnecessary. Undesirable, because US opposition to such a scheme had been made abundantly clear during Dillon's tour of European capitals.[13] Unnecessary, because EFTA itself was not regarded as a long-term threat to Germany's export performance since it was expected to disintegrate due to the heterogeneous interests of its members.[14] With continued threats being voiced by leading British politicians, London was still regarded as essentially hostile towards the EEC.[15] Emphasizing the need to safeguard the Community, Foreign Minister Brentano claimed 'that it remains the goal of British policy to prevent the unification of Europe'.[16]

It was in this context that the resolution of the 'Special Economic Conference' injected a note of caution.[17] In order to avert the perceived danger of the combined efforts of the Economics Ministry and the British government, the *Auswärtiges Amt* advocated the participation of the Commission in the ensuing talks as well as recommending a breathing space of at least two years before renewed negotiations between the two trade blocs.[18] The ministry was alarmed by the prospect of EFTA/EEC negotiations creeping back up the European agenda, in particular if the Ministry of Economics was to be given responsibility for the Trade Committee discussions which had been initiated in Paris.[19]

However, the institutional muddle following the duplication of fora for discussing EEC/EFTA relations offered an opportunity to neutralize such dangers. In collusion with the French Foreign Ministry and supported by the US government, the *Auswärtiges Amt* now argued that the proposed EEC/EFTA Contact Committee should discuss short-term problems only, while the Trade Committee of the 'Special Economic Conference' was to debate the consequences of the existence of two blocs for world trade.[20] The participation of the European Commission in the former was thought to ensure that real negotiations would not develop, while the presence of US representatives was to prevent a Six plus Seven agreement to emerge from the latter.

With regard to both means and ends, the position of the Ministry of Economics was the exact opposite of that of the *Auswärtiges Amt*.[21] Although it agreed that the prospects of an immediate restart of negotiations were limited, the ministry regarded pragmatic solutions to short-term problems as evolutionary steps towards a wider agreement.[22] The long-term feasibility of a European-wide solution was given some substance by the possibility of accepting tariff harmonization which was now openly debated in EFTA countries, in particular in Sweden and Britain.[23] However, the ministry's approach of slowly progressing towards a wider solution was promising only if an appropriate Six plus Seven forum could be formed and dominated by the ministry.[24] With US participation seemingly ruling out compromises in the Trade Committee, the Ministry of Economics favoured the Contact Commission.[25] Its officials therefore not only lobbied for representative competencies therein but also sought to exclude the Commission.[26] Therewith, the interministerial struggle with the *Auswärtiges Amt* had resurfaced.

A truce followed in February, after State Secretaries van Scherpenberg and Müller-Armack had worked out a compromise which appeared to give both sides the means with which to achieve their respective ends.[27] The *Auswärtiges Amt* was to be in charge of the reorganization of the OEEC and was to chair the interministerial preparations for the Trade Committee negotiations, while the Economics Ministry was given full responsibility for the Contact Committee. However, this truce was of limited duration, as Erhard and his officials soon found it impossible to achieve their aims of turning the Contact Committee into a forum for real negotiations. The ministry had clearly backed the wrong horse, in so far as Britain and other EFTA countries simply ignored the offer of a Contact Committee, themselves seemingly favouring the Trade Committee as a forum for Six plus Seven talks.[28]

While the prospect of an agreement between the two organizations thus seemed remote, the attention shifted onto the issue of acceleration, a plan to move forward the EEC's internal tariff cuts originally envisaged for 1961. The Six debated this proposal throughout the winter of 1959/60, and it was formally floated as the Hallstein plan in March 1960.[29] The interest of the *Auswärtiges Amt* in its adoption stemmed primarily from the fact that, on French initiative, these tariff cuts were to be supplemented by the first move towards the common external tariff. However, this first move towards the reality of the customs union was expected to meet strong criticism from two sources. Once again, it was Erhard, and his ministry, who was expected to oppose the measures since they implied tariff increases for Germany as a low-tariff country among the Six.[30] In addition to pressure from industrial interests, Erhard's argument would derive strength from the advent of real discrimination at a time when there was still some residual hope for a Six plus Seven agreement.[31] In this regard, the German Foreign Ministry once again expected a coalition to be formed between the Economics Ministry and the British government; a force which had proved disruptive to the cohesion of the Six during the FTA negotiations.[32] And indeed, British tactics and Erhard's fierce criticism of acceleration now led to a period of open conflict within the German government.[33] A powerful opposition to the Hallstein plan had been formed between industrial circles and the Ministry of Economics, and had also attracted the support of large sections of Conservative members in the *Bundestag* and *Bundesrat*.[34] Their case was based not only on the negative effects of German tariff increases but also on the necessity of a wider European arrangement. A heated debate followed, in which Erhard became ever more outspoken in his criticism of acceleration.[35] However, immediately after the US government had fully endorsed the Hallstein plan, Brentano urged the Chancellor to intervene so as to avoid endangering Germany's entire foreign policy in advance of the summit conference, which was due to bring together de Gaulle, Eisenhower, Macmillan and Krushchev in Paris.[36] Adenauer complied immediately, sending a telegram from San Francisco to Erhard, in which he stated that he:

cannot permit any utterances by yourself or your ministry which throw doubts on the unity of the Cabinet. I am determined to fulfil the EEC-treaty in its spirit and content. Acceptable shortenings of the transition phases are to be welcomed.[37]

Though this intervention somewhat calmed the debate, a formal Cabinet decision on acceleration was still due. Here, the outcome was far from predictable, for Erhard could count on the support of the Ministers of Finance and Interior, Franz Etzel and Gerhard Schröder. It was into this situation that Prime Minister Macmillan injected perhaps the most outspoken comments about the Common Market, which more than affirmed the impression of British hostility towards the project. In his talks with Eisenhower, he was quoted in the German press as claiming that:

it was Britain's historical role to prevent Napoleon's planned economic integration of Europe. If the attempt should be repeated by France and Germany, Britain would have no choice but to lead an alliance against them.[38]

Moreover, Macmillan also raised the issue of anti-Semitism and the possibility of a nazified post-Adenauer Germany. German enthusiasm for European integration and sensibility about the latter issues now ensured the adoption of the acceleration proposals by the Cabinet.[39] How narrow the passing of the proposals had been was evident not only in the postponement of tariff changes until 1 January 1961 but also in that the Cabinet's resolution included a call for renewed EEC/EFTA talks. Describing the impact of Macmillan's pronouncements on the Cabinet meeting, the Head of the Economics Ministry's Department E, Ulrich Meyer-Cording, very diplomatically informed the British embassy that:

the Prime Minister's reported remarks from Washington about the political danger of a split had no doubt to some extent helped certain members of the Cabinet to see how seriously [the British] viewed the situation. Equally it is true that their forcefulness had been taken by others in an unfriendly spirit.[40]

Once again, therefore, British tactics seem to have had the undesired effect of strengthening German commitment to the Common Market.

Rethinking British policy towards Europe

The combination of American and European reactions to Macmillan's outburst and the acceleration decision of the German Cabinet had a profound effect on the internal deliberations of the British government by demonstrating that an arrangement with the EEC was imperative not only economically but also politically.[41] At the same time, the German Cabinet's call for a renewed attempt at solving the Six plus Seven problem appeared to increase the chances of a new British initiative.[42] Though some officials warned of overoptimism in this respect, reports from the British embassy in Bonn reaffirmed that pressure for a solution of the trade problem was mounting in the press, among industrialists as well as in the *Bundestag*.[43] However, the European Economic Questions Committee recognized that the concept of a free trade treaty between the two organizations had finally to be buried, and that Britain required a new policy for accommodation with the Common Market.[44]

Such was the anxiety of ministers about Britain's relations with the EEC that, although a new economic policy had yet to be formulated, the need for improved political relations was addressed first. The deterioration of relations with Europe and the US had come after increased political co-operation had been contemplated by the Six for some time. If such proposals were now to come to fruition, there was the danger of Britain being excluded from Continental political decision-making.[45] Something clearly had to be done to restore confidence in British intentions.[46] Taking up a suggestion made in a letter by the Conservative MP Peter Kirk to *The Times*, Foreign Secretary Selwyn Lloyd informed Macmillan that, in his view, Britain should join the ECSC and Euratom.[47] The Prime Minister was swiftly convinced and instructed officials to study this option further.[48] The latter in turn asked British embassies to assess the likely reactions of their host governments to an application to the two lesser Communities.[49] Responses were on the whole discouraging, with the Belgians described as suspicious, the Italians unimpressed and the French most certainly opposed.[50] With the exception of Luxembourg, it was once again only the German government which offered some hope.[51] The British Ambassador to Bonn claimed that 'such dramatic evidence of our good faith in our professions to Europe would ... turn the scale if anything could'.[52] On this evidence, officials concluded that while a British application to join the ECSC and Euratom would help to improve the atmosphere, it was unlikely to overcome political objections to a wider European economic agreement. Ministers were therefore advised that such an application could only be a step in a longer term strategy which might involve signing the Treaty of Rome.[53]

Nonetheless, the Cabinet gave permission to the President of the Board of Trade to introduce the issue to EFTA ministers gathering in Lisbon in late May, and for the proposals to be officially floated at the forthcoming WEU meeting in early June.[54] Instrumental in the decision to overrule the advice of officials was the failure of the summit meeting in mid-May, which had the double effect of, on the one hand, increasing the necessity of Western cohesion in the face of deteriorating relations with the Soviet Union, while, on the other hand, seemingly improving Britain's relations to France and the United States.[55] In order to make it more forthcoming with regard to Britain's willingness to join the two Communities, Macmillan personally ordered an alteration of the draft of a speech given by Foreign Office Minister, John Profumo, to the WEU.[56]

In the event, the pessimism of officials was more justified than the optimism of ministers. EFTA members were concerned about the integrity of their organization and the US government was openly hostile to a British application, while most European governments showed themselves unimpressed.[57] Perhaps most unexpected was the negative reaction of the German government, which argued that, at a time when the amalgamation of the European Communities was being considered, it would be impossible for any country to be a member of two out of the three.[58] In all, the result of ministerial activism had only given further substance to the idea that only British membership in the Common Market itself would solve the political problem.

In the meantime, very similar conclusions were being reached by British officials concerned with the economic problem of finding a wider European trade arrangement. In mid-April, the Economic Steering Committee on Europe concluded that the concept of a free trade link between the two organizations had been buried by the decision in favour of acceleration.[59] In the search for an alternative approach, Sir Frank Lee submitted a personal memorandum to his colleagues, in which he argued that only the wholesale acceptance of tariff harmonization would secure Britain's future economic well-being in Europe. As a long-term aim of British policy, he therefore recommended 'near identification' of Britain and EFTA with the Common Market, a policy which would involve the formation of an all-European customs union by accepting 'most of the essential features of the Common Market without formal participation in it'.[60]

Although officials agreed on the submission of Lee's memorandum to ministers, they questioned whether the US government would welcome a discriminatory bloc.[61] Moreover, even with regard to the Continentals, there was considerable doubt about the negotiability of any new British proposals, despite the fact that the Six had complemented their decision in favour of acceleration with a declaration of intent to discuss EEC/EFTA problems within the Trade Committee. Maudling, in particular, questioned whether 'EEC countries possessed the real will to negotiate', and interpreted the declaration merely as a consequence of 'the need to reconcile the rigid attitude of France and the EEC Commission with the changing situation in Germany'.[62] Although Erhard's success in securing a postponement of acceleration to 1 January 1961 and in pressing for the Cabinet statement in favour of renewed EEC/EFTA discussions had been welcomed in Whitehall, there was little hope that Adenauer would actually press the French into opening real negotiations.[63] Again, it was the failure of the summit conference which appeared to increase both the necessity for a wider agreement and the chances of success of a renewed British initiative. In a letter to his Foreign Secretary, Macmillan argued that the Western Alliance had to be strengthened in response to the summit failure, and his suggestions included further 'economic arrangements in Europe'.[64] At the same time, it was speculated in Cabinet that 'the present circumstances ... might make it possible to consider solutions which would otherwise have been unacceptable to the United States'.[65] Even the French were said to be more favourably inclined towards solving European trade problems as a result of the summit experience. The British Ambassador to Bonn added: 'As far as Germany is concerned, I think the atmosphere continues good. The prospect of an intensified cold war makes the idea of a trade war as well all the more unpalatable.'[66]

It was under these changed circumstances that ministers finally considered the 'near identification' proposal. Most participants in the (Ministerial) European Economic Questions Committee still seemed to disapprove of the idea. However, it was once again a measure of Macmillan's anxieties that he himself decided that further consideration be given to the ideas contained in the memorandum. He even went beyond the original proposition, arguing that:

> policies of 'near identification' and of joining the Common Market were so similar that one might well lead to the other, and if we were ready to contemplate near identification, it might be preferable to contemplate full membership. The basic choice for the Government, therefore, was between a dramatic change in direction in our domestic, commercial and international policies, and maintaining our traditional policy of remaining aloof from Europe politically, while doing all we can to mitigate the economic dangers of a divided Europe.[67]

In itself, this certainly did not represent a decision in favour of membership, but it did mean that the cumulative effect of his outburst in Washington, of the acceleration of the EEC and of the summit failure, had led the British Prime Minister to break the 'taboo' which had hitherto constrained British thinking on policy towards European integration. The list of questions concerning the effects of the Treaty of Rome, which Macmillan put to his officials after the committee meeting, set in motion the first in-depth examination of potential benefits and dangers of British membership of the European Community since 1955.[68]

Macmillan's questions relating to the effects of membership on Britain's foreign policy, Commonwealth relations, trade performance, agriculture and horticulture were divided among the respective departments, and the answers discussed by officials in the Economic Steering Committee, before being submitted to Cabinet in July 1960.[69] In essence the report recommended consideration to be given to full membership on political grounds, arguing that:

> if the Six 'succeed', we should be greatly damaged politically if we were outside; if we were inside, the influence we would wield in the world would be enhanced; while still retaining in some degree the right to speak on our own account, we should also be speaking as part of a European bloc.[70]

Simultaneously, the political difficulties of relinquishing sovereignty no longer seemed as insurmountable following President de Gaulle's speech of May 1960, in which he had envisaged the EEC developing on confederate rather than federal lines.[71] Further political considerations produced a re-run of the arguments used in favour of the FTA. Only from within would Britain be in a position to stabilize the EEC so as to counteract German hegemony, or alternatively to prevent a possible collapse of the organization which was expected to result in disintegration of the Western Alliance and a neutral or communist Germany. In economic terms, Britain was expected to benefit from 'participating in a vigorous and rapidly expanding market' and from attracting inward investment, though membership was also expected to be detrimental to agricultural, Commonwealth and EFTA trade interests.[72] Accordingly, it was not suggested to simply sign the Treaty of Rome as it stood, but to attempt to negotiate satisfactory arrangements for these interests. Economic benefits and compensatory arrangements could conceivably be realized by a policy of 'near identification', but the political benefits clearly could not. Hence, the report recommended a pause of from 12 to 18 months in which 'to ensure by some appropriate preliminary approach that the Six... would be willing to see us join or move to close association with them on terms which we could accept'.[73]

However, during the preparation of the report, it had become clear that any announcement following its conclusion would produce great uncertainty in Europe. Other governments were undoubtedly aware of the fact, if not the content, of the re-appraisal under way in Britain. The unfortunate ECSC and Euratom initiative had already aroused great suspicion on the part of EFTA governments of a 'desertion' by Britain, while it had reinforced European and American doubts about the sincerity of British motives, with the German press describing British policy as 'shilly-shallying'.[74] Hence, the dilemma facing the British government lay in that there was an obvious need for both a cautious approach to membership and an authoritative statement of British policy.

In early July, the Cabinet's discussion of the report revealed the differences prevailing among ministers. While the Chancellor and the Commonwealth Secretary appeared principally in favour of membership of the Community, the Foreign Secretary and the President of the Board of Trade were more reserved. Given the anxiety shown by the Prime Minister in starting the inquiry, the latter two could not openly dismiss the option recommended in the report.

Opposition to membership was therefore masked with a reference to the apparent reluctance of the Six to negotiate and to the need to prepare domestic public opinion and Commonwealth and EFTA governments. Maudling, in particular, seized on the difficulties of timing and tactics highlighted by the report, and argued that all that was possible and required at this stage was

> an authoritative statement in which the Government would make it clear that this was not a suitable moment for negotiations with the Community and, while expressing readiness to work towards a single trading system in Europe, would emphasize the fundamental objections to United Kingdom membership of the Community.[75]

Obviously, his proposal amounted to little more than a restatement of some form of Six-plus-Seven deal. Yet, Cabinet instructed Maudling to draft such a statement after the opponents of membership had managed to impress their colleagues by exploiting the only weakness of a report which had otherwise strongly favoured British membership of the Community. It appeared that the decision had thereby been postponed well into the next year.

Arguably, the issue of British membership would indeed have disappeared until the completion of the GATT round of 1961 had it not been for signs in the summer of 1960 that the German government was becoming increasingly anxious to find a solution to the problem of Britain's relations with the Community.[76] The continued interest of the Ministry of Economics was apparent, but was now complemented by the fact that *Auswärtiges Amt* officials had approached their British counterparts in an effort to initiate exploratory talks.[77] Furthermore, the German Ambassador to London, Hans Heinrich von Herwarth, informed the Foreign Secretary of a change of opinion within his government.[78] Ambassador Steel added that Chancellor Adenauer was becoming increasingly disenchanted with the continued division as well as with the Commission. He claimed that the German Chancellor now rejected 'Hallstein and all his works' and that 'his express discounting of a supranational European State is a turning point and may make things much easier for us'.[79]

However, given previous disappointments there was some residual doubt about the strength of Adenauer's conversion.[80] Officials in the Foreign Office argued that 'as long as the Germans believe that we are bound in the long-run to join the EEC unconditionally, there is little prospect of enlisting German support against the French'.[81] An opportunity to examine German views was soon to arise with Macmillan's visit to Bonn in August 1960.

Macmillan's visit to Bonn – a converted Chancellor?

In the four months prior to Macmillan's visit to Bonn, there had indeed been a change in the German position on EEC/EFTA relations in general, and Anglo-German relations in particular. While the German Economics Ministry continued to press for a European-wide arrangement, following their partial success in postponing acceleration and in placing EEC/EFTA relations back onto the agenda, a more dramatic shift took place in the attitudes of the *Auswärtiges Amt* and of the Chancellor himself – a change inconceivable at the time of the acceleration debate.

In April 1960, domestic parliamentary and public pressure for some form of economic accommodation with Britain still had to be balanced against the continued French reluctance to enter into real negotiations. The Economics Ministry and the Trade Policy Department of the *Auswärtiges Amt* therefore advocated an evolutionary approach, in which the formulation of a common European position for the forthcoming GATT negotiations would help to reduce trade friction.[82] Officials in Erhard's ministry clearly hoped that in the process of identifying a list of products important to intra-European trade new opportunities for a restart of real negotiations would emerge.[83] Their hopes as well as part of the remaining reluctance on the part of the political authorities in the Foreign Ministry to force early formal negotiations were both based on the assumption that Britain would soon be prepared to accept tariff harmonization.[84] For the Economics Ministry, these changing circumstances seemed to point to the possibility of a limited customs union.[85] Despite the similarities in the approach of the two ministries, the Department 'West I' of the *Auswärtiges Amt* remained fearful of Erhard's intervention until acceleration was accepted by the EEC, and therefore sought to limit his public appearances as well as diplomatic contacts.[86] Moreover, any new initiative was to be discussed in the Trade Committee in order to curtail the Economic Ministry's involvement. Concentrating on the committee also ensured that pressure on France would be balanced with US opposition to a discriminatory agreement.[87]

More important than the internal dispute were the political developments of spring 1960 which increasingly seemed to rule out any compromise. Despite the efforts of the German embassy in London to limit the impact of Macmillan's remarks in Washington, Anglo-German relations were at an all-time low.[88] Adding to the impression of Britain as an unreliable partner was the Prime Minister's summit policy, in which – so Adenauer feared – Berlin and the German question would be used as a bargaining chip to improve East–West relations. In this context, the reliability of the US was also in question, given their continued flirtations with the idea of a neutrality zone in central Europe.[89] In the event, it proved somewhat reassuring to Adenauer that the East–West summit broke down after an American U2 spy plane had been shot down over Soviet territory. Yet, the Chancellor's preparatory meeting with de Gaulle, Macmillan and Eisenhower on 15 May 1960 had appeared to confirm his scepticism regarding the unity of the West.[90] Expecting increasing East–West tensions and further problems over Berlin, the Chancellor's trust in allied support had remained intact only with regard to de Gaulle. After the meeting he noted that: 'The overall impression... was depressing and strengthened my decision to fasten the ties with France... even more.'[91] Macmillan's motives, by contrast, were viewed with suspicion, exemplified by Adenauer's swift and complete endorsement of the Foreign Ministry's dismissive response to a possible British application to the ECSC and Euratom.[92]

The reliance placed on the French President by an insecure Adenauer was not to survive for long. First, in a public speech in May 1960, de Gaulle appeared to threaten the integration achievements of the EEC, while giving substance to the suspicion that France was set to transform NATO. The weight of Europe in the decision-making process of the Western Alliance would have to be increased relative to that of the USA, or France would leave the organization. In de Gaulle's thinking, increased European weight meant increased French influence, for his policy of a national independent nuclear deterrent would relegate Germany to the status of a 'satellite state', as argued by the French Prime Minister, Michel Debré.[93] Strongly disapproving of this new French line, Adenauer's suspicions were further heightened by the visit of Antoine Pinay, recently dismissed from his post as Finance Minister in de Gaulle's Cabinet. He reaffirmed the picture of the General as a nationalist, bent on breaking with NATO, loosening ties with America and slowing down the Common Market.[94]

De Gaulle had become aware of the Chancellor's anxieties which led him to forward an invitation for Adenauer to meet him at Rambouillet in July 1960.[95] Although the records of these discussions are incomplete, it appears that the French President was once again able to charm Adenauer into accepting not only that there was a need to reform NATO but also that the European Commission had been too determined in its application of the principle of supranationality. A reform of European institutions was therefore also necessary, and de Gaulle argued for political co-operation to be organized on intergovernmental lines, with regular meetings of Foreign Ministers as well as Heads of Governments of the Six. Adenauer's acceptance of the need to make NATO less American-centred appears to have been the result of the insecurity following the summit, now heightened by the uncertainty of impending presidential elections which threatened to return the allegedly more isolationist Senator John F. Kennedy. The Chancellor's unexpected agreement on the need to reduce supranationality in Europe seems to have stemmed from his deteriorating personal relations with Hallstein, whose swift endorsement of Erhard as the future Chancellor had greatly upset Adenauer during the presidential candidacy episode of 1959.[96]

While the Rambouillet meeting may have reassured Adenauer of the reliability of the French President, the *Auswärtiges Amt* was not convinced.[97] In Brentano's view, de Gaulle's ideas simultaneously threatened two tenets of German foreign policy: European integration and security in the North Atlantic Alliance. A Six-power Europe abandoned by the US and acting as a 'third force' with its intergovernmental decision-making dominated by a nuclear France was clearly not in the interest of Germany at a time of growing tensions with the communist bloc.[98] The Foreign Ministry managed to impress the danger of this scenario on the Chancellor, who, by the early autumn of 1960, was said to 'have completely lost confidence in the General and... that he would not regain it too quickly'.[99]

In the meantime, the cumulative effect of impending presidential elections in the US, mistrust of de Gaulle, disenchantment with Hallstein and the anticipation of intensified Soviet aggression had led to a reassessment of the importance of the crisis in Anglo-German relations, which was now no longer seen as a minor irritation but as part of a wider problem of a lack of cohesion of the Western Alliance.[100] The issue chosen by Adenauer to restore the relationship was, not surprisingly, that of EEC/EFTA relations, since Britain's place in Europe had been one of the main causes of friction between the two countries, following the abandonment of the FTA negotiations and culminating in Macmillan's outburst. When the two Heads of Governments met in August 1960, Adenauer and Brentano therefore suggested bilateral talks between representatives of the two governments with a view to solving the EEC/EFTA problem.[101]

As had been the case in previous meetings during the FTA negotiations, the Chancellor's initiative did not represent a direct response to British warnings, but instead it was the result of an element of insecurity in Franco-German relations and in the Western Alliance at large. This time, however, he made sure to clarify his position on Macmillan's habitual reference to the possibility of troop withdrawals in the case of the continued exclusion of Britain, interjecting that 'the British people knew quite well that the troops in Germany were there for the defence of the United Kingdom and not for that of Germany'.[102] Nevertheless, Adenauer's initiative was to ensure that the issue of British membership had not disappeared from the agenda.

Anglo-German bilateral talks

The technical bilateral consultations which followed Macmillan's visit to Bonn examined the problems associated with Britain's possible acceptance of tariff harmonization, and agricultural provisions, as well as their effect on the system of Commonwealth preferences. In approaching these problem areas, the two sides agreed not to formulate solutions but merely to explore possible consequences. Yet, the shape of an ultimate agreement could not be ignored altogether, for it would undoubtedly determine the types of problems which were expected to arise. Here, it was agreed that expert discussions could only work under two hypothetical assumptions, membership or association.[103]

This more than vague remit for the bilateral talks was in the interest of the *Auswärtiges Amt* whose motives with regard to Anglo-EEC relations were ambiguous. On the one hand, a sincere desire to overcome the economic division in Europe characterized the view of its Trade Policy Department, supported by the agreement of 'West I' on the need to improve Anglo-German political relations at a time of mounting Franco-German tensions. It was in particular the French reference to Germany as a 'satellite state' which had stimulated van Scherpenberg's decision in favour of Anglo-German bilateralism.[104] On the other hand, however, there was growing anxiety in Department 'West I' that the Franco-German crisis, and in particular the Adenauer–de Gaulle relationship, should not be allowed to deteriorate too far.[105] After Macmillan's visit to Bonn, Adenauer's distrust in de Gaulle had been fuelled by the latter's public announcements of his plans to reform both NATO and the EEC.[106] The combination of these reform plans and the growing unpopularity of Hallstein with the Chancellor now posed a real threat to the integration policy of the *Auswärtiges Amt*. Here, it was deemed imperative to at least keep the French government informed about Anglo-German bilateral talks, and furthermore to have the Commission associated in any such discussions. However, Adenauer's dislike of Hallstein was now deep-seated, so that Brentano's efforts to secure the latter objective led to an unusual disagreement between Chancellor and Foreign Minister in the presence of their British counterparts. After it had been decided by the two Heads of Governments that the Commission should not be associated with the talks, Brentano was reported to have warned that

> if we were too negative about the change of attitude towards the Commission there would be trouble with the rest of the Six. Dr. Adenauer said he did not quite share Herr von Brentano's point of view . . . There was in fact a basic and fundamental change and this should be brought out clearly.[107]

Not able to secure the participation of the Commission, the *Auswärtiges Amt* only partially welcomed the bilateral expert talks as a measure to sustain the more European-minded attitude in Britain, but not as a means to arrive at any wider agreement.[108] This attitude was strengthened by the growing expectation that Britain would ultimately accept membership of the Community. The changes in the British Cabinet, which had seen Foreign Secretary Selwyn Lloyd move to the Treasury, Lord Alec Douglas Home take over the Foreign Office, Edward Heath appointed Lord Privy Seal with special responsibilities for European policy and Peter Thorneycroft re-enter Cabinet as Minister of Aviation, were interpreted as a move towards membership by 'weakening the retarding forces originating from Maudling'.[109] Throughout the autumn and winter of 1960, press coverage, diplomatic exchanges as well as ministerial speeches seemed to give further substance to this interpretation.[110]

The assessment and objectives of the *Auswärtiges Amt* formed a stark contrast to those of the Ministry of Economics. Here, the

Anglo-German talks were seen as a real chance to formulate a wider European trade arrangement. Britain was not expected to declare its intention to join the Community, and in any case the ministry's free trade philosophy seemed to favour a wider arrangement including the 'liberal' EFTA members over the narrow concept of British membership.[111] After a number of schemes had been contemplated, including EEC joining EFTA or vice versa, negotiators of the Economics Ministry sought to convince their British colleagues to accept that tariff harmonization would not pose a serious threat to either agricultural provisions or the Commonwealth preference system.[112] Ultimately, this exercise seemed to have been successful, leading Müller-Armack to draw up a plan for a partial customs union between the two organizations, with problematic Commonwealth produce being subject to a separate free trade arrangement which would include compensatory taxes.[113] However, the formulation of the German position in the expert talks lay with the Foreign Ministry's Trade Policy Department, and any attempt by Erhard to intervene directly in order to press on with the 'Müller-Armack plan' met determined internal resistance.[114] In any case, it had been made abundantly clear by the French government that no wider European agreement would be negotiable.[115] By prematurely leaking the Müller-Armack plan to the press, the *Auswärtiges Amt* appears to have put an end to any hopes for such an agreement.[116]

Perhaps surprisingly, the British government was not unduly concerned about the apparent failure of the talks. German hopes for the talks to provide a real chance to restart negotiations on a wider agreement had been misplaced. The British side had never worked towards any such scheme to emerge from the discussions, displaying a remarkable realism with regard to both the French government's readiness to negotiate and to the motives and distribution of power within the German government.[117] While British officials noted Adenauer's increased anxiety, Erhard's continued enthusiasm as well as Müller-Armack's customs union idea, they had also recognized the scepticism prevailing in the *Auswärtiges Amt*.[118] Nevertheless, entering into such talks had been motivated not merely by the desire to improve Anglo-German relations. The discussions were also deemed useful in two other respects. First, they provided an opportunity to examine the possibilities for safeguarding Commonwealth and agricultural interests for the hypothetical case of British membership, and to identify the concessions necessary towards this end. Secondly, the inevitable failure of expert talks to deliver a European-wide scheme could be used to demonstrate to the remaining opposition in Cabinet and party that a purely economic scheme was no longer a realistic possibility and, hence, that only full membership would safeguard the political interests identified in the Lee report.[119] Hence, the efforts of the German Economics Ministry towards an all-European customs union were clearly not sufficient: 'While our immediate task must be to find solutions to the complex of economic difficulties, we must not lose sight of our political objective of being "inside the councils of the Six".'[120] The political dimension came to dominate British thinking in the new year, when the plans for foreign policy co-operation among the Six were finally taking shape.

Overcoming internal opposition to membership – the political dimension

The Heads of Governments of the Six were due to meet in February 1961 to work out the arrangements for political co-operation. Although there was still considerable disagreement about the supranational content, it appeared that the option of co-operating within WEU (thereby including Britain) had been rejected by most of the Six during the months preceding the meeting.[121] In combination with the continuing Anglo-German, Anglo-French, Anglo-Italian and Franco-German expert talks, which all seemed to rule out an economic arrangement for the Six plus Seven problem, the anticipated exclusion from these new arrangements led the political dimension of Anglo-European relations to become paramount in the eyes of most British officials and ministers.[122] Indeed, both the Foreign Office and the Treasury were now thinking in terms of membership, and officials from the two departments jointly formulated a memorandum, in which they described membership as the only option to secure Britain's continued influence on the Continent and in the world at large.[123] In their efforts to press for an early decision in favour of membership, however, they faced considerable opposition from the Board of Trade, headed by the FTA enthusiast Reginald Maudling.[124]

A temporary reprieve came with the decision of the Six to refer discussions on the arrangements for political co-operation to a group of experts, after the February meeting had seen the Dutch delegation argue for supranational organization and lobby on behalf of British participation.[125] However, the failure of the Six to find agreement on this issue masked a *rapprochement* of Adenauer and de Gaulle who, after the former had successfully opposed those elements of the French plan which threatened NATO and the EEC, now seemed to agree that only membership would allow for Britain's participation in political co-operation. The Foreign Office's awareness of this development increased the necessity for an early decision in favour of membership.[126] Hence, Whitehall officials obtained ministerial permission for studying the impact of membership in a Treaty of Rome Working Group established for this purpose.[127]

However, if anything, the obstacles to British membership seemed to be increasing at the time. Not only was EFTA seen as a potential source of opposition, but there was also great uncertainty about the willingness of the French to agree to any exceptional treatment of British agricultural or Commonwealth concerns.[128] In his meeting with Macmillan, President de Gaulle had denied the possibility 'for the Commonwealth and the Six to make an economic community without destroying one or the other'.[129] In the expert talks, the chief negotiator Olivier Wormser had countered Lee's argument that the inclusion of agriculture would make the Commonwealth problem insurmountable with a simple but uncompromising 'tant pis'.[130]

Most importantly though, an announcement to Cabinet of the intention to seek membership was expected domestically to 'lead to a resurgence of opposition on the grounds of principle rather than practice'.[131] Meeting at Chequers in February, Prime Minister Macmillan, Chancellor Selwyn Lloyd, Foreign Secretary Lord Home and Lord Privy Seal Heath therefore agreed not to circulate the joint memorandum of Treasury and Foreign Office.[132] Nevertheless, Macmillan argued that 'we must press on' and that Cabinet would have to decide on the issue before his forthcoming visit to Washington.[133] The main obstacle here was the continued opposition to membership shown by Maudling who had deliberately been excluded from their meeting.[134]

Given the ongoing internal debate, ministers and the Prime Minister himself were clearly unable to issue an authoritative policy statement on the question of membership. In the absence thereof, there was some confusion with Heath and Selwyn Lloyd appearing to hint at an imminent decision in favour, while the Prime Minister appeared to rule out this possibility in his meetings with de Gaulle and Adenauer in the early months of the year.[135] Not surprisingly, the ambiguity of ministerial statements led not only to the expected disunity in Cabinet but also to some confusion about British intentions on the Continent.[136] Indeed, in the spring of 1961, second-guessing British intentions was widespread in the principle German ministries. Most officials in the Department E of the Ministry of Economics saw no possibility of an imminent application, and in any case preferred a wider, and purely economic, arrangement which would allow the 'liberal' EFTA members to participate, thereby providing a counterweight to protectionist influences in the EEC.[137] However, any initiatives formulated towards this end met the resistance of the *Auswärtiges Amt* which even sought to prevent Erhard from meeting his British counterpart.[138] In Department 'West I' of the Foreign Ministry, there was some speculation about an ultimate British decision in favour of membership.[139] However, others were not convinced and argued that, until an application materialized, there should be no compromise solution on the issue of British participation in the process of political co-operation.[140] The ambiguity of ministerial statements prolonged the fear of Brentano and his officials of the possibility of Britain taking part in these deliberations while attempting to secure a wider agreement, thereby undermining both, the economic and political process of further integration in Europe. On the occasion of the London visit of Adenauer and Brentano, Prime Minister Macmillan had fuelled the latter's suspicions by continuing his references to a wider arrangement and to the need for British participation in the political co-operation among de Gaulle's *Europe des patries*.[141] Despite contrary assurances given to the British government, the *Auswärtiges Amt* remained opposed to a Six plus Seven agreement as well as to political consultations in WEU.

It was only due to the intervention of the new US President John F. Kennedy that the internal debate within the British as well as the German government finally moved towards acceptance of British membership in April 1961. After his visit to Washington, the British Prime Minister reported that he was told by his host that he was 'anxious ... for us to get into the Six' and that 'politically [the Americans] hoped that if we were in the Six we should be able to steer them'.[142] Thereby, Macmillan invoked third-party confirmation of the long-held belief that Britain could determine the future course of integration. In contrast, it was made 'explicit for the first time [sic] ... that the United States Government do not favour, and will not help to bring about, a purely economic association of the Six and the Seven'.[143] Thus, 'steering from within' was now the only option, if there was to be any British 'steering' at all.

The effect of the Washington meeting was felt on the ministerial as well as the official level. The frankness with which the Americans had expressed their view allowed Macmillan to reintroduce the membership issue in Cabinet in April, arguing that 'nothing would now be gained by delaying a decision'.[144] However, the President of the Board of Trade as well as the new Minister of Education, David Eccles, remained unconvinced, which was not surprising given that both had been closely associated with the purely economic FTA negotiations. Given their continued opposition, Cabinet could only agree to a further study of the impact of British membership.

On the official level, the reluctance to contemplate full membership, which had hitherto been shown mainly by Board of Trade officials in the Treaty of Rome Working Group and the European Economic Questions Committee, could now be overruled with reference to the impossibility of a Six plus Seven agreement. Hence, the American dimension featured prominently in their report submitted in late April, which concluded that 'the decision which Ministers have to take is essentially a political one of first importance'.[145] Though not recommending any particular course of action, the tenor of the report clearly favoured a British application.

Adenauer and his Foreign Minister were also notified about the explicit American support for British membership during their visit to Washington, which immediately followed that of Macmillan. The effect of their encounter with the new President was immediate. The Chancellor was impressed by Kennedy's argument that British membership was necessary not only for the unity of Europe but also as a means to strengthen the Atlantic Alliance.[146] In an official government statement following his return from the US, Adenauer described the EEC as open to applications for membership and expressed the hope that 'others will decide in favour of taking such a step. This applies in particular to Great Britain.'[147] However, some doubts about British sincerity were still harboured in the *Auswärtiges Amt*.[148] Foreign Minister Brentano, however, appeared reassured about the intentions of the British government which in his view was now on the whole 'aware of the economic *and* political significance of the European Economic Community', though he still questioned whether this applied to all Cabinet ministers.[149]

The reaction of the Economics Ministry to the new developments was, perhaps surprisingly, less enthusiastic. Although the prospect of British membership was generally welcomed and Müller-Armack now admitted that his customs union plan had been overtaken by events, the ministry was concerned about the status of EFTA members.[150] Though Denmark and Norway were widely expected to follow Britain's lead and simultaneously apply for membership, there were doubts about the possibility of finding a solution for the association of the neutral countries, especially after US representatives argued that such discussions should be postponed until membership negotiations were completed.[151] Erhard's free-trade, rather than anglophile, motivation found its reflection in an interview for the Swedish *Dagen Nyheter*, in which he argued that only the simultaneous accession of all EFTA members would support his view that 'the customs wall [of the EEC] towards the outside... has to be substantially lowered'.[152] Despite these concerns, the Minister of Economics intervened on behalf of London, by convening a meeting of the EEC's Comité Spécial which declared itself in favour of British membership.[153]

Though Erhard's initiative as well as the positive reactions of Brentano and Adenauer were welcomed in Britain, the attitude of the Six was, perhaps remarkably, not Macmillan's main concern at the time.[154] The period between the Washington visit in April and the announcement of Britain's intention to apply for membership in July had to be used by the Prime Minister to overcome internal opposition. In doing so, Macmillan continuously sought to present the problem of membership as a fundamental choice between becoming the 'dominating influence in Europe... [or]... being marginalized'.[155] Correspondingly, he attempted to present the economic problems associated with membership in a customs union as surmountable. Most notable in this context was the decision to send his more 'europhile' ministers on a tour of Commonwealth capitals under the pretext of sounding out their likely reaction to a possible application for membership in the EEC.[156] By putting a positive gloss on their subsequent reports to Cabinet, Heath and Thorneycroft, as well as the Secretaries for the Colonies, for Commonwealth Relations and the Minister of Labour – Iain Macleod, Duncan Sandys and John Hare – clearly pursued the ulterior motive of their visits, namely to pacify the domestic opposition based on Commonwealth relations.[157] Macmillan furthermore initiated a personal dialogue with the main opponents of a British application. While he was successful in muting the objections raised by David Eccles and Defence Minister Harold Watkinson, Maudling persisted in his efforts to prevent the application.[158] Though the

President of the Board of Trade skilfully used the continued ambiguity of the French position as well as the American reluctance to contemplate association agreements for the EFTA neutrals, to argue for abandoning the project, Macmillan's other efforts had ensured the passage of the Cabinet resolution in which it was agreed that:

> a formal application to join the Treaty of Rome should now be made for the purpose of enabling negotiations to take place with a view to ascertaining whether the special needs of the United Kingdom, the other Commonwealth countries and the other members of the European Free Trade Association could be met.[159]

After the governments of EFTA and EEC members, as well as that of the US administration, had been given advance information, Macmillan was finally able to make a statement in the House of Commons on 31 July, declaring the government's intention to enter into negotiations for membership of the Community.

However, it is important to recognize that the preoccupation with domestic opposition to membership had been at the expense of a thorough examination of the attitudes of the Six. The only step taken in this respect had been to request an assessment of British Ambassadors in the capitals of the EEC member countries. These had confirmed that the French government remained reluctant to compromise on special arrangements for British agriculture and Commonwealth relations.[160] In contrast, Ambassador Steel had once again anticipated that British membership would be enthusiastically welcomed in Germany.[161] Despite this information, no tactical recommendations were formulated by officials. Hence, ministers reverted to the fall-back position, and the similarity to the 1958 tactics was striking: without recognizing earlier mistakes, Macmillan's Private Secretary, Philip de Zulueta, argued that the Germans could be 'bullied' while the French had to be 'bribed'. With regard to the latter, Britain could pressure the US for an extension of tripartite talks, while German support could be stimulated by pointing out 'to Dr. Adenauer that if the Six do not make it possible for us to join them on reasonable terms we shall find it impossible to support anything like the existing financial burden arising from our troops in Germany'.[162] Hence, the way in which the British government expected to stimulate German support in the coming membership negotiations remained the very same which had proven counterproductive in the past six years.

Towards Britain's first application

A number of political and economic factors appear to have played a part in the fundamental change of British policy towards European integration – from the failure of 'bridge-building' to the first application for membership of the European Economic Community. In short: the cumulative effect of the summit failure, the acceleration of the EEC timetable, the crisis in Anglo-European relations following Macmillan's outburst in Washington, and the plans for political co-operation among the Six had convinced the Treasury and the Foreign Office as well as the Prime Minister himself not only of the economic but also, more importantly, the political necessity to take part in the EEC.

However, the process of policy change has been shown to have come to an abrupt halt in the summer of 1960, when internal government opposition thwarted the plan for an early application drawn up by the Lee working group. The subsequent 12 months saw Prime Minister Macmillan as well as Foreign Office and Treasury officials seeking to overcome this opposition, which was led by the departments under the former FTA-enthusiasts, Maudling and Eccles. While a Cabinet reshuffle had boosted the ranks of 'europhile' ministers, it still had to be demonstrated to the remaining sceptics that EEC membership was indeed the only way to solve the problem of economic and political isolation from Europe. The opposition in Cabinet held their ground until the early part of 1961, when the combination of political co-operation of the Six and unequivocal American support for British membership finally tipped the balance in favour of Macmillan and his supporters.

Anglo-German relations have been shown to have played an important part in both the initial reappraisal of summer 1960 and Macmillan's efforts to overcome the opposition in Cabinet. A complex set of factors had played a part in the former episode. In the early months of 1960 the British desire to continue to be seen by EFTA members to work for a Six plus Seven solution led to a misconception about British motives on the Continent. In Germany, this fuelled the debate about acceleration versus a wider agreement, leading to open interministerial conflict. The continued pressure exerted by the Ministry of Economics for the latter was interpreted by the *Auswärtiges Amt* as furthering the perceived intention of the British government to undermine the progress of European integration. The suspicions of Brentano and his officials seemed to be validated by Macmillan's unfortunate remarks on the occasion of his visit to Washington. Combined with the support for acceleration expressed by the US administration, this outburst led the German Cabinet to narrowly accept the acceleration proposals. Later, British overtures with regard to ECSC and Euratom membership were ignored for the very same reason. Ironically, Anglo-German relations, and in particular Macmillan's hyperbolical reference to the political division of Europe, thereby helped to give rise to the very factors which caused the reappraisal of British policy.

After this reappraisal had been halted by internal opposition in the summer of 1960, Adenauer's suggestion of bilateral expert talks helped to keep membership on the British domestic agenda. Motivated by the desire to improve Anglo-German relations in a period marked by temporary difficulties in Franco-German relations, uncertainty about the future of European integration, and anxiety about the cohesion of the Western Alliance, Adenauer's initiative inadvertently contributed to the success of the proponents of membership within the British Cabinet. However, deep-seated suspicions about British sincerity continued to be held in the *Auswärtiges Amt*, so that no effort was made towards British participation in political co-operation without membership of the Community. Again, therefore, the *Auswärtiges Amt* unintentionally strengthened the position of the pro-membership forces in the British government.

It is noteworthy in this context that there were no illusions among British officials as to the ability, or indeed the willingness, of the German government to deliver agreement on either EEC/EFTA relations or political co-operation. Instead, the efforts of the Economics Ministry towards attaining a wider agreement were politely ignored in the knowledge that the more suspicious Foreign Ministry was now in charge of the bilateral expert talks. Furthermore, officials were well aware of the temporary nature of Adenauer's conversion, given his *rapprochement* with de Gaulle in February 1961. In any case, external factors such as the expert talks, the progress of political co-operation among the Six, and even Kennedy's intervention, were no longer changing the attitude of Macmillan and others, but acted to reinforce their earlier decision of 1960. Indeed, he successfully used these external factors in the internal debate about membership.

Finally, the preoccupation with domestic opposition has been shown to have prevented a thorough examination of the impact of the British application on the Continent. There was only a very general awareness of the positive attitude of Adenauer and his Foreign Minister following their own meeting with the new American President, as well as of the obstructionist efforts to be expected from the French government. However, officials made no recommendation for a new approach in the forthcoming negotiations in which these two governments were to play an important part. By default, therefore, the tactic of 'bullying the Germans' and 'buying the French' was allowed to continue. The failure to adjust tactics in accordance with the new policy supports the interpretation of the first British application as a response to perceived political and economic necessities, rather than as a fundamental change in outlook on European integration as such.

Conclusion: Intersection or Periphery?

A decade after Winston Churchill had depicted the United Kingdom as being at the intersection of the infamous 'three circles' – (the Atlantic Alliance, the Commonwealth and Europe), the framework of international politics he was referring to had changed in some of its more important features. Though one cannot – not even for the early 1960s – speak of a disappearance of these circles, or any fundamental realignment of the partners therein, it would be equally misleading to regard as essentially unchanged the respective weight of these arrangements to Britain's foreign policy.

Her privileged position in the Atlantic Alliance – epitomized by the so-called special relationship to the superpower United States – had been called into doubt during the Suez débacle, the apparent loss of influence subsequently confirmed not only by the failure of Prime Minister Macmillan's summit diplomacy but also by the increasingly obvious dependency of Britain's nuclear deterrent on delivery systems supplied by the Americans.[1] Again, it would be grossly misleading to argue that the special relationship was dissolved or beyond repair, or that Britain now ranked merely as one among many American partners within the Alliance. The efforts of Macmillan and his Foreign Secretary to mend Anglo-American relations after 1956 did have some measure of success; yet, the above mentioned factors no longer allowed for the view that the leaders of the two nations were dealing with one another as equals – a trend accentuated by the generational change in the US presidency in 1961.

With regard to the Commonwealth, it is imperative to emphasize the continued premium that Britain could and did derive from her privileged trading relations. The role of sterling as a reserve currency had been somewhat diminished, yet the system of trade preferences continued to ensure cheap imports of raw materials and temperate foodstuffs into Britain, while giving her manufactures a competitive advantage in what consequently were fairly secure markets. In contrast by the early 1960s, it could no longer be ignored that the political status the Commonwealth had hitherto conferred to Britain was eroding rapidly. While the process of decolonization had again gathered force in the second half of the 1950s, the Suez crisis had seen some reluctance to follow Britain's lead even on the part of the dominions. In 1961, the bitter row over the apartheid regime in South Africa only confirmed mounting difficulties in the Commonwealth.

The third and hitherto least important of the 'three circles' undoubtedly witnessed fundamental changes in the 1950s. Though political union had proven elusive after the failures of the EDC and EPC, by 1960, the consolidation of Western Europe brought about by the integration successes of the Coal and Steel Com munity and the Common Market had clearly surpassed expectations that had been held at the beginning of the decade. In essence, Western Europe was consolidating around a Franco-German core and, in doing so, enjoyed near unfailing support from Washington. In economic terms, the European market was gaining in weight, with growth rates significantly above the British level.[2] In political terms, the immediate effect was less marked, given the overwhelming importance of superpower relations, coupled with the protraction of attempts to coordinate foreign policy in the EEC. Nonetheless, persistent US support for the integration venture did seem to enhance the value of the Community as a political entity within the Western Alliance. Late in the decade, some doubt may have been cast by de Gaulle's efforts to establish the European Community as an independent player (or indeed as a vehicle for France's return to world-power status). Winston Churchill's metaphor can be customized regardless; the centre of the 'European circle' had shifted since the end of World War II, and the expectation of British preeminence in this arena slowly gave way to the realization that 'intersection' might mean 'periphery' in the longer term.

Britain readjusting

Given these latter changes, one may – and many did at the time – argue that the government should primarily aim at strengthening Britain's position at the intersection of the other two circles, cultivating the special relationship to the US and preserving her privileged trading relations with the Commonwealth. Others, however, warned that European integration could not simply be ignored, as Britain's position in these two circles was expected to weaken – and to do so partly as a result of the consolidation of Europe. Economically, the customs union clearly provided the more vibrant and innovative market than the Commonwealth. Additionally, the latter's long-term economic value to the more developed dominions was doubtful, given that Canada and Australia were no longer complementary to but increasingly in competition with British manufactures. These countries were expected to look elsewhere – that is to the United States and not least to Europe – to improve their trading relations independently, leaving Britain as the 'leader' of the less developed, less innovative markets of Africa, Asia and the Carribean. The consolidation of the 'European circle' without Britain was also expected directly to undermine the special relationship. Once the plans for foreign policy coordination and ultimately political integration would come to fruition, the United States was expected to look to Europe as the preferred partner. In the longer term, the linguistic and cultural propinquity to America – so it was feared – would not suffice to offset the sheer weight of a united Europe in international diplomacy.

In the latter half of the 1950s, it was this second, more pessimistic outlook that was gaining currency in governmental circles. The recognition of the possible consequences of Continental European integration led to some adjustment, though there was no sweeping overhaul of British foreign policy. Instead, as the previous chapters have illustrated, appreciation of these long-term trends seemed to allow for a number of approaches, with Britain's EEC membership being at the end of only one of these paths. As has been shown, the initial reaction to the *relance* of Europe at Messina was marked by the conviction that British influence over Continental governments – and over Bonn in particular – would be sufficiently powerful to either halt the project, or to guide the efforts of the Six so as to minimize the adverse effects on Britain's standing in world trade and international politics. What followed over the six years after the Messina conference has been described as a slow learning process regarding the inability to 'steer from without' in this manner. The policies advocated during this period are well known and have been analyzed in detail. From early attempts to prevent the establishment of the Common Market, these evolved to the Free Trade Area scheme meant to attach Britain and other nations to the emerging Community, to the application of economic pressure for an all-European trading arrangement by way of creating a rival trading bloc and, finally, to seeking acceptable terms in advance of the first application for membership.

The need to convince two audiences: presentation and negotiation tactics

What was of interest to this study was rather the tactical approach chosen by the British government in the pursuit of the various initiatives. Archival evidence suggests that while policies were adapted whenever they had proven ineffective or had otherwise run their course, surprisingly, the presentation of British policy did not vary significantly. For much of the period discussed, the 'selling' of the various initiatives was addressed above all to an uneasy domestic public and to hesitant – at times dissenting – members of the Cabinet and the Conservative parliamentary party. Following initial attempts to stop the creation of the Common Market, proponents of policy change placed emphasis first and foremost on the need somehow to associate with the Continentals in order to avoid having to suffer the trade discrimination the customs union was thought to entail. This wholly defensive case for some form of link with the emerging Community was supplemented by countless assurances to safeguard agriculture, horticulture and other industries, and by a more general pledge not to endanger traditional ties to the Commonwealth (and later to accommodate EFTA members).

Thereby, the British government successfully carried with it public and party – a considerable achievement, considering that the policy reversal was indeed radical if the beginning and the end of the period are contrasted, and given the humiliating set-backs the government had suffered along this route. Yet, the flipside of this success was that what appeared prudent at home was most unsuitable to dealing with foreign governments in what was after all a complicated exercise in multilateral diplomacy. Regarding the economics of European integration, the defensive case not only seemed to signify reluctance rather than enthusiasm but also made the British government vulnerable to the charge of seeking 'the best of both worlds' – Commonwealth and Europe. In addition, the reassurances given to domestic interests severely restricted the room for compromise in the negotiations. Of even more consequence was the defensive political case when dealing with Continental governments. Here, the concern over the exclusion of Britain which featured prominently in internal debates – particularly at Cabinet level – translated into repeated warnings being issued to the Six that trade discrimination in Europe would cause economic and political friction, ultimately undermining the cohesion of the Western Alliance.

Preaching to the converted – alienating the sceptics – lacking credibility

To be sure, the idea of somehow associating Britain with the continental integration effort did have its supporters among the Six. The motivation behind such support was both economic and political, with the British market providing attractive export opportunities to some, while her involvement promised to stabilize the emerging Community.

Yet, the various policy initiatives on Europe, and more importantly the tactics used to advance the respective negotiations, did not further the cause of Britain's supporters on the Continent. Indeed, the resulting inflexibility of Britain's negotiation position and the residual doubts about her motives – during the Free Trade Area negotiations for example – seriously impeded their efforts to convince other, less interested parties. Furthermore, the threat of economic division and retaliatory measures in trade policy failed to have an impact on the very government Britain needed to convince. Thus, the strongest supporters of a free trade arrangement with Britain – Belgium, the Netherlands and Germany – stood to lose from an economic division of Europe; France simply did not. In this sense, economic pressure for an arrangement amounted to 'preaching to the converted'.

Moreover, and perhaps more importantly, British tactics took little account of the fact that the economic dimension of the integration process was not the definitive Continental ambition. There was a sizeable and influential group of European politicians for whom the Common Market represented the beginning of an irrevocable fusion of national economies, which itself was seen only as a precursor to some form of political integration – however imprecise and disputed in its outline at the time. Even with regard to this political motive, British involvement in the venture did seem of some importance. Including one of the victorious Allied powers within its ranks – and one with particularly close relations to the United States – would undoubtedly have enhanced the Community's standing in what otherwise remained an East–West conflict between superpowers. Internally, the Community would have been more evenly balanced, with Britain providing a counterweight to the Franco-German 'axis' which had come to dominate the course of integration since the ECSC treaty. Yet again, however, British policy and tactics tended to be counterproductive. Those who supported her inclusion were hampered in their efforts to devise schemes acceptable to others by the fact that British politicians did little to confirm that they were ready to support let alone play an active part in political integration. On the contrary, from the winter of 1955 on, their tactics rather supported the view that Britain was reacting with some hostility to political integration. Even after the more obvious attempts at sabotaging the Common Market project had been abandoned, the main British argument for a 'non-political trading arrangement' did extend into the political realm, in so far as any such proposals were combined with the warning that continued economic division would undermine the cohesion of the West and would ultimately lead to a reappraisal of security policy. This argument – though perhaps an understandable inversion of British fears about the possibility of political marginalization – proved disastrous when used in bi- and multilateral exchanges. It represented the direct opposite of what 'Euro-enthusiasts' thought they were aiming at. Integration – particularly when extended to include foreign policy – was generally seen as a contribution to stability on the Continent, and as contributing to the cohesion of the West. The strenuous support shown by the United States confirmed this view. Thus, British warnings were interpreted not as a reference to regrettable but unintended consequences of European integration, but as indicating a readiness to deliberately risk irritating security partners in order to undermine the Common Market. In so doing, London appeared unreliable, an impression alienating still further those sceptical about Britain's European credentials.

'Preaching to the converted' and 'alienating the sceptics' among the Six were not the only flaws in Britain's negotiation performance. In addition, the spectre of trade discrimination and political division plainly lacked credibility. Though her market was of considerable importance to many a Continental exporter, the scope of possible retaliatory measures in Britain's commercial policy was severely restricted by her membership in other international trading regimes, such as GATT and OEEC. As long as the customs union of the Six was not in contravention of the regulations of these organizations – and there were few signs that it would be – its direct effect on the economies of non-members did not warrant any retaliation.[3] Even if these legal barriers had been ignored, Britain simply stood to lose any 'trade war', considering that European markets became increasingly important to her export economy, let alone the adverse consequences even extra-European foreign trade would have to suffer in the case of any serious disruption of GATT and OEEC.

A similar 'credibility gap' distinguished British warnings of possible readjustments of security policy, since the threat of weakening NATO was so obviously out of sync with her own national interest. If it had ever needed confirmation, the impossibility of a solitary stance in defence matters became readily apparent in the Suez conflict. There was, however, some scope with regard to British troop commitments to the Continent. Yet, Continental politicians were well aware – as was Foreign Secretary Selwyn Lloyd – that these troops were posted there primarily for the defence of Britain rather than protecting the territories to the east of the Rhine. Overriding all such considerations was, of course, the US position on conditionally linking integration and defence. Washington's support for the Community as a contribution to Western cohesion had a double effect on the credibility of British warnings. On the one hand, it seemed remote that London would endanger the special relationship, deliberately weakening the first of Churchill's circles. On the other hand, even in the unlikely event that the British government would opt for this course, Continental governments were assured of the unfailing support of their most important security partner.

In all, therefore, the presentation and tactics of British policy on Europe were unsuited to further an arrangement with the Community. It targeted the wrong parties, it increased doubts about Britain's sincerity and it used implausible scenarios to threaten the Continentals into compliance. Nowhere was this more obvious than in the attempts of the British government to persuade the German government to support its policy.

Seeking German support

As this study has attempted to demonstrate, British efforts to generate support for her policies among the Six were often aimed directly at the German government. In contrast to other accounts, however, it has been argued here that the conviction that Germany represented a natural ally willing and capable to further British interests was not based on the much quoted 'basic miscalculation' regarding the relative strength of the factions associated with Chancellor Konrad Adenauer on the one hand and his Economics Minister Ludwig Erhard on the other. Instead, Whitehall appears on the whole to have accurately assessed the balance of power in Bonn, leaving little doubt as to who was in charge of European integration policy there.

The way in which the British lobbied the German government – in some sense – followed logically from this assessment. Officials had determined in autumn 1955 that the outcome of the dispute over European integration policy within the German Cabinet hinged on the determination of Adenauer to overrule economic interests in the name of Franco-German reconciliation, rather than on the ability of Erhard to deliver on his many declarations of intent regarding world- or European-wide trade liberalization. Thus, in order to generate German support, it was deemed necessary to impress the German Chancellor by emphasizing the political significance of amicable Anglo-European relations.

Though this may have been the logical conclusion to be drawn from the assessment of the divisions in Bonn, the actual arguments used did not take the motives of the Chancellor into account. As outlined above, the wholly negative approach, stressing the potential disruption of bilateral relations and even defence arrangements, did not correspond to any of the convictions held by 'Euro-enthusiasts' such as Adenauer. Neither did free trade proponents like Erhard need a reminder of the importance of good trade relations. In this, the two protagonists in the German debate were little different from any other European politician. However, what distinguished the impact of British tactics in Bonn from that in other capitals was their effect on the dynamics and outcome of the internal dispute there. Thus, at crucial junctures, Adenauer's hand was strengthened inadvertently, enabling him to dismiss Erhard's genuine plea for accommodating British interests with reference to the dubious motives behind London's approach. The decision in autumn 1956 to continue unaltered the EEC negotiations despite the British Free Trade Area initiative as well as the narrow vote in favour of the acceleration proposals in the spring of 1960 are perhaps the most telling examples of this effect.

Hence, if the 'selling' of British policy on the Continent was ineffective, it proved nothing less than counterproductive in Germany. It is noteworthy that, despite repeated indications to the contrary, British politicians remained steadfast in their conviction that Adenauer was susceptible to warnings or threats. So much so that, when contemplating the tactics to be used in the up-coming membership negotiations, the idea that Germany could be 'bullied' had survived the disappointments of the preceding six years. This remarkable example of 'cognitive dissonance' may be seen as the result of a combination of two factors.[4] First, it was part of the overall failure to examine European attitudes. Why no such in-depth study – going beyond the few paragraphs contained in the reports of the Clarke and Lee working groups – was ever produced was the result of a transfer of categories. Given that 'turning European' – be it in the form of the Free Trade Area or membership – constituted a historic decision at home, requiring considerable effort to convince the public, industry and the Conservative parliamentary party, it was simply assumed that it would also be perceived as such abroad and that Britain would be enthusiastically welcomed on the Continent.

The second factor relates to the difficulties faced by the one department best informed about the motives behind Adenauer's policies. The often more realistic tactical recommendations of the Foreign Office simply appeared invalidated by the German politicians concerned. On the occasions of the Erhard–Butler meeting of autumn 1955, and more importantly the Anglo-German summits of April and October 1958, the Germans indeed seemed to respond to British warnings. Face-to-face top-level encounters appear to have been more important in shaping the views of government ministers than their briefing by officials. Furthermore, an apparent lack of communication often prevented the Foreign Office from later countering the impressions thus formed. It has emerged, however, that the assurances of support forthcoming from Adenauer and his Foreign Minister Heinrich von Brentano were not given in response to British warnings, but reflected nothing but a temporary concern about relations to France or the cohesion of the Western Alliance. German politicians can thus be said to have on occasion misled their counterparts in London, though this was at least as much the result of the timing of meetings and of a general desire to please as it constituted a deliberate attempt to deceive.

Evaluating British policy

In examining British attempts to 'steer Europe from without' between 1955 and 1961, the idea of 'missed opportunities' has not featured prominently in this study. Rather than seeking to identify the occasion at which the government could have joined the integration effort, but failed to grasp the importance of this alleged choice, it has been argued here that Britain did actively try to lead the Europeans prior to the first application, but that she simply did not succeed. And yet, even if the notion of 'missed opportunities' has been rejected and the focus has thus been on the policy Britain did follow, any attempt to evaluate the propriety thereof still has to envisage feasible alternatives. Such scenarios cannot take the form of colourful counterfactuals, but serve their purpose of underpinning historical judgement only if possessing some plausibility.[5] Though British entry into Europe could perhaps have been effortless, it should be obvious that conceiving of a government that had remained in the Spaak Committee, signed the Treaty of Rome and had wholeheartedly subscribed to the goal of supranational integration is of little use to a critical evaluation of Reginald Maudling's negotiation performance, Harold Macmillan's mind set or the workings of the governmental machinery.[6]

Of course, the more interesting question arising from the findings of this study is whether different tactics could have persuaded Continental governments to agree to – and the administration in Bonn to press more forcefully for – a European-wide trading arrangement, or an association agreement acceptable to Britain. *Prima facie*, there is nothing implausible about a corresponding alternative scenario, given the terms Britain had secured with the ECSC only a year before the Messina conference. Had the government candidly welcomed the positive contribution of the Six to the cohesion of the West and promised non-participatory support to political integration in the same vein as the US government did, the request for non-discrimination in foreign trade may well have been met. Though such a positive political approach would perhaps have needed some effort to win over interest groups and to carry along domestic public and parliamentary opinion, it would certainly have calmed Continental anxieties about British motives, leading to a more resolute search for compromises on economic detail.[7] This applies in particular to the potential support of Bonn, as it would have significantly changed the course and outcome of the interdepartmental dispute there. Had the political authorities around Adenauer and Brentano not been able to refer to British initiatives as a potential danger, they would have found it far more difficult to dismiss Erhard's arguments about Germany's national economic interest, which were on the whole forcefully seconded by industrial pressure groups. Furthermore, the initial assumption of the *Auswärtiges Amt* that Britain would eventually associate with the Common Market, the economic interest of its Trade Department, as well as Chancellor Adenauer's apparent lack of dogmatism with regard to the form of economic integration, all suggest that their opposition to British initiatives were not of principle. All they were in need of was reassurance that accommodating British interests did not threaten the achievement and future progress of European integration.

However, if antecedent developments, such as Britain's association with the ECSC, suggest that a purely economic arrangement might have been attainable with a more positive approach in the early stages of the period discussed here, subsequent events seem to indicate the contrary for the later part thereof. In view of the two vetos in the following decade, French opposition – personified by President Charles de Gaulle – does not appear to have been due to British negotiation tactics. De Gaulle regarded the Community primarily as a vehicle for enhancing France's status and leverage in international diplomacy – and one for which the price in the form of the opening of her economy was not only worth paying but ultimately proved a bargain given the provisions for harmonization, overseas territories and later the Common Agricultural Policy. It certainly was not a concern that Britain might pose a threat to the Community that provided the reason for French delaying tactics in the later stages of the Free Trade Area negotiations, for the rejection of any Six plus Seven deal, the refusal to accept British participation in foreign policy co-ordination or the lukewarm attitude towards the first application. For the French President, Britain did not endanger *the* Community, but she did compromise *his* Community.

Personifying the conflict of interests in this way is not to suggest that a positive British approach would have been unreservedly welcomed before de Gaulle's coming to power. Due to structural

Conclusion: Intersection or Periphery? 173

problems of French industry, a deal with Britain carried little appeal as it meant further competition without the benefits the Treaty of Rome promised. Yet, while it is at least conceivable that special safeguards for French industry as well as market access to Britain for her agricultural exports could have overcome these problems before 1958, it appears very unlikely that such concessions would have altered the position of the General thereafter. Indeed, de Gaulle's own plans for the Community meant that however intense the pressure from the Adenauer government and any other government among the Six, it would not have been sufficient to reverse his blank refusal to accommodate British interests. Instead, had the other five been more assertive in these formative years of the Community, the French President could and perhaps would have decided not to honour the Treaty of Rome.[8]

In view of plausible alternative scenarios, a judgement about British policy on Europe between 1955 and 1961 has to be qualified in temporal terms. Before Charles de Gaulle's coming to power in 1958, a more positive 'selling' of an Anglo-European deal based on a *bonafide* evaluation of Continental motives could have been successful – thereafter, negotiating tactics made little difference. However, even if it is appreciated that the General was able and determined to keep Britain out, her government cannot be fully exonerated, as the attitude which continued to be taken towards Continental governments in general, and towards Bonn in particular, proved to have longer-term implications, not least in reducing the chances of the first application. Between 1955 and 1961, British attempts to 'steer from without' evoked a basic mistrust of her intentions which, until recently, successive governments did little to dispel. Instead, British politicians time and again appeared to verify the doubts harboured in Continental capitals.

Notes

Introduction

1. Perhaps most influential in shaping this view was the early study by M. Camps, *Britain and the European Community, 1955–1963* (Oxford University Press: London, 1964), pp. 506–7. Other examples include A. Deighton, 'Missing the Boat: Britain and Europe 1945–61', in: *Contemporary Record* (February 1990), pp. 15–17, or R. Denman, *Missed Chances: Britain and Europe in the Twentieth Century* (Cassell: London, 1996). For an argument that the said opportunity was missed in the early 1950s, see E. Dell, *The Schuman Plan and the British Abdication of Leadership in Europe* (Oxford University Press: Oxford, 1995), esp. chapter 11, 'Could Britain Have Taken the Initiative?' and A. Nutting, *Europe Will Not Wait: a Warning and a Way Out* (Hollis & Carter: London, 1960), p. 32.
2. One of the rare, explicit rejections of this claim is found in J. W. Young, *Britain and European Unity, 1945–1992* (Macmillan: London, 1993), pp. 52–6. This is, of course, in line with the main contention of Young's study, that Britain had a far more sophisticated European policy after 1945 than hitherto assumed.
3. Comment by an official of the Foreign Office on the chances of influencing German economic and monetary policy from within or without the Common Market, 11 June 1956, FO371/124587 (London: Public Record Office). All subsequent references to the Foreign Office (FO), the Prime Minister's Office (PREM), the Treasury (T) and the Cabinet (CAB) are also to files held here.
4. See draft by the Foreign Office, 22 June 1960, FO371/150361, and the final report submitted to Cabinet as C (60) 107, 6 July 1960, CAB129/102.
5. Prime Minister John Major's promise to the German Chancellor Helmut Kohl in March 1991, as quoted in Young, *Britain and European Unity*, p. 162, and Robin Cook's first policy statement as Foreign Secretary, 2 May 1997, on the FO Internet site: http://www.fco.gov.uk/keythemes/europe, 1997.
6. Denman, *Missed Chances*, p. 233.
7. Quotes taken from 'Messina! Messina! or the Parting of Ways', Radio 3 programme, written and presented by M. Charlton, transmitted 9 March 1981, transcript held at BBC Script Library.
8. For the recent salience of counterfactual historical writing and its uses, see N. Ferguson (ed.), *Virtual History: Alternatives and Counterfactuals* (Picador: London, 1997). For traditional scepticism, compare E. H. Carr's discussion of this '"might-have-been" school of thought', in *What is History?* (Penguin: London, 1990), pp. 96–8.
9. A. S. Milward, *The European Rescue of the Nation State* (Routledge: London, 1992), p. 356.

10 See Churchill's Cabinet memorandum C (51) 32, 29 November 1951, CAB 129/48. See also, K. Larres, 'Integrating Europe or Ending the Cold War? Churchill's Post-War Foreign Policy', in: *Journal of European Integration History* (1996/1), pp. 15–49.
11 Hugh Gaitskill at the 1962 Labour Party Conference, as quoted – among many – in: W. Kaiser, *Using Europe, Abusing the Europeans: Britain and European Integration, 1945–1963* (Macmillan: London, 1996), p. 148. Rab Butler's comment as quoted in Young, *Britain and European Unity*, p. 46.
12 See W. Lipgens, *A History of European Integration, 1945–1947. Vol. 1: The Formation of the European Unity Movement* (Clarendon Press: Oxford, 1982). See also the concluding chapter of W. Loth, *Der Weg nach Europa: Geschichte der europäischen Integration 1939–1957*, 2nd edn (Vandenhoeck & Ruprecht: Göttingen, 1991).
13 Among many examples, see Dell, *Schuman Plan*, ascribing to the British government 'lack of leadership, of imagination, of analytical and diplomatic skills' (p. 299), and A. Shlaim, P. Jones and K. Sainsbury, *British Foreign Secretaries since 1945* (David and Charles: Newton Abbot, 1977), portraying Ernest Bevin as 'a roadblock on the path to European unity' (p. 67), Anthony Eden as being 'out of touch with reality' (p. 90) and blind 'to the real opportunity . . . of assuming the leadership of a united Europe' (pp. 108–9), Harold Macmillan as 'slow to realizing the importance of Messina' (p. 115) and Selwyn Lloyd as displaying the very same 'deficiencies in this respect' (p. 142). Most damning in its criticism of individuals, Kaiser, *Using Europe, Abusing the Europeans*, esp. its concluding chapter.
14 Compare R. T. Griffiths, 'A Slow One Hundred and Eighty Degree Turn' (Unpublished paper, European University Institute conference: Florence, 17–19 February 1994), p. 2, and S. Burgess and G. Edwards, 'The Six Plus One: British Policy-Making and the Question of European Economic Integration, 1955', in: *International Affairs* 64(3) (1988), pp. 393–414 (393–4).
15 Milward, *European Rescue*, p. 431.
16 For more detailed discussions of Britain's relations to the Continent before 1955, see for example: M. Beloff, *New Dimensions in Foreign Policy: a Study in British Administrative Experience, 1947–1959* (Allen & Unwin: London, 1961); R. Bullen, 'Britain and "Europe", 1950–1957', in: E. Serra (ed.), *The Relaunching of Europe and the Treaties of Rome* (Bruylant: Brussels, 1989), pp. 315–38; S. Greenwood, *Britain and European Cooperation since 1945* (Blackwell: Oxford, 1992); R. Lamb, *The Failure of the Eden Government* (Sidgwick and Jackson: London, 1987); and D. C. Watt, 'Großbritannien und Europa, 1951–1959; die Jahre Konservativer Regierung', in: *Vierteljahreshefte für Zeitgeschichte* 28 (1980), pp. 389–409. See also J. W. Young (ed.), *The Foreign Policy of Churchill's Peacetime Administration, 1951–1955* (Leicester University Press: Leicester, 1988) and, by the same author, *Britain, France and the Unity of Europe, 1945–51* (Leicester University Press: Leicester, 1984).
17 Though in the longer term this policy may not have been in Britain's economic interest, as recently suggested by A. S. Milward and G. Brennan,

176 *Notes*

Britain's Place in the World: a Historical Enquiry into Import Controls, 1945–60 (Routledge: London, 1996). See also Loth, *Der Weg nach Europa*, pp. 66–7, Shlaim et al., *British Foreign Secretaries*, pp. 52–3, and D. Barbezat, 'The Marshall Plan and the Origin of the OEEC', in: R. T. Griffiths (ed.), *Explorations in OEEC History* (OECD: Paris, 1997), pp. 33–44.

18 See, among many, W. Loth, 'The Process of European Integration: Some General Reflections', in: C. Wurm (ed.), *Western Europe and Germany: the Beginnings of European Integration 1945–1960* (Berg: Oxford, 1996), pp. 208–10. See also Loth, *Der Weg nach Europa*, pp. 72–8.

19 For the French 'ultimatum' and early British attempts to water down the plan to an intergovernmental arrangement, see R. Bullen, 'The British Government and the Schuman Plan', in: K. Schwabe (ed.), *Die Anfänge des Schuman-Plans, 1950/1* (Nomos: Baden-Baden, 1988), pp. 199–210, Dell, *Schuman Plan*, ch. 8, and Loth, *Der Weg nach Europa*, pp. 83–4. On the concept of 'supranationality', see G. Thiemeyer, 'Supranationalität als Novum in der Geschichte der internationalen Politik der fünfziger Jahre', in: *Journal of European Integration History* (1998/2), pp. 5–21. For staunch US support, see K. Schwabe, '"Ein Akt konstruktiver Staatskunst" – die USA und die Anfänge des Schuman-Plans', in: Schwabe, *Die Anfänge des Schuman-Plans*, pp. 211–40.

20 See Loth, *Der Weg nach Europa*, pp. 98–101. For the resulting 'sense of betrayal', see Shlaim et al., *British Foreign Secretaries*, p. 100.

21 An exhaustive documentation of the EDC negotiations is contained in L. Köllner et al. (eds), *Anfänge westdeutscher Sicherheitspolitik, 1945–1956*, Vol. 2 (Oldenbourg: München, 1990). See also E. Fursdon, *The European Defence Community: a History* (Macmillan: London, 1980), and W. Lipgens, 'EVG und Politische Föderation: Protokolle der Konferenz der Aussenminister der an den Verhandlungen über eine europäische Verteidigungsgemeinschaft beteiligten Länder am 11. Dezember 1951', in: *Vierteljahreshefte für Zeitgeschichte*, 32 (1984), pp. 637–88.

22 For the former view, see, for example, J. Wright, 'The Role of Britain in West German Foreign Policy since 1949', in: *German Politics* 5 (April 1996), pp. 26–42 (28–9). For a different view on the evolution of British policy, see S. Dockrill, *Britain's Policy for West German Rearmament, 1950–55* (Cambridge University Press: Cambridge, 1991). Whether or not the charge of sabotage is being supported, many seem to share the view of Shlaim et al., *British Foreign Secretaries*, which portrays British abstention as 'the single most important factor in its [the EDC's] eventual defeat' (p. 56).

23 Macmillan before the House of Commons, 2 August 1961, as quoted in Deighton, 'Missing the Boat', p. 17.

24 Exemplary thereof are: Camps, *Britain and the European Community*, W. Kaiser, *Grossbritannien und die europäische Wirtschaftsgemeinschaft, 1955–1961* (Akademie: Berlin, 1996), or J. Moon, *European Integration in British Politics, 1950–63: a Study of Issue Change* (Gower: Aldershot, Hants., 1985).

25 Examples include R. T. Griffiths and S. Ward (eds), *Courting the Common Market: the First Attempt to Enlarge the European Community* (Lothian Foundation: London, 1996), and A. Deighton (ed.), *Building Postwar Europe: National-Decision-Makers and European Institutions, 1948–1963* (Macmillan:

London, 1995). Going beyond this national perspective on multilateral issues is the multi-archival study by N. P. Ludlow, *Dealing with Britain: the Six and the First UK Application to the EEC* (Cambridge University Press: Cambridge, 1997).

26 See, for example, Milward and Brennan, *Britain's Place in the World*, or W. Kaiser, 'The Bomb and Europe: Britain, France and the EEC Entry Negotiations (1961–1963)', in: *Journal of European Integration History* (1995/1), pp. 65–85.

27 See F. R. Willis, *France, Germany and the New Europe, 1945–1967* (Stanford University Press: Stanford, 1968), and H. J. Küsters, *Die Gründung der europäischen Wirtschaftsgemeinschaft* (Nomos: Baden-Baden, 1982). See also K. Kaiser, *EWG und Freihandelszone: England und der Kontinent in der europäischen Integration* (Sythoff: Leiden, 1963), D. C. Watt, *Britain looks to Germany: British Opinion and Policy towards Germany since 1945* (Oswald Wolff: London, 1965), and Watt, 'Großbritannien und Europa'.

28 Camps, *Britain and the European Community*, p. 155. For the divisions in Bonn, see U. Enders, 'Integration oder Kooperation? Ludwig Erhard und Franz Etzel im Streit über die Politik der europäischen Zusammenarbeit', in: *Vierteljahreshefte für Zeitgeschichte*, 45 (1997), pp. 143–71; H. J. Küsters, 'Adenauers Europapolitik in der Gründungsphase der europäischen Wirtschaftsgemeinschaft', in: *Vierteljahreshefte für Zeitgeschichte*, 31 (1983), pp. 646–73, and by the same author, 'Der Streit um Kompetenzen und Konzeptionen deutscher Europapolitik, 1949–1958', in: L. Herbst, W. Bührer and H. Sowade (eds), *Vom Marshallplan zur EWG: die Eingliederung der Bundesrepublik Deutschland in die westliche Welt* (Oldenbourg: München, 1990), pp. 395–70. See also Herbert Müller-Roschach, *Die deutsche Europapolitik, 1949–1977* (Europa Union Verlag: Bonn, 1980).

29 The only exception is S. Lee, *An Uneasy Partnership: British–German Relations between 1955 and 1961* (Brockmeyer: Bochum, 1996).

30 To enhance fluidity and avoid a prohibitive presentation, all quotations from primary German sources have been translated into English by the author.

1 From Indifference to Hostility: Britain, Germany and the Messina Project

1 See Monnet's so-called action programme of 14 April 1955, filed in *AA: PA*, Vol. 900 (Political Archive of the German Foreign Ministry: Bonn). All subsequent references to the *Auswärtiges Amt (AA)* are also to the Political Archive in Bonn. PA denotes files of the *AA*'s *Politische Abteilung* (Political Department), *LA* refers to its *Länderabteilung* (Foreign Relations by Country), while *HPA* denotes *Handelspolitische Abteilung* (Trade Policy Department). *BStS* and *MB* refer to *Büro des Staatssekretärs* (State Secretarial Office) and *Ministerbüro* (Minister's Office) respectively. For Monnet's plan and the initial German reaction, see Loth, *Der Weg nach Europa*, pp. 114–17, and W. Bührer, 'Die Montanunion – ein Fehlschlag? Deutsche Lehren aus der EGKS und die Gründung der EWG', in: G. Trausch (ed.), *Die europäische Integration vom Schumanplan bis zu den*

178 *Notes*

Verträgen von Rom (Nomos: Baden-Baden, 1993), pp. 75–90 (here pp. 86–7).
2 See also Enders, 'Integration oder Kooperation?'
3 See Erhard to Adenauer, 25 March 1955, B136/1310 Vol. 1 *Bundeskanzleramt (BuKa)* (Bundesarchiv: Koblenz). Subsequent references to the Chancellor's Office *(BuKa)*, the Ministry for Economics *(BMWi)*, the Ministry for Economic Co-operation *(BMWZ)* and to the private papers *(Nachlaß* NL239) of Foreign Minister, Heinrich von Brentano, and Germany's Ambassador to Paris, Herbert Blankenhorn *(Nachlaß* NL351), are also to documents held in Koblenz.
4 See for example *Vereinigung Deutscher Elektrizitätswerke* to Adenauer, 25 April 1955, and *Vereinigung Industrielle Kraftwirtschaft* to Adenauer, 28 April 1955, both B136/1310 *(BuKa)*.
5 See, for example, *Bulletin des Presse- und Informationsamtes der Bundesregierung*, Bonn, 22 September 1954.
6 See Hallstein to Erhard, 30 March 1955, B136/1310 Vol. 1 *(BuKa)*.
7 As early as April, there was a fierce internal debate within the *BMWi*: see, for example, Josef Rust (Head of *BMWi* Department III 'Mining, Energy, Water') to Erhard, 18 April 1955, as well as Hans von der Groeben to Rust, 21 April 1955, both B102/022137 *(BMWi)*.
8 See A. Müller-Armack, *Auf dem Weg nach Europa: Erinnerungen und Ausblicke* (Wunderlich/Poeschel: Tübingen/Stuttgart, 1971), pp. 99–101, and Küsters, *Die Gründung der europäischen Wirtschaftsgemeinschaft.*
9 Müller-Armack, *Auf dem Weg*, p. 100. See also protocol of an interministerial meeting of 26 May 1955, and Ophüls to Hallstein, 24 May 1955, both *AA: PA* Vol. 900.
10 See memorandum and German protocol, 2 June 1955, B102/022137 *(BMWi)*.
11 See telephone report by Westrick, 1 June 1955, B102/022160 *(BMWi)*.
12 See Rust to press office, 7 July 1955, B102/022137 Vol. 2 *(BMWi)*.
13 See Ophüls's comments during an interministerial meeting, 20 June 1955, B102/022160 *(BMWi)*.
14 For the following paragraph, see the *BMWi*'s position paper, 6 July 1955, B102/022160 *(BMWi)*, and interministerial meeting, 25 June 1955, B102/022160 *(BMWi)*.
15 The *BMWi*'s opposition to harmonization was shared by the Ministry of Finance *(BMF)* under Fritz Schäffer. See Schäffer to all other departments, 27 May 1955, B102/022160 *(BMWi)*.
16 See Sir G. Allchin (HM Ambassador to Luxembourg) to the Foreign Office, 18 May 1955, FO371/116038.
17 Allchin to the Foreign Office, 18 May 1955, FO371/116038.
18 See minutes by Edden, 14 May 1955, FO371/116038, and 11 June 1955, FO371/116039.
19 See Allchin to FO, 18 May 1955, FO371/116038, Cecil Weir (Head of UK delegation to ECSC) to Coulson, 8 June 1955, FO371/116039, and also Allchin to Foreign Secretary Macmillan, 8 June 1955, FO371/116039.
20 See Ellis-Rees to Strath, 21 April 1955, Edden's minute of 14 May 1955, Allchin to FO, 18 May 1955, and James Majoribanks (UK delegation to ECSC) to Edden, 2 June 1955, all FO371/116038. See also Weir to Coulson,

8 June 1955, Allchin to Macmillan, 8 June 1955, both FO371/116039, as well as HM embassy, Brussels, to Western Organization Department, FO, 21 June 1955, FO371/116040. See also Commercial Department, HM embassy, Paris, to FO, 15 June 1955, T232/430.
21. See Ellis-Rees to Strath, 21 April 1955, Edden's minute of 14 May 1955, Allchin to FO, 18 May 1955, and Majoribanks to Edden, 2 June 1955, all FO371/116038.
22. See Allchin to FO, 18 May 1955, and Edden's minute of 14 May 1955, both FO371/116038.
23. Edden's comment on Ellis-Rees to FO, 7 June 1955, FO371/116038.
24. As reported by Ophüls to Brentano, 29 June 1955, *AA*: *PA* Vol. 902. See also Butler's slightly regretful comments during 'Messina! Messina! or the Parting of Ways', Radio 3 programme, written and presented by M. Charlton, transmitted 9 March 1981, transcript held at BBC Script Library.
25. The Treasury did, however, file some FO correspondence in advance of the conference, including the translation of a newspaper article of the *Handelsblatt* of 1 June 1955, in which Erhard outlined his opposition to the sector approach, 2 June 1955, T232/430.
26. See memorandum by Strath, 29 June 1955, T232/430.
27. See Strath's memorandum, 15 June 1955, and also draft statement for Butler, 21 June 1955, both T232/430.
28. The Chancellor supported Strath's view: see his comments on instructions to Ellis-Rees, 29 June 1955, T232/430.
29. For the former comment, see Edden's memo of 11 June 1955, FO371/116039, for the latter, see Strath's memorandum of 29 June 1955, T232/430. See also Treasury memo to the MAC (MAC [55] 123), T232/430.
30. MAC (55) 23rd meeting, 28 June 1955, CAB134/1026.
31. FO draft, 1 July 1955, and changes suggested, T232/430; see also MAC (55) 23rd meeting, 28 June 1955, CAB134/1026.
32. FO to representatives abroad, 7 July 1955, T232/430.
33. See the protocol of the meeting, 7 July 1955, B136/1310 (*BuKa*) and the account in *BMWi* files, 7 July 1055, B102/022160 (*BMWi*).
34. See Adenauer, 6 July 1955, B136/1310 (*BuKa*); see also 89th Cabinet meeting, in which Erhard had provoked Adenauer's statement with his criticism, 6 July 1955, in: Bundesarchiv (ed.), *Die Kabinettsprotokolle der Bundesregierung*, Vol. 8, 1955 (R. Oldenbourg: München, 1997), pp. 405–6.
35. See Hallstein's comments at the meeting of 7 July 1955, B136/1310 (*BuKa*) and the account in *BMWi* files, 7 July 1055, B102/022160 (*BMWi*).
36. For Hallstein's speech, see 9 July 1955, B102/022160 (*BMWi*).
37. See record of interministerial debate, 11 July 1955, B102/022160 (*BMWi*). The conflict over competences before June 1955 is well documented in Küsters, 'Der Streit um Kompetenzen'.
38. Warner to FO, 9 July 1955, FO371/116041.
39. Edden's comment on a report sent by Basil Boothby (Councillor, HM embassy, Brussels) to Coulson, 11 July 1955, FO371/116041.
40. Edden's comment on Warner's report, 9 July 1955, FO371/116041.
41. Coulson to Boothby, 22 July 1955, FO371/116041.
42. See reports on committee meetings by Ellis-Rees, 16 July 1955, Charles de Peyer (UK delegation to ECSC), 19 July 1955, Warner, 19 July 1955,

180 Notes

21 July 1955, 22 July 1955, Boothby, 3 August 1955, Bretherton, 4 August 1955, Andrew Collier (Principal, Treasury), 5 August 1955, all T232/431.
43 See reports by Warner, 21 July 1955, Boothby, 3 August 1955, Collier, 5 August 1955, all T232/431.
44 See FO telegrams to embassies in Bonn and elsewhere, 9 August 1955, and HM embassy, Bonn to FO, 3 September 1955, both T232/431.
45 See von der Groeben on expert talks, 1 September 1955, B102/022160 (*BMWi*).
46 See *Bulletin des Presse- und Informationsamtes der Bundesregierung*, Bonn, 6 September 1955.
47 See report on Noordwijk conference, 6 September 1955, B102/022161 (*BMWi*).
48 See Westrick, 9 September 1955, B136/1310 (*BuKa*).
49 The *AA* clearly supported Spaak's renewed choice of von der Groeben as part of the small drafting committee for the interim report: see Brentano to Erhard, 14 October 1955, *AA: PA* Vol. 899.
50 See joint Cabinet memorandum, 9 November 1955, B102/022161 (*BMWi*).
51 Erhard's remarks put him in conflict with his own staff: see von der Groeben to Dankmar Seibt (*Persönlicher Referent* [private secretary] to Erhard), 18 November 1955, B102/022161 (*BMWi*), and von der Groeben to Erhard, 24 November 1955, B102/022161 (*BMWi*).
52 See for example *Bund Deutscher Industrie* (*BDI*) to *BMWi*, 3 November 1955, and *Eschweiler Bergwerksverein* to von der Groeben, 13 December 1955, both B102/022161 (*BMWi*). With the explicit consent of the *AA*, von der Groeben and Rust of the *BMWi* used their high-level contacts with industrialists to prevent the *BDI* from passing a resolution against the Common Market: see Karl Carstens (Deputy Head of Political Department, *AA*) to Hallstein, 9 November 1955, *AA: PA* Vol. 899.
53 See Schäffer in Cabinet meeting, 25 November 1955, B136/1310 (*BuKa*), also in: Bundesarchiv (ed.), *Kabinettsprotokolle*, 1955, pp. 689–9. Of course, his opposition to the funds was not new (see Schäffer to *AA* and *BMWi*, 27 May 1955, *AA: PA* Vol. 900), but he now received support from three other Cabinet Ministers (Siegfried Balke, Hans-Joachim von Merkatz and Hermann Schäfer – Ministers of the Post Service, of Federal Relations [*Bundesrat*] and without portfolio, respectively). Hallstein cut the debate short, assuring all dissenters that the expert committee deliberations were non-binding for the government – the very same tactic he had already used during the Messina conference: see Hallstein to *BMF*, 2 June 1955, and to *BML*, 3 June 1955, both *AA:PA* Vol. 901.
54 See internal *BMWi* meeting, 20 December 1955, B102/022161 (*BMWi*).
55 See Jackling to Coulson, 4 August 1955, FO371/116044.
56 Jackling to Coulson, 4 August 1955, FO371/116044.
57 See, for example, minutes by Gerald Rodgers (Assistant Head of the Mutual Aid Department, FO), 20 August 1955, FO371/116046, and 4 August 1955, FO371/116044.
58 See Warner to FO, 22 July 1955, T232/431, and Jackling to FO, 19 August 1955, FO371/116046.
59 Edden, 4 October 1955, FO371/116035A.

Notes 181

60 Record of conversation, 14 September 1955, T232/433.
61 Strath to Frank Turnbull (Under-Secretary, Treasury), 19 September 1955; see also Boothby, 16 September 1955; both T232/432.
62 Nichols to Strath, 10 October 1955, T232/433.
63 Sir Edward Bridges to Butler, 20 September 1955, T232/432.
64 As reported to Strath, 14 September 1955, T232/432.
65 Nichols to Strath, 10 October 1955, T232/433; see also Turnbull to Collier, 21 September 1955, draft brief for Butler by Collier, 28 September 1955, Turnbull to Strath, 4 October 1955 (all T232/432), as well as Strath's minute, 10 October 1955, T232/433.
66 Draft brief for Butler by Collier, 28 September 1955, T232/432.
67 Quotes from the Schäffer meeting refer to the protocol MAC (55) 193, 12 October 1955, CAB134/1030.
68 See MAC (55) 28th meeting, 15 July 1955, CAB134/1026.
69 See the two memoranda, MAC (55) 135 (Board of Trade), 13 July 1955, and MAC (55) 136 (Treasury), 14 July 1955 (both CAB134/1029). For the instruction to representatives, see MAC (55) 28th meeting, 15 July 1955, CAB134/1026.
70 MAC (55) 135, 13 July 1955, CAB134/1029.
71 MAC (55) 136, 14 July 1955, CAB134/1029 (emphasis in original).
72 For the discussion about withdrawal, see Strath to Butler, 20 September 1955, and Sir Edward Bridges to Butler, 20 September 1955, as well as Harry Crookshank (Lord Privy Seal and Leader of the House of Commons) to Butler, 21 September 1955, Macmillan to Butler, 23 September 1955, and Peter Thorneycroft (President of Board of Trade) to Butler, 23 September 1955 (all T232/432). For the ongoing dispute about the departure of the British representative, see conflicting comments by Bretherton and the *Chef de Cabinet* of Spaak, Robert Rothschild, during 'Messina! Messina! or the Parting of Ways'.
73 Quotes taken from the Trend report, MAC (55) 199–201, 24 October 1955, CAB134/1030.
74 See ES (55) 8th meeting, 1 November 1955, CAB134/889; the ES report itself is contained in EP (55) 53–5, CAB134/1228.
75 ES (55) 8th meeting, 1 November 1955, CAB134/889.
76 MAC (55) 211, 11 November 1955, CAB134/1030. Clarke was Third Secretary in the Treasury.
77 EP (55) 11th meeting, 11 November 1955, CAB134/1226. Wolfram Kaiser attributes this comment to Macmillan, which is central to his argument that the Foreign Secretary had caused the diplomatic 'fiasco'. See Kaiser, *Grossbritannien*, p. 60. The same argument is extended forcefully in his 'To Join, or Not to Join: the "Appeasement" Policy of Britain's First EEC Application', in: B. Brivati and H. Jones (eds), *From Reconstruction to Integration: Britain and Europe since 1945* (Leicester University Press: Leicester, 1993), pp. 144–65, in particular p. 149 and his footnote 22. The relevant protocol does not, however, list Macmillan among those present. Curiously, Kaiser himself acknowledged this in his earlier writings: see his 'Selbstisolierung in Europa – die britische Regierung und die Gründung der EWG', in: C. Wurm (ed.), *Wege nach Europa: Wirtschaft und Außenpolitik Großbritanniens im 20. Jahrhundert* (Brockmeyer: Bochum,

182 *Notes*

1992), pp. 125–53 (133, footnote 20). Indeed, the comment is found in the summing-up section of the document and can thus not be attributed to any committee member in particular. Liz Kane, by contrast, claims that the whole idea of sabotage is a 'myth' and that the British government was taken by surprise when faced with angry reactions on the Continent: see L. Kane, 'European or Atlantic Community? The Foreign Office and "Europe": 1955–1957', in: *Journal of European Integration History* (1997/2), pp. 83–98. However, she seems to overlook not only the November telegrams but also the sustained British effort to persuade the US administration to withdraw its support: see chapter 2, below.

78 See Lord Reading (Minister of State, FO) relaying the EP Committee's conclusions to the FO, and Edden's draft of the two telegrams, 11 November 1955, FO371/116035A.
79 See Edden, 9 July 1955, FO371/116041.
80 See protocol of the meeting of 22 December 1955, B102/022161 (*BMWi*).
81 Protocol of the meeting of 22 December 1955, B102/022161 (*BMWi*).
82 Hallstein to Erhard, 30 March 1955, B136/1310 (*BuKa*). For the persistence of this *AA* view, see also comments made by Ophüls to the ECSC Committee of the *Bundestag*, 29 September 1955, B102/022161 (*BMWi*).
83 Protocol of the meeting of 22 December 1955, B102/022161 (*BMWi*).
84 See also footnote 53 in this chapter.
85 See Müller-Armack, *Auf dem Weg*, pp. 91–3.

2 Entering Wedge or Counterblast? Britain's Plan G

1 See K. Adenauer, *Erinnerungen, 1955–1959* (DVA: Stuttgart, 1967), pp. 252–5 (quote p. 254). While German Ministers are accountable for the running of their departments (*Ressortprinzip*) as well as for the joint formulation of policy (*Kabinettsprinzip*), the German Chancellor has the constitutional right to issue binding guidelines. This *Richtlinienkompetenz* is laid down in Art. 65 of the basic law. For Adenauer's skilful use of this provision, see W. Hennis, *Richtlinienkompetenz und Regierungstechnik* (Mohr: Tübingen, 1964).
2 See BDI to Adenauer, 28 May 1955, *AA*: *PA* Vol. 905, *Geschäftsvereinigung Eisen- und Stahlindustrie* to Erhard, 16 January 1956, B102/022161 (*BMWi*) and *Wirtschaftsvereinigung Bergbau* to Erhard, 10 March 1956, B146/1845 (*BMWZ*). For the electricity generating industry, see *Verband Deutscher Elektrizitätswerke* to Erhard, 23 May 1956, *AA*: *PA* Vol. 905.
3 For the perhaps most prolific example, see Erhard's comments during a press conference following his visit to London in February 1956, in: *Bulletin of the Press and Information Office of the Federal Government*, English Version Vol. 4, No. 10, 8 March 1956, filed in FO371/122024.
4 See Carstens to diplomatic outposts, 14 February 1956, *AA*: *PA* Vol. 904, and report of the German embassy in Paris, 17 May 1956, *AA*: *PA* Vol. 905. See also memo by Herbert Müller-Roschach (Head of *AA* Sub-Department 'European Political Integration'), 23 May 1956, *AA*: *PA* Vol. 905.
5 See Hallstein to Brentano and Adenauer, 29 May 1956, *AA*: *PA* Vol. 905.

6 Adenauer, *Erinnerungen, 1955–1959*, p. 257.
7 See René Sergeant to Hallstein, 31 January 1956, and memo by Müller-Roschach, 1 March 1956, both *AA: PA* Vol. 926.
8 See the *BMWZ* study of 26 May 1956, *AA: PA* Vol. 926.
9 See German embassy, London, to *AA*, 8 February 1956, *AA*: LA Sub-Dept. 301, Vol. 65.
10 German embassy, Washington, to *AA*, 14 May 1956, *AA: PA* Vol. 905.
11 See memorandum by Müller-Roschach, 23 May 1956, *AA: PA* Vol. 905.
12 Hallstein at Venice conference, as quoted in Müller-Roschach's memo of 31 May 1956, *AA: PA* Vol. 905. The desire to appease Britain had also characterized earlier meetings: see, for example, Carstens to diplomatic outposts, 14 February 1956, *AA: PA* Vol. 904.
13 See *The Times*, 29 May 1956, filed in *AA: PA* Vol. 905. An early indication of a change in the British position came with the idea to include Western Europe in the Commonwealth system: see German embassy, London, to *AA*, 1 June 1956, *AA: PA* Vol. 925.
14 For the British OEEC statement, see Ellis-Rees, 6 December 1955, T234/182. For the run-up to the meeting, see memo by Ellis-Rees, 24 November 1955, MAC (55) 219, CAB134/1030, and Figgures to Clarke and Denis Wright (Assistant Under-Secretary, FO), 25 November 1955, T234/182. For the aftermath, see also Ellis-Rees reporting to MAC, 12 December 1955, MAC (55) 233, CAB134/1030. See also Kaiser, *Grossbritannien*, pp. 60–1, and – disagreeing – Kane, 'European or Atlantic Community?'.
15 See reports by HM Ambassador to The Hague, Sir Paul Mason, 10, 10, 13 and 14 December 1955. In defence, Ellis-Rees quoted other Dutch politicians to the contrary effect: see Ellis-Rees to FO, 12 December 1955, 17 December 1955, 21 December 1955 (all FO371/116035b). See also Sir Paul Mason to FO and minutes by Robert Munro (Mutual Aid Department, FO) and Rodgers acknowledging that the meeting had backfired, 8 December 1955, FO371/122044.
16 Quoted in Hoyer-Millar to FO, 31 December 1955, and HM embassy, Bonn, to Edden, 31 December 1955 (both FO371/122044).
17 Munro's comment on HM embassy, Bonn, to Edden, 31 December 1955, FO371/122044.
18 See Roger Makins (HM Ambassador, Washington) to FO, 23 December 1955. See also minutes by Munro, Rodgers, C. H. Johnston (Head of Western Department, FO) and Edden (all FO371/115999).
19 MAC (56) 2nd meeting, 10 January 1956, CAB134/1282. See also Wright to Clarke, 11 January 1956, FO371/122022.
20 MAC (56) 6, 13 January 1956, CAB134/1283.
21 For examples of the growing literature on American support for European integration, see P. Winand, *Eisenhower, Kennedy and the United States of Europe* (Macmillan: London, 1993), and K. Schwabe, 'Die Vereinigten Staaten und die europäische Integration: Alternativen der amerikanischen Außenpolitik (1950–55)', in: G. Trausch (ed.), *Die europäische Integration vom Schumanplan bis zu den Verträgen von Rom* (Nomos: Baden-Baden, 1993), pp. 41–54.
22 CM (56) 13th meeting, 9 February 1956, CAB128/30.

184 *Notes*

23 For an early example of concern about Britain's negative approach, see proposals by FO Minister of State, Anthony Nutting, of extending the Commonwealth preference system to cover Europe, 10 January 1956, FO371/122023.
24 For his claim, see H. Macmillan, *Riding the Storm, 1956–1959* (Macmillan: London, 1971), pp. 74–7.
25 See, for example, Macmillan to Sir Leslie Rowan (Second Secretary, Treasury), 23 January 1956, T234/183, and to Sir Edward Bridges, 1 February 1956, and 24 February 1956, both T234/100.
26 Sir Alec Cairncross, *Years of Recovery: British Economic Policy 1945–51* (Methuen: London, 1985), p. 55.
27 Macmillan to Sir Edward Bridges, 24 February 1956, T234/100. For the records of the Clarke working group, see T234/101 and FO371/122025. Substantive work only began in March 1956: see Clarke to Caccia, 1 March 1956, and record of first meeting, 7 March 1956, both FO371/122024.
28 See report by Clarke working group, 21 April 1956, FO371/122025.
29 For precursors to alternative C, see W. A. Brusse, 'The Failure of European Tariff Plans in GATT (1951–1954)', in: G. Trausch (ed.), *Die europäische Integration vom Schumanplan bis zu den Verträgen von Rom* (Nomos: Baden-Baden, 1993), pp. 99–114.
30 Note by Clarke, 29 May 1956, T234/101, not citing any evidence for the latter claim. The working group had not asked for a FO assessment at this stage.
31 See record of the meeting, 31 May 1956, FO371/122028.
32 See Thorneycroft to Macmillan, 22 May 1956, FO371/122028.
33 See Bretherton's four-page memo on the advantages of an industrial Free Trade Area, undated (received in registry 15 March 1956); see also Bretherton's note to Clarke working group, 4 April 1956 (both FO371/122044).
34 For the two articles by Meade, see *Manchester Guardian*, 14 and 15 March 1956; for Bretherton's claim see M. Charlton, *The Price of Victory* (BBC: London, 1983), pp. 177–87. For the suspicion of official encouragement, see Camps, *Britain and the European Community*, p. 95. For advance information, see Figgures to FO, passing on Meade's letter to Bretherton, 25 January 1956, FO371/122044.
35 See Macmillan to Sir Edward Bridges, 1 February 1956, T234/100, and Thorneycroft to Macmillan, 22 May 1956, FO371/122028. For the November telegram, see Chapter 1, above.
36 See, for example, Clarke to Sir Leslie Rowan, 16 January 1956, T234/182, and Macmillan complaining about this attitude to Sir Edward Bridges, 1 February 1956, T234/100.
37 For indications of increased chances of the Common Market in French politics, see Johnston to Lord Hood (Head of Western Organisation Department, FO), 23 January 1956; for the opponents of the Common Market in Germany keeping a 'low profile', see HM embassy, Bonn, to FO, 24 January 1956, both FO371/122022. For the view on German industry, see Treasury brief for Eden's visit to the US, 6 January 1956, T234/182, and UK delegation to the ECSC reporting

Notes 185

on the views of the Chairman of the *BDI*, Fritz Berg, 10 January 1956, FO371/122022.
38 See papers of the Clarke working group, T234/100 *passim*, and its report, 21 April 1956, FO371/122025.
39 See, for example, Greenwood, *Britain and European Cooperation since 1945*, especially chapters 4–6.
40 Brief for the PM's visit in MAC (56) 6, 13 January 1956, CAB134/1283.
41 For the following argument, see Wright to Clarke, 11 January 1956, FO371/122022, Nutting's memo of 10 January 1956, FO371/122023, and the report of Clarke's working group, 21 April 1956, FO371/122025.
42 Wright's memorandum, 17 May 1956, FO371/122028.
43 Caccia's comment on an ES EI report, 30 May 1956, FO371/122028.
44 See Clarke to Sir Leslie Rowan, 16 January 1956, T234/182.
45 Macmillan to Sir Edward Bridges, 1 February 1956, T234/100.
46 See Clarke's memo, 29 May 1956, T234/101.
47 See report of Clarke's working group, 21 April 1956, FO371/122025.
48 HM embassy, Bonn, to FO, 24 January 1956, FO371/122022.
49 See Munro's comment on the report, 24 January 1956, FO371/122022.
50 See brief for Erhard visit, MAC (56) 27, CAB134/1283, discussed in the Mutual Aid Committee 7th meeting, 17 February 1956, CAB134/1282.
51 Note on the discussion between Macmillan and Erhard on 23 February 1956. See also note on earlier discussion, 21 February 1956, both T234/27. Erhard also made his views public in the official *Bulletin of the Press and Information Office of the German Federal Government*, Vol. 4 No. 10, 8 March 1956 (English Version), filed in FO371/122024.
52 Hoyer-Millar to Prime Minister's Office, 4 April 1956, PREM11/1365; see also report on Adenauer's speech, 23 March 1956, FO371/122024.
53 The Treasury and FO briefs for Brentano's visit, T234/67 and FO371/122025 respectively.
54 Note of conversation by Figgures, 2 May 1956, T234/67.
55 Clarke's memo on the report of his working group, 29 May 1956, T234/101. The 'collective approach' referred to the 1952 plan to move towards limited convertibility within the sterling area, as part of the wider policy of removing worldwide barriers to trade. It had been formulated jointly by the then head of the Treasury's Overseas Finance Division, Sir Leslie Rowan, and Sir George Bolton, Governor of the Bank of England. For a discussion thereof, see Milward, *European Rescue*, pp. 358–84.
56 See Thorneycroft to Macmillan, 22 May 1956, FO371/122028, and memo by Board of Trade, 22 May 1956, T234/195. For Foreign Office preference for the first alternative, see MAC (56) 14th meeting, 27 April 1956, discussing FO memorandum MAC (56) 64 on the merger of institutions of the Council of Europe and OEEC, described by Figgures as a 'counter-blast to the Messina proposals', CAB134/1282. For FO fear that E will encounter US opposition, see Wright's minute, 17 May 1956, FO371/122028. Interestingly, this correct prediction of US reactions was ignored.

186 *Notes*

57 See record of the ministerial meeting in the Treasury, 31 May 1956, FO371/122028.
58 See Clarke's opening paper to the working group, 2 June 1956, T234/102.
59 The first meeting was on 2 June 1956. Minutes of 1st to 6th meetings are in T234/102; all memoranda and the interim report are in T230/336. The Sub-Committee's minutes and memoranda were given the code ES (EI), contained in CAB134/1238 and CAB134/1239 respectively.
60 See conclusions of the ministerial meeting in the Treasury, 31 May 1956, FO371/122028, and Clarke's note to the Sub-Committee, EP (EI) (56) 1, 18 June 1956, T230/335.
61 See, for example, report by the Board of Trade's (BoT) tariff division, 21 June 1956, FO371/122029.
62 See 'United Kingdom Initiative in Europe, Plan G', CP (56) 191, 27 July 1956, CAB129/82. Also as ES (EI) (56) 2, 1 August 1956, CAB134/1239.
63 See Figgures to Clarke, 8 June 1956, T234/184, Boothby to FO, 7 June 1956, and Ellis-Rees to FO, 15 June 1956 (both FO371/122050).
64 See Ellis-Rees to Figgures, sending draft letter containing this suggestion, 7 July 1956. Sent to Sergeant, 12 July 1956. Both FO371/122050.
65 It is noteworthy that other than testing likely European reception, there were at least two other motives for the British OEEC initiative, the first of which was to keep the OEEC 'vital during the months when the initiative in the trade field may be felt to lie with the Messina Powers': Cabinet memorandum by the Chancellor, CP (56) 171, 9 July 1956. The second motive was that with the achievement of 90 per cent quota liberalization, there was mounting pressure in the OEEC to reduce tariffs, which was not acceptable to Britain at this stage, suggesting the Free Trade Area was therefore also a holding operation. See joint Cabinet memorandum by the Chancellor and the President of the Board of Trade, CP (56) 172, 9 July 1956 (all CAB129/82).
66 Quoted by Ellis-Rees to Wright, 11 August 1956, T234/196.
67 Bretherton's memorandum, 23 July 1956, FO371/122051, referring to the German representative at OEEC, Karl Werkmeister, and the Head of the *AA*'s Trade Policy Department, Hilgar van Scherpenberg.
68 See Ellis-Rees to Wright, 11 August 1956, T234/196.
69 'United Kingdom Initiative in Europe, Plan G', CP (56) 191, 27 July 1956, CAB129/82. Also as ES (EI) (56) 2, 1 August 1956, CAB134/1239.
70 See Federation of British Industry (FBI) to FO, 3 September 1956, FO371/122033. See also the resolution sent to FO by the British National Committee of the International Chamber of Commerce, 29 October 1956, FO371/122038.
71 See Figgures's draft questionnaire, 27 July 1956, FO371/122032. The letter itself is in ES (EI) (56) 3, CAB134/1239.
72 See comments by Colonial Secretary in Cabinet, CM (56) 66th meeting, 18 September 1956, CAB128/30. For the benefits of a renewed Anglo-Australian wheat agreement to the reception of Plan G, see EP (56) 71, 31 August 1956, CAB134/1231
73 See HM embassy, Washington, to FO, 11 August 1956, FO371/122033.

74 Jebb, in ES (EI) (56) 18, 17 August 1956, CAB134/1239. The same argument was, however, restated by Clarke, 3 September 1956, T234/197, and it also entered into the report of 31 August 1956, EP (56) 70, CAB134/1231.
75 Within a free trade area, the definition of origin refers to the circumstances under which a product can be regarded as having been produced within that area, and which should hence enjoy freedom from tariffs if sold in another member country. The origin of goods traded between member countries of the free trade area has to be controlled at the border in order to avoid possible deflections of trade flows. These occur if one free trade area country has a lower external tariff on certain products. Imports into this country may then be re-exported free of tariffs to another member country, thereby undermining the latter's tariff protection and hence tariff autonomy *vis-à-vis* third countries. The practical advantage of a customs union lies in the fact that the common external tariff prevents this effect, thereby allowing for real integration in the form of the abolition of border controls. However, when seeking to include only some and not all members of a customs union into a free trade area, the problem of definition of origin is aggravated. A product may be produced in or enter a low tariff member country of the free trade area, be re-exported tariff free to a member country of both customs union and free trade area, and finally enter – again tariff free – the customs union country not participating in the free trade area. The latter country would by default become a member of the free trade area. The only measure to avoid this effect lies in re-introducing border controls between those customs union members which are also members of the free trade area, and those which are not. This, in turn, would mean that there is no real customs union any longer. There is no historical precedent for a solution to this problem.
76 See HM embassy, Bonn, to Wright, 11 August 1956, FO371/122033.
77 See the final report, 31 August 1956, EP (56) 70, CAB134/1231.
78 See CM (56) 65th meeting, 14 September 1956, and CM (56) 66th meeting, 18 September 1956, both CAB128/30. The same scaring tactic was used to convince Commonwealth Finance Ministers: see draft letter, 10 September 1956, FO371/122033.
79 For the text of Macmillan's news conference, see ES (EI) (56) 50, 4 October 1956, CAB134/1240. See also press release, 3 October 1956, FO371/122052.
80 See Brentano's Cabinet memorandum of 7 May 1956 seeking approval for the opening of negotiations and also Erhard's advance approval of the above, 6 May 1956 (both *AA: PA* Vol. 909). For Erhard's suggestion that the Economic Cabinet should be given responsibility, see his Cabinet memorandum of 15 June 1956, *AA: PA* Vol. 909. While supporting the *AA* view, even the *Bundeskanzleramt* was at this stage concerned about Brentano's attempts to secure all responsibilities: see minute by Franz Haenlein (Head of Chancellory Department B 'Economics, Social Policy and Finances'), 22 May 1956, B136/1312 (*BuKa*).
81 Brentano to Adenauer, copied to Erhard, 5 June 1956, B136/1312 (*BuKa*),

188 Notes

based on Müller-Roschach to Brentano, 4 June 1956, *AA: PA* Vol. 909. For the continued conflict about the Economic Cabinet, see Erhard to Adenauer, 13 July 1956, and Adenauer to Franz Blücher (Minister for Economic Co-operation), 19 July 1956, both B136/1312 (*BuKa*). See also Haenlein to Erhard, 23 July 1956, B102/12616 (*BMWi*).

82 For the controversy surrounding von der Groeben, see Carstens to Hallstein, 4 May 1956, *AA: PA* Vol. 904, Ophüls to *AA*, 5 June 1956, *AA: PA* Vol. 909, Brentano to Erhard, June 1956 (undated), *AA: PA* Vol. 909. See also Ophüls to Brentano, 12 June 1955, *AA: PA* Vol. 909, Etzel to Brentano, 7 June 1956, *AA: PA* Vol. 909, and Erhard to Brentano, 16 June 1956, *AA: PA* Vol. 909. The Chancellor finally settled the question in favour of the *AA*: see Hallstein's comments at an interministerial meeting, 25 June 1956, B136/1312 (*BuKa*).

83 See Hallstein to Brentano and Adenauer, 29 May 1956, *AA: PA* Vol. 905.

84 For the proposals, see report of *BMWi* working party, 12 June 1956, and the *AA*'s assessment, 20 June 1956. See also interministerial meeting, 22 June 1956 (all *AA: PA* Vol. 909).

85 Confidential *AA* report (unsigned), 13 July 1956, *AA: PA* Vol. 927.

86 Confidential *AA* report (unsigned), 13 July 1956. For a later statement to this effect, see van Scherpenberg's report on the meeting of the Franco-German Economic Council, 11 January 1957 (both *AA: PA* Vol. 927).

87 Press service of the Federal Government to all ministries, undated, reporting on the Common Market debate in the French National Assembly in which this view featured strongly, B146/1845 (*BMWZ*). See also account of the French Assembly debate on EDC, 17 October 1952, in Fursdon, *European Defence Community*, pp. 200–3.

88 Protocol of a meeting between State Secretaries of Foreign Ministries of the Six, Carstens, 20 July 1956. See also Dept 4 report, 15 August 1956 (both *AA: PA* Vol. 927). For further such indications, see French Assembly debate in early July as described by Camps, *Britain and the European Community*, pp. 67–8.

89 Hartlieb's memorandum, 25 July 1956. See also Hallstein's comments at the meeting of State Secretaries of Foreign Ministries of the Six, 20 July 1956, both *AA: PA* Vol. 927.

90 See, for example, Dept 4 report, 15 August 1956, *AA: PA* Vol. 927, Ophüls reporting that Spaak shared this impression after a visit to London, 7 September 1956, *AA: PA* Vol. 926, and report from German embassy, London, 30 October 1956, *AA: PA* Vol. 925.

91 This argument was used later by Hallstein at a meeting with Erhard and the Economic Ministers of the *Länder*, 30 November 1956, *AA: PA* Vol. 914.

92 See Hartlieb's report on the first meeting of the Common Market committee, 5 July 1956, *AA: PA* Vol. 911.

93 See comments made by Günther Harkort (Head of *AA* Sub-Department 40 'General Trade Policy') and by Müller-Armack at interministerial meeting, 30 June 1956, B136/1312 (*BuKa*).

94 For the reservations of Dept 4, see Harkort, 2 October 1956, *AA: PA*

Vol. 913. For those of Dept 2, see Hartlieb, 16 August 1956, and Brentano to the foreign policy committee of the *Bundestag*, Hartlieb's draft, 14 July 1956 (both *AA: PA* Vol. 911).
95 Adenauer's comment at Cabinet meeting, 20 July 1956, B136/1313 (*BuKa*).
96 Brief (*Sprechzettel*) for the Chancellor, September 1956 (undated), *AA: PA* Vol. 912.
97 For the opposition voiced by the *BMWi* and the *BMA*, see interministerial debates of 25 July 1956 and 27 July 1956, in the first of which Erhard described the French demands as 'a step towards disintegration' (both *AA: PA* Vol. 911). See also Storch to Brentano and Adenauer, 27 September 1956, *AA: PA* Vol. 912. Finally, see 'theses' on the Spaak report and French demands, drafted by Rolf Gocht (Head of *BMWi* Sub-Department 1A1, 'General Questions of Economic Policy'), 13 August 1956, as well as Cabinet memorandum by Erhard, 2 October 1956 (both B102/12616 [*BMWi*]).
98 See Müller-Armack at interministerial debate, 1 September 1956, *AA: PA* Vol. 911.
99 See *BMWi* Cabinet memorandum, 2 October 1956, *AA: PA* Vol. 913, and B102/12616 (*BMWi*). See Hartlieb's comments on the Cabinet memorandum, 4 October 1956, *AA: PA* Vol. 913. See also his comments on the working party report, 6 September 1956, *AA: PA* Vol. 911, and 11 July 1956, *AA: PA* Vol. 912.
100 See Erhard to Adenauer, 25 September 1956, and Storch to Adenauer, 27 September 1956 (both *AA:MB* Vol. 48).
101 Adenauer to Brentano, passing on the two letters, 28 September 1956, *AA:MB* Vol. 48.
102 A translation of Macmillan's Washington statement was later printed in *Bulletin*, Vol. 188. Quote taken from Erhard to Brentano (copy to Adenauer), 4 October 1956, *AA:MB* Vol. 48. There was also a renewed conflict over competences, this time with regard to the OEEC working party No. 17. Erhard objected to the *AA*'s choice of van Scherpenberg as a representative, arguing that this was a purely economic scheme. In the end, the *BMWi* and the *AA* settled for joint representation: see *BMWi*'s official complaint, 29 August 1956, Brentano to Blücher, 30 August 1956, and reports on the working party meetings, 19 October 1956, 7 November 1956, 15 November 1956 (all *AA: PA* Vol. 927). Further to Erhard's attempts to wreck the Common Market, see Loth, *Der Weg nach Europa*, pp. 124–5.
103 See Etzel to Adenauer, 4 October 1956, *AA:BStS* Vol. 350. The *BMWZ* apparently supported this interpretation of British motives: see minute on *AA* and *BMWi* Cabinet memoranda, 4 October 1956, B146/1845 (*BMWZ*).
104 Cabinet, 5 October 1956, as reported by Carstens at an interministerial meeting, 6 October 1956, *AA: PA* Vol. 913.
105 See German embassy, Luxembourg, to *AA*, 9 October 1956, Carstens's memo, 11 October 1956, and Hartlieb to Wilhelm Grewe (Head of Political Department, *AA*), 18 October 1956 (all *AA: PA* Vol. 907).
106 See Carstens to Hallstein, 22 October 1956, *AA: PA* Vol. 907.

107 See Brentano to Adenauer, 31 October 1956, sending Lefèvre's letter, *AA:MB* Vol. 48. The US State Department also blamed the Germans for the failure in Paris: see report of German embassy, Washington, 30 October 1956, *AA: PA* Vol. 907.
108 See Carstens's minute of 29 October 1956, *AA: PA* Vol. 913.
109 Reference to Macmillan's public comments and Adenauer's interpretation thereof was made in an internal, unsigned *BMWZ* minute on the Cabinet memoranda of the *AA* and the *BMWi*, 4 October 1956, B146/1845 (*BMWZ*).
110 Carstens's report to an interministerial meeting, 13 November 1956. Further to the Hungarian and Suez Crises and the resulting willingness to compromise in Paris, see Adenauer reporting to the German Federal President, Theodor Heuss, 12 November 1956, in: K. Adenauer and Th. Heuss, *Unter vier Augen: Gespräche aus den Gründerjahren 1949–1959* (Siedler: München, 1997), pp. 214–15. The German embassy, Washington, reported the US administration's prompt congratulations for the compromise reached, 15 November 1956 (both *AA: PA* Vol. 914).
111 See, for example, meeting between Erhard and the Economic Ministers of the *Länder*, 30 November 1956, *AA: PA* Vol. 914.
112 Etzel to Erhard (copies to Adenauer and Brentano), 17 November 1956, *AA:MB* Vol. 48; confirmed by German embassy, London, 26 October 1956 and 30 October 1956 (both *AA: PA* Vol. 925).
113 Reference to this meeting is found only in Erhard to Etzel, 16 November 1956, and Etzel's reply, 17 November 1956 (both *AA:MB* Vol. 48). Erhard claimed to have bowed to this political pressure, while Etzel accuses him of continuing sabotage attempts regarding the Common Market.
114 See record of ministerial meeting, 31 May 1956, FO371/122028. See also Clarke's opening paper to the Sub-Committee, 2 June 1956, T234/102.
115 See, for example, Ellis-Rees to Wright, 11 August 1956, T234/196.
116 See, for example, Hoyer-Millar to FO, 23 October 1956, and HM embassy, Paris, to FO 24 October 1956 (both FO371/122036). See also HM embassy, The Hague, to FO, 25 October 1956, and Hoyer-Millar to FO, 27 October 1956 (both FO371/122037). The Foreign Office, however, did not share their gloomy outlook on the chances of the Common Market: see FO to HM representatives abroad, 30 October 1956, T234/199.
117 See HM embassy, Paris, to FO, 24 October 1956, and comments by Rodgers and Edden, FO371/122036. Enthusiasm for the Free Trade Area without a customs union was also found among German industrialists: see Martin Liebes (*Industriekreis für Auslandsbeziehungen*) to FO, 23 October 1956, FO371/122038.
118 See HM embassy, The Hague, to FO, 25 October 1956, FO371/122037.
119 Edden at ES (EI) (56) 16th meeting, 8 November 1956, CAB134/1238.
120 This argument was based on the assumption that the customs union would discriminate against Commonwealth exports, whereas the Free Trade Area would allow countries of the Six to determine their individual

Notes 191

tariff policy, which was expected to be on balance more favourable to Commonwealth products. It derived additional strength from the plan of the Six to include overseas territories: see ES (EI) (56), 17th meeting, 15 November 1956, CAB134/1238.
121 See first version of the Sub-Committee's memorandum ES (EI) (56) 79, 9 November 1956, T234/200.
122 Clarke's memorandum to Roger Makins (now Joint Permanent Secretary, Treasury), 7 November 1956, T234/104. See also ES (EI) (56) 17th meeting, 15 November 1956, CAB134/1240.
123 See FO to HM representatives abroad, 23 October 1956, T234/199.
124 See first version of the Sub-Committee's memorandum ES (EI) (56) 79, 9 November 1956, T234/200.
125 See ES (EI) (56) 79 (final), discussed in the Sub-Committee's 17th meeting, 15 November 1956, CAB134/1240.
126 See Hoyer-Millar to FO, 8 November 1956, FO371/122038.
127 See ES (EI) (56) 79 (final), discussed in the Sub-Committee's 17th meeting, 15 November 1956, CAB134/1240. See also Macmillan's speech on BBC European Services, 30 November 1956, FO371/122040.
128 See Cabinet meeting, 13 November 1956, CAB128/30. For a general account of the crisis, see D. Carlton, *Britain and the Suez Crisis* (Oxford: Basil Blackwell, 1988).
129 Among those regarding the FTA plan as 'sabotage', see, in particular, Greenwood, *Britain and European Cooperation*, chapter 6, in which he argues that 'behind the trappings of a modest conversion to "Europeanism" lay nothing much more than a common British reflex urge to wreck the Spaak proposals' (p. 78). See also Lamb, *Failure of the Eden Government*, pp. 87–99, and *The Macmillan Years, 1957–1963: the Emerging Truth* (London: John Murray, 1995), chapter 7. Finally, see Griffiths, 'A Slow One Hundred and Eighty Degree Turn'.
130 For the *BMF*'s opposition, see interministerial meeting, 24 November 1956, *AA*: *PA* Vol. 914, and also Schäffer's comments, 2 February 1957, *AA*: *PA* Vol. 929.
131 See 'position paper' after the Venice conference, 23 June 1956, *AA*: *PA* Vol. 910.
132 See debate between ministers, 2 February 1957, *AA*: *PA* Vol. 929, and meeting between Erhard/Müller-Armack and the Economic Ministers of the *Länder*, 30 November 1956, *AA*: *PA* Vol. 914. See also interministerial debate, 24 November 1956, *AA*: *PA* Vol. 914, and the debate within the German delegation, 20 November 1956, *AA*: *PA* Vol. 929.
133 See, for example, Thorneycroft's comments to Spaak, 21 October 1956, FO371/122037. The demand for the inclusion of overseas territories were first made at the Venice conference: see Boothby to FO, 20 September 1956, FO371/122033. News of detailed Franco-Belgian proposals reached the Foreign Office in November: see George Labouchère (HM Ambassador to Brussels) to FO, 19 November 1956, FO371/122039.
134 See Macmillan to Spaak, 16 October 1956, T172/2127. His fears were shared by all government departments: see record of a meeting in the Treasury, 17 October 1956, FO371/122038, and ES (EI) (56) 79, discussed in its 17th meeting, 15 November 1956, CAB134/1240.

192 Notes

135 See Ellis-Rees to FO, 18 February 1957, FO371/128337. Hong Kong was the only colony in favour of joining.
136 See Hoyer-Millar to Erhard, passing on a letter from Macmillan, 30 November 1956, *AA: PA* Vol. 929 and B102/11155 (*BMWi*).
137 See, for example, Hoyer-Millar to FO, 18 December 1956, FO371/122042. See also ES (EI) (56) 22nd meeting, 20 December 1956, CAB134/1238.
138 See *BMWi* Cabinet memorandum, 7 January 1956, B146/1845 (*BMWZ*). See Müller-Armack at interministerial debate, 8 December 1956, *AA: PA* Vol. 915.
139 See Hartlieb's minute for Hallstein, 7 December 1956, *AA: PA* Vol. 915, as well as Freiherr Wolfgang von Welck (Head of *AA* Department 3 'Foreign Relations by Country') to Erhard, 10 December 1956, *AA: PA* Vol. 927.
140 Compare *BMI* Cabinet memorandum, 10 January 1957, B146/1845 (*BMWZ*) with debate of ministers, 2 February 1957, *AA: PA* Vol. 929.
141 See, for example, minute by Hartlieb, 17 December 1956, *AA: PA* Vol. 928
142 Hartlieb not only refused a meeting suggested by the *BDI* but also argued against negotiation documents to be passed on to the organization, 17 December 1956, *AA: PA* Vol. 915.
143 Brentano to Adenauer, 8 December 1956, *AA: PA* Vol. 915, and B136/1313 (*BuKa*). This argument was also used by State Secretary Hallstein: see meeting with Economic Ministers of the *Länder*, 30 November 1956, *AA: PA* Vol. 914, and by Carstens: see interministerial meeting 24 November 1956, *AA: PA* Vol. 914.
144 See Hoyer-Millar to FO, 11 December 1956, FO371/122041. After several had been planned and postponed, a meeting finally took place on 15 February 1956, at which the Six showed little response to British concerns: see FO371/128337.
145 Statement of Erhard read out at lunch with Thorneycroft, Paris, 14 February 1957, FO371/128336.
146 See Jebb to FO, 20 February 1957, FO371/128336.
147 For Dutch reservation, see Foreign Minister Joseph Luns to Brentano, 11 February 1957, *AA:MB* Vol. 48. See also record of the meetings of Foreign Ministers and Heads of Governments, 20 February 1957, *AA:MB* Vol. 48.
148 See FO to Ellis-Rees, advising that 'any charge of British objection should be denied', 23 February 1957, FO371/128338.
149 Support for the scheme was especially marked in the *Economist* (see 8 September 1956 and 22 September 1956), but also found in *The Times*, 18 July 1956 and 21 September 1956. For a positive reaction of the FBI, see CP (56) 256, 6 November 1956, CAB129/84. Representatives of both FBI and the Trade Union Congress (TUC) indicated their support at a meeting of the Economic Planning Board, see ES (EI) (56) 69, 30 October 1956, CAB134/1240.
150 For the debate and Macmillan's argument, see *Hansard House of Commons*, 26 November 1956, 5th series, Vol. 561. Both kinds of scepticism persisted even after the debate. For examples of such lobbying, see *Hansard House of Commons*, 21 February 1957 and 26 February 1957, 5th series, Vol. 565, col. 91 and cols 1014–15 respectively.

151 See, for example, Ellis-Rees to FO, 31 October 1956, FO371/122054, and Bretherton's memorandum, 23 July 1956, FO371/122051.
152 Extracts of the Eisenhower speech sent by Douglas McKean (Assistant Secretary, Treasury) to Edden, 12 November 1956. See also Caccia (now HM Ambassador to Washington), 10 November 1956 (both FO371/122039). For Canadian reaction, see note by Chancellor to Cabinet, CP (56) 261, 12 November 1956, CAB129/84.
153 For a summary of European reactions, see CP (56) 256, 6 November 1956, CAB129/84.
154 See meeting between Bretherton and Majorlin, 18 October 1956, FO371/122037, HM embassy, Brussels, to FO, 12 October 1956, and Ellis-Rees to Bretherton, 23 October 1956 (both FO371/122046).
155. This was transmitted to OEEC capitals: see Figgures's draft message, 30 November 1956, FO371/122040. Criticism, however, persisted: see Sir Roderick Barclay (HM Ambassador to Copenhagen) to FO, 3 December 1956, and Sir Robin Hankey (HM Ambassador to Stockholm) to FO, 1 December 1956 (both FO371/122040). For French and Italian objections, see respective HM embassies to FO, both dated 12 December 1956, FO371/122042.
156. See, for example, Carstens's at an interministerial meeting, 8 December 1956, *AA*: *PA* Vol. 915.
157. Erhard to OEEC, 14 February 1957, official English translation, B102/11154 (*BMWi*).
158. Report on the meeting of the Ministerial Council of the OEEC, 18 February 1957, *AA*: *PA* Vol. 926.
159. See OEEC's information division on a press conference with Thorneycroft, 15 February 1957, and report of the *DPA* (German Press Agency), 20 February 1957 (both B102/11154 [*BMWi*]); see also internal *BMWi* report, 22 February 1957, B102/11155 (*BMWi*). For Erhard's attempt to capitalize on Thorneycroft's statement, see *Manchester Guardian*, 13 February 1957.
160. See OEEC information division, 15 February 1957, B102/1154 (*BMWi*). For substantiation of this view, see Figgures to Clarke, 7 February 1956, T234/200.
161. See ES (EI) (56) 2nd and 3rd meeting, 8 January 1957 and 24 January 1957, CAB134/1855, discussing the publication of the White Paper. The draft paper is dated 21 January 1957, FO371/128375.
162. See White Paper entitled, *A European Free Trade Area: United Kingdom Memorandum to the Organisation for European Economic Co-operation*, Cmnd. 72 (HMSO: London, 1957). The Danish government, for example, approached the *AA* in an effort to persuade the latter to oppose the opening of OEEC negotiations: see Danish embassy to *AA*, 31 January 1957, *AA*: *PA* Vol. 927.
163. The Ministry of Agriculture's changes to the British memo, 18 January 1957, T172/2136.
164. As anticipated in the final brief for the OEEC meeting, ES (EI) (57) 26, 6 February 1957, T234/200.
165. See minute by Hans Globke (State Secretary, Chancellory), 16 March 1957, B136/1313 (*BuKa*).

194 *Notes*

166. See 'post-mortem' reports by Müller-Armack (28 February 1957) and Gocht (12 March 1957 and 20 March 1957) (all three B102/12617 [*BMWi*]).
167. For the re-emergence of the conflict over competences, see meeting between Erhard, Blücher and Heinrich Lübke (Minister for Agriculture), 8 March 1957, B102/11155 (*BMWi*).
168. See, for example, Sir Christopher Steel (new HM Ambassador to Bonn) to FO, reporting on a meeting with Erhard, in which the latter suggested a meeting between Thorneycroft and Adenauer, 27 February 1957. The Foreign Office apparently pressed for such a meeting but the Treasury declined due to scheduling difficulties: see Wright to Paul Gore-Booth (Deputy Under-Secretary, FO) 22 March 1957 (both FO371/128337). See also Edden to Jackling, 22 March 1957, FO371/128337, Steel to Gore Booth, 11 March 1957, and various minutes thereon, FO371/128338.
169. While there was some fear of waning support at home, see Thorneycroft to Butler (now Home Secretary), trying to postpone House of Commons debate, 20 March 1957, T172/2136. The main obstacle to the FTA was seen in France: see record of a meeting between Macmillan and Faure, 9 March 1957, FO371/128338. See also Gladwyn Jebb to FO, 14 March 1957, FO371/128339.

3 Mistaken, Misled or Misguided? British Hopes for German Mediation during the FTA Negotiations

1. For the English translation of Erhard's speech, see 14 February 1957, B102/11154 (*BMWi*).
2. See, for example, Steel to Paul Gore-Booth about conversation with Erhard, 27 February 1957, FO371/128337.
3. For the following arguments, see meeting between Erhard, Blücher and Lübke, 8 March 1957, B102/11155 (*BMWi*), and memoranda by van Scherpenberg, 3 May 1957, 14 May 1957, and Carstens, 20 May 1957 (all *AA: PA* 200/456) (the reorganization of *AA* departments in 1958 meant that files dated 1957 and thereafter were given a prefix denoting the respective department or sub-department, in this case the Political Department 200. For the reorganization itself, see footnote 132 in this chapter).
4. See Adenauer's guideline, 16 March 1957, *StBKAH* III 23 and *AA: PA* 200/456. See also Erhard to Adenauer 17 March 1957, and Adenauer to Erhard, 17 March 1957 (both *StBKAH* III 23).
5. See memorandum by Sub-Department B 6 (responsible for relations to the *BMWi* and the *BMA*), 3 August 1957, B136/2596 (*BuKa*).
6. Reports of working parties no. 21 (29 July 1957) and no. 22 (31 July 1957), B 102/11156 (*BMWi*), and FO371/128389.
7. See, for example, Hartlieb to Carstens, 17 May 1957, *AA: PA* 200/456.
8. For the former, see memorandum by *AA* Sub-Department 215 'ECSC', 3 May 1957, *AA: PA* 200/348. For the grand design argument, see memorandum by Carstens, 30 March 1957, *AA: PA* 200/89a.

9 See Hartlieb to Carstens, 17 May 1957, *AA: PA* 200/456. See also Erhard's submission to Cabinet, 2 July 1957, and Hartlieb memorandum of 6 July 1957, both AA: *PA* 200/244.
10 See Bretherton to Figgures, 29 March 1957, FO371/128380, and Figgures to Wright, 28 February 1957, FO371/128378.
11 Treasury brief for Chancellor's meeting with Erhard, 25 March 1957, FO371/128340.
12 See record of discussions in memorandum of Sub-Committee on Closer Association with Europe, ES (EI) (57) 91, 1 April 1957, CAB134/1858. For the charge of 'ignorance', see minutes of 16th meeting of the Sub-Committee, 2 April 1957, CAB134/1855.
13 Treasury brief for Chancellor's meeting with Erhard, 25 March 1957, FO371/128340.
14 Figgures to Bretherton, 23 April 1957, FO371/128343.
15 See memorandum ES (EI) (57) 83, 27 March 1957, CAB134/1858. For Brentano's opposition, see FO to HM embassy, Bonn, 17 April 1957, PREM11/1841.
16 Peter Tennant's (Overseas Director, Federation of British Industry) report on Königswinter conference, 14 April 1957, FO371/128341.
17 Peter Tennant's report, 14 April 1957, FO371/128341.
18 Steel to FO, 6 May 1957, PREM11/1829A. See also Philip de Zulueta (Private Secretary to Prime Minister) to Macmillan, 28 April 1957, PREM11/1841.
19 McKean to Edden, 2 May 1957, FO371/128342.
20 McKean to Edden, 2 May 1957, FO371/128342. See also Cabinet's 37th meeting, 2 May 1957, CAB128/31.
21 See, for example, minute by Lord Hood, 18 June 1957, FO371/128351, or Gore-Booth's note, recording Macmillan's argument that the FTA should go ahead even if there was no customs union, FO371/128350.
22 See record of *ad hoc* meeting between Macmillan, Thorneycroft, Eccles and others, 18 April 1957, PREM11/2133. See also Figgures's draft paper, 3 April 1957, FO371/128341, and Cabinet paper by Chancellor, C (57) 106, 30 April 1957, CAB129/87.
23 See record of the meeting, ES (EI) (57) 142, 15 May 1957, CAB134/1860 and Cabinet's 37th meeting, 2 May 1957, CAB128/31.
24 Figgures's account of the meeting, 9 May 1957, FO371/128344 and T234/706.
25 Minute by Clarke, 20 May 1957, T234/201. For French assurances, see Foreign Secretary to HM embassy, Brussels, 6 May 1957, FO371/128343. See also Chancellor's report on meeting Maurice Faure, Economic Policy Committee, 10th meeting, 8 May 1957, CAB134/1674.
26 Protocol of interministerial meeting, 29 June 1957, B102/11156 (*BMWi*).
27 See protocol of interministerial meeting, 29 June 1957, B102/11156 (*BMWi*).
28 See Freiherr von Mahs (Chairman of the working group and Head of the *BMWi* Sub-Department 'Economic relations to EPU countries') to Chancellory, 5 September 1957, enclosing his report, B136/2596 (*BuKa*).
29 Freiherr von Mahs to Chancellory, 5 September 1957, B136/2596 (*BuKa*). See also van Scherpenberg to Adenauer, 8 February 1957, B136/2596 (*BuKa*).

196 *Notes*

30 Memorandum by Graf von Hardenberg (Head of the *AA*'s Trade Policy Sub-Department 401 'Intergovernmental and Supranational Organizations'), 13 August 1957, *AA: PA* 200/351.
31 Brief for Brentano's meeting with Maudling, 1 October 1957, *AA: PA* 200/351.
32 For the French ratification debate, see report by HM embassy, Paris, sent to FO, 11 July 1957. For the *Bundestag*'s unanimous vote in favour, see reports by HM embassy, Bonn, 9 July 1957 and 23 July 1957. For the German election and the FTA, see also HM embassy, Bonn, to FO, 13 July 1957 and 16 July 1957, and Edden's minute of 17 July 1957 (all FO371/128351). For postponement, see Makins to Clarke, 11 July 1957, T234/202.
33 Minute by the Head of the FO's Western Department, Patrick Hancock, 30 July 1957, FO371/128388.
34 Chancellor's comment in the Cabinet Committee (Ministerial) 'The Free Trade Area' (established March 1957), 3rd meeting, 29 July 1957, CAB130/123.
35 Makins to Clarke, 11 July 1957, T234/202.
36 See Macmillan to Thorneycroft, 15 July 1957, PREM11/2133, and Thorneycroft's reply, 22 July 1957, PREM11/2132. The final decision was taken by the Cabinet: see 61st meeting, 2 August 1957, CAB128/31.
37 See records of meetings, 22 August 1957, FO371/128356, and 28 August 1957, ES (EI) 224, CAB134/1861. See also HM embassy, Paris, to FO, 26 September 1957, FO371/128361.
38 Bretherton to Figures, 2 October 1957, T234/373.
39 See, for example, Steel to FO, 26 July 1957, FO371/128353, and 6 September 1957 and 12 September 1957, FO371/128358. For the hope being shared by other departments, see Figures to Clarke, 18 September 1957, FO371/128360.
40 Macmillan's minute on Adenauer's reply to his congratulations to re-election. Therein Adenauer had referred to 'our joint policy for the consolidation of Europe', FO371/130732.
41 Ellis-Rees to Gore-Booth, 30 September 1957 and 2 October 1957, FO371/128361 and FO371/128392 respectively.
42 See minute by Coulson (Assistant Under-Secretary, FO, now seconded to Paymaster-General's Office) that Maudling had seen the letter, on Ellis-Rees to Gore-Booth, 30 September 1957, FO371/128361.
43 Minute by J. M. Heath (Mutual Aid Department, FO) on Ellis-Rees to Gore-Booth, 30 September 1957, FO371/128392.
44 For the following argument see ES (EI) (57) 236, FO paper on possible inducements, 16 September 1957, CAB134/1826.
45 For the following argument, see brief for Maudling visit, prepared for Erhard by his ministry's Foreign Trade Department, 1 October 1957, B102/11156 (*BMWi*). Anglo-German identity of interest was also diagnosed by the *Financial Times* on 7 August 1957.
46 See letter by *Bauernyerband* to Adenauer, 9 September 1957, B136/2596 (*BuKa*).
47 Protocol of Maudling's visit, 4 October 1957, B102/11156 (*BMWi*) and *AA:MB* 156.

48 Protocol of Maudling's visit, 4 October 1957, B102/11156 (*BMWi*) and *AA:MB* 156.
49 See record of the meeting sent by James Majoribanks (now Economic Minister at HM embassy, Bonn) to Edden, 5 October 1957, FO371/128362, later circulated as ES (EI) (57) 275, 9 October 1957, CAB134/1863, respectively.
50 Protocol of Maudling's visit, 4 October 1957, B102/11156 (*BMWi*) and *AA:MB* 156.
51 Compare Ellis-Rees to FO, 28 October 1957 and 30 October 1957, FO371/128394 and FO371/128392, with Steel to FO, 4 October 1957, FO371/128362, and Majoribanks to Gore-Booth, 4 November 1957, FO371/128366, respectively.
52 See Carstens to Hallstein, 13 September 1957, *AA: PA* 200/244.
53 See Adenauer to Erhard, 27 October 1957, and Adenauer's address to the new *Bundestag* (*Regierungserklärung*) of 29 October 1957, both quoted in a summary of the struggle over competences, 28 January 1958, B102/11032 (*BMWi*). See also Adenauer to Brentano, 27 October 1957, *AA:MB* 49, and his dismissal of the idea of a European ministry, in Adenauer and Heuss, *Unter vier Augen*, pp. 227–8.
54 See Brentano to Adenauer and Brentano to Erhard, both dated 25 October 1957, *AA: PA* 200/244.
55 See Brentano to Erhard, 12 November 1957, *AA:MB* 49.
56 See Hartlieb (in Paris) to *AA*, 30 November 1957, *AA: PA* 200/244.
57 See, for example, Brentano to Adenauer, 10 January 1958 and 29 January 1958, position paper on competencies by the *BMWi*, 22 January 1958, Erhard to Adenauer, 6 February 1958, and Brentano to Adenauer, 7 February 1958 (all *AA:MB* 49). See also Erhard to Adenauer, 7 November 1957, B136/2596 (*BuKa*). Adenauer was clearly annoyed with both ministries, see Adenauer and Heuss, *Unter vier Augen*, p. 263.
58 See Majoribanks to Müller-Armack, 17 October 1957, B102/11156 (*BMWi*).
59 These vague promises of agricultural concessions had been agreed well before the Bonn visit: see Cabinet's 62nd meeting, 27 August 1957, CAB128/31, discussing C (57) 188, 24 August 1957, CAB129/88.
60 See report of the interim committee, 10 October 1957, B136/2596 (*BuKa*).
61 Erhard's speech to OEEC, 16 October 1957, B102/11156 (*BMWi*).
62 See Maudling's memoranda C (57) 219 and C (57) 221, both 4 October 1957, CAB129/89. Approved by Cabinet, 72nd meeting, 8 October 1957, CAB128/31.
63 See reports by Ellis-Rees to FO, 17 October 1957 and 19 October 1957, both FO371/128394.
64 See Maudling to Erhard, 30 October 1957, B102/11156 (*BMWi*) and B136/2596 (*BuKa*).
65 See report by Gocht, 8 November 1957, B102/11156 (*BMWi*).
66 See protocol of interministerial meeting on 9 November 1957, B 136/2596 (*BuKa*).
67 On the pivotal role of Faure in the EEC and FTA negotiations, see B. Riondel, 'Itinéraire d'un fédéraliste: Maurice Faure', in: *Journal of European Integration History* (1997/2), pp. 69–82.
68 Handwritten comment by the Deputy Head of Chancellery

198 Notes

   Sub-Department B 6 on *BMWi* invitation for interministerial meeting, 7 January 1958, B136/2597 (*BuKa*).
69 Chancellory report on interministerial meeting of 9 November 1957, B136/2597 (*BuKa*).
70 See Chancellory memorandum quoting Erhard, 7 January 1958, B 136/2597 (*BuKa*). See also Hartlieb about OEEC Ministerial Council meeting 15–16 January 1958, *AA*: *PA* 200/149.
71 For the new arrangement of competencies, see memorandum by Gocht, 2 December 1957, B102/11156 (*BMWi*).
72 See Majoribanks to Gore-Booth, 4 November 1957, FO371/128366, Steel to FO, 15 November 1957, FO371/130732, Wright to Hancock, 19 November 1957 FO371/130733, and HM embassy, The Hague, to Edden, 6 December 1957, FO371/128371.
73 FO brief for Brentano's visit to London, undated, PREM11/1839, also noting Brentano's and Hallstein's political preference for the Common Market. The brief was based on a report by HM embassy, Bonn, 2 December 1957, FO37 1/130734. In the event, the focus of the meeting was on NATO matters and not on the FTA, though Macmillan again employed vague threats of political division on Europe: see record of meeting, 4 December 1957, PREM11/1839.
74 Draft FO brief for PM, undated (late November 1957), FO371/128369.
75 See Steel to FO, 30 November 1957, FO371/130734.
76 Undated minute by Prime Minister (November 1957), FO371/128369.
77 See protocol of the first meeting of the EEC Council of Ministers, 25 January 1958, B136/1296 (*BuKa*). Apparently, Hallstein had been nominated by the French: see Adenauer and Heuss, *Unter vier Augen*, p. 258. See also Brentano to Hans Furler (President of the Common Assembly of the ECSC), 8 January 1958, *AA:MB* 49. The other Commissioner playing an important part in the remainder of the FTA negotiations was Jean Rey, who was responsible for the Community's external relations.
78 Although the Treaty of Rome stipulated that the Commission was to take part in the formulation of Community policy towards third countries, it was not clear whether this applied to the FTA negotiations, which had started well before the establishrnent of the Community itself: see protocol of the first meeting of the EEC Council of Ministers, 25 January 1958, B136/1296 (*BuKa*).
79 Van Scherpenberg to Brentano, 22 January 1958, *AA*: *PA* 200/149. See also – disagreeing – Hartlieb to Carstens, 9 January 1958, *AA*: *PA* 200/149. Van Scherpenberg's appointment strengthened Erhard's hand, a fact which he was only too happy to communicate to the British: see note for the record by H. S. Lee (Private Secretary to Paymaster-General), 12 March 1958, FO371/134494.
80 See, for example, Hartlieb to *BMWi* and *BuKa*, 7 February 1958, B136/1296 (*BuKa*).
81 *Handelsblatt*, 14 February 1958. See also Chancellory memorandum, 11 February 1958, B 136/1296 (*BuKa*).
82 See report by Kiesswetter (*BMWi* permanent representative at the FTA negotiations in Paris), 14 January 1958, B102/11157 (*BMWi*).

83 See record of conversation between Foreign Secretary Selwyn Lloyd and van Scherpenberg, 21 February 1958, FO371/134491.
84 See Ophüls (now permanent representative to EEC) to *AA*, reporting on consultations among the Six, 18 January 1958, B 136/1296 (*BuKa*), and report on the meeting between Maudling and representatives of Denmark and the Six, 30 January 1958, B136/2597 (*BuKa*), protocol in B102/11157 (*BMWi*).
85 See record of meeting between representatives of the Six, UK and Denmark, 30 January 1958, T234/202.
86 See German translation of French memorandum, 3 March 1958, B136/2597 (*BuKa*).
87 See Economic Steering Committee, 5th meeting, 4 March 1958, CAB134/1863.
88 Economic Steering Committee, 5th meeting, 4 March 1958, CAB134/1863. See also Coulson reporting on a conversation with Hallstein, 5 March 1958, FO371/134493, and Maudling's meeting with French representatives, 12 March 1958, FO371/134497.
89 For the summary passed to the British, see Ellis-Rees to FO, 6 March 1958, FO371/134492. For Maudling's meeting with Erhard, see H. S. Lee, 12 March 1958, FO371/134494.
90 Quoted in Ellis-Rees to FO, 11 March 1958, FO371/134493.
91 See memorandum of Economic Steering Sub-Committee on Closer Association with Europe, ES (EI) 53, 26 February 1958, CAB134/1866, discussed in 11th meeting, 4 March 1958, CAB134/1864.
92 For the *AA*'s view, see record of telephone call from Carstens to *BuKa*, 14 March 1958; for the position of the Chancellory, see Haenlein's memorandum of 6 March 1958, which in substance reiterated an undated memorandum by Kiesswetter (all B 136/2597 [*BuKa*]).
93 Hartlieb's memorandum, 23 January 1958, *AA*: PA 200/149.
94 Hartlieb to Carstens, 22 March 1958, *AA*: PA 200/149.
95 See protocol of Maudling Committee, 12 March 1958, and revised Carli plan (OEEC document No. CIG [58] 30), 19 March 1958, both B102/11161 (*BMWi*). See also F. Fauri. 'Italy and the Free Trade Area Negotiations', in: *Journal of European Inrtegration History* (1998/2), pp. 5–21.
96 See meeting of permanent delegates of the Six, protocol date 13 March 1958, B136/1297 (*BuKa*).
97 See memorandum of the Secretariat of the Council of Ministers, 15 March 1958, B102/10905 (*BMWi*); see also EEC General Secretariat to *AA*, 17 March 1958, B136/2597 (*BuKa*).
98 See Chancellory Sub-Department B 6 to Haenlein, 19 March 1958, B136/2597 (*BuKa*).
99 Ellis-Rees to FO, 18 March 1958, T234/375.
100 For the following argument, see memorandum by Sub-Department 'Coordination of Foreign Trade Problems Regarding the Private Sector', 22 March 1958, B102/11161 (*BMWi*).
101 On the meeting with French representatives, see Müller-Armack, 3 April 1958, B102/11161 (*BMWi*), and Gocht to Kiesswetter, 8 April 1958, B102/12121 (*BMWi*).

102 See Carstens's report on the Franco-German bilateral talks, 22 March 1958, *AA: PA* 200/149.
103 Gocht to Kiesswetter, 8 April 1958, B102/12121 (*BMWi*).
104 Secret note by Macmillan on his meeting with Maudling, 17 March 1958, PREM11/2531.
105 See Edden's minute on his discussion with Majoribanks, 28 March 1958, FO371/1334496.
106 Steel to Selwyn Lloyd, 21 March 1958, FO371/134501.
107 See brief for Adenauer visit ES (EI) (58) 72, 26 March 1958, CAB134/1866. See also Maudling's memorandum to Cabinet C (58) 64, 21 March 1958, CAB129/92, discussed in 27th meeting, 27 March 1958, CAB128/32.
108 See Steel to Selwyn Lloyd, 10 April 1958, PREM11/2341.
109 See Gore-Booth to Caccia, 10 April 1958. An official did indeed convey this to the Americans; see HM embassy, Washington, to FO, 17 April 1958, both FO371/134496. For earlier signs of increasing American support for the FTA scheme, see Caccia to FO, 21 March 1958, FO371/134495, and Ellis-Rees, 27 March 1958, FO371/134496.
110 For Erhard's intervention, see Haenlein to Adenauer, 10 April 1958, B136/2597 (*BuKa*).
111 See reports by German embassy, 20 March 1958, and Herwarth himself, 26 March 1958, both *AA: PA* 200/351. For the intervention of the British embassy, see note for the record by Harkort (who had replaced van Scherpenberg as Head of the *AA*'s Trade Policy Department), 3 March 1958, *AA: PA* 200/149.
112 See anonymous and undated paper entitled 'Informal U.S. Views on Free Trade Area', which diagnosed a 'key role of Germany in an effort to moderate French position', *AA: PA* 200/149.
113 See Hartlieb's memorandum, 28 March 1958, *AA: PA* 200/344, and report by the German embassy, Copenhagen, about threats made by Maudling on the occasion of his visit there, 16 April 1958, *AA: PA* 200/349.
114 See report on 9th Königswinter conference 28–30 March 1957, *AA: LA* 304/99. See also Albert Menne (*Farbwerke Hoechst* and Vice-Chairman of the *BDI*) to Brentano, 14 April 1958, *AA:MB* 49.
115 Hartlieb (undated, early April 1958), *AA: PA* 200/149.
116 See Carstens's report on the meetings, 18 April 1958, B102/11158 (*BMWi*), and also *AA: PA* 200/351. A great number of very optimistic British press reports followed the meetings: all *AA:LA* 304/86. For the meetings of officials, see ES (EI) (58) 81, 83 and 85, dated 18 April 1958, 21 April 1958 and 23 April 1958, respectively: all CAB134/1866.
117 Hartlieb's scribble on Carstens's report, 19 April 1958, *AA: PA* 200/351.
118 Werkmeister to Erhard, 7 May 1958 B102/11159 (*BMWi*).
119 See, for example, Steel to FO, 30 April 1958, FO371/134500, and Ellis-Rees to FO, 7 May 1958, FO371/134501.
120 For details of the solution to the support cost problem, see Cabinet's 34th meeting, 24 April 1958, CAB128/32. See also *The Times*, 13 March 1958.
121 See Haenlein to Adenauer, 24 April 1958, B136/2597 (*BuKa*).

122 Quoted in Haenlein to Adenauer, 24 April 1958, B136/2597 (*BuKa*).
123 See Werkmeister to *AA*, 23 May 1958, B102/11158 (*BMWi*) and *AA*: *PA* 200/149. See also Steel to FO, 23 May 1958, T234/367, and Coulson to FO, 23 May 1958, FO371/134501.
124 As reported by Sub-Department 'General Questions of Foreign Trade Policy' to Erhard, 10 May 1958, B102/11159 (*BMWi*).
125 Report on the meeting of 22 May 1958, B102/11159 (*BMWi*); see also report by Sub-Department 41 'Trade Policy Relations to Foreign Countries' to van Scherpenberg, 27 May 1958, *AA*: *PA* 200/149 and *AA:MB* 49. Compare British impressions in Coulson's report, 27 May 1958, FO371/134502.
126 Coulson to FO, 22 April 1958, FO371/134500.
127 See, for example, 26th meeting of the European Free Trade Area Steering Group (interdepartmental forum for officials, established October 1957, chaired by Clarke and concerned with technical details of the FTA), 18 April 1958, CAB130/132. See also Maudling to Erhard, 5 May 1958, T234/376.
128 Steel to Gore-Booth, 10 April 1958, FO371/134498. See also Maudling about his meeting with van Scherpenberg, 2 April 1958, FO371/134497, Ellis-Rees to Coulson, 14 April 1958, FO371/134498, Clarke to H. S. Lee, 16 April 1958, T234/375, and Maudling to Erhard, 5 May 1958, T234/376.
129 The Treasury obtained copies of the relevant sections of the Ockrent report (presumably from the Belgian delegation to OEEC), both dated 16 May 1958, T234/708 and T234/709.
130 See memorandum by Makins, 21 May 1958, T234/376.
131 Macmillan to Foreign Secretary, 24 June 1958, PREM11/2315.
132 See Müller-Roschach to Carstens, 26 April 1958, *AA*: *PA* 200/149. In a reorganization of the *Auswärtiges Amt*, the 'Political Department' 2 had been renamed Department 2 'West I', covering European integration and co-operation as well as relations to the countries of Western Europe. Department 3, formerly 'Foreign Relations by country' (*Länderabteilung*) became Department 3 'West II' covering international organizations such as the UN, as well as the Americas, Southern Africa and, significantly, Great Britain, Ireland, Australia and New Zealand. Following the appointment of Grewe as Ambassador to Washington, Carstens had been promoted to Head of Department 2, with Müller-Roschach as his Deputy.
133 See reports by German embassy, Paris, 23 May 1958 and 19 June 1958, both *AA:MB* 55.
134 Hartlieb memorandum, 4 July 1958, *AA*: West I, 200/1.
135 See report on the meeting between Müller-Armack and British representatives, 25 June 1958, B102/11159 (*BMWi*).
136 See report on the meeting between Erhard and Maudling, 25 June 1958, B102/11159 (*BMWi*). See also British record, 26 June 1958, T234/377.
137 See press conference given by Maudling and Erhard (protocol 26 June 1958), B102/11159 (*BMWi*). See also *Handelsblatt* 27 June 1958 and *Frankfurter Allgemeine Zeitung (FAZ)*, 27 June 1958.
138 This had been advocated by the Germans as early as April 1958, in

202 *Notes*

their confidential talks with French representatives: see footnotes 101 and 102 in this chapter.
139 This proposed interim agreement should not be confused with the 'interim arrangement' which was to be debated at the end of the year. While the latter was merely an offer by the Six to extend their tariff cuts, the interim agreement proposals of the summer of 1958 envisaged a multilateral agreement of tariffs. There were, in fact, two such proposals. Yet, that of the Commission had been rejected by the *BMWi* negotiators and had led to the formulation of an alternative German proposal, which, over and above tariff cuts, envisaged a contractual obligation to complete the FTA negotiations. Both were rejected by Britain and France. For the Commission proposal, see protocol of the Council of Ministers, 23 June 1958, B102/11162 (*BMWi*); for *BMWi* proposals, see memorandum by Meyer-Cording, 28 July 1958, B102/11159 (*BMWi*).
140 See memorandum by de Zulueta, 20 June 1958, PREM11/2531. On Maudling's tactics for Erhard's visit, see EA (58) 5th meeting, 23 June 1958, CAB130/123.
141 De Zulueta to Macmillan, 20 June 1958, PREM11/2531.
142 See meeting between Rey and Müller-Armack, 19 July 1958, B136/2597 (*BuKa*).
143 See Werkmeister's report on the meeting between Erhard and Couve de Murville, 23 June 1958, *AA*: West I 200/149.
144 See memorandum by Meyer-Cording, 18 July 1958, B102/11159 (*BMWi*).
145 See record of the meeting, 29 June 1958, PREM11/2326.
146 Macmillan's report to Cabinet, 1 July 1958, 51st meeting, CAB128/32.
147 See Macmillan to de Gaulle, 30 June 1958, and de Gaulle's reply, 5 July 1958, both PREM11/235 1. De Gaulle recalled Macmillan threatening a trade war, while he himself remained unimpressed. For the brief section on the FTA, de Gaulle employed 'combat vocabulary', depicting the British scheme as an 'offensive' against the Common Market: see C. de Gaulle, *Memoiren der Hoffnung: die Wiedergeburt 1958–1962* (Molden: Wien 1971), pp. 231–3.
148 See brief for Maudling Committee meeting. ES (EI) (58) 132, 22 July 1958, CAB134/1867.
149 See Macmillan to de Gaulle, 19 July 1958, PREM11/2351. See also Adenauer congratulating Macmillan, 4 August 1958, PREM11/2607.
150 The proposals of the Steering Board of Trade and those of Maudling were included in the *BMWi* brief for the Maudling Committee meeting on 25 July 1958, B102/11159 (*BMWi*).
151 *BMWi* brief for the Maudling Committee meeting, 18 July 1958, B 102/11159 (*BMWi*). See also *AA* memorandum, 17 July 1958, *AA*: West I 200/149. The report of the Steering Board of Trade, 10 July 1958, is contained in *AA*: West I 200/150.
152 See Harkort's report on the meeting, 25 July 1958, and *AA* memorandum, 28 July 1958, both *AA*: West I 200/149. See also advance meeting of the EEC's Council of Ministers, 23 July 1958, *AA*: West I 200/150.
153 Erhard's speech to the OEEC Council, 1 August 1958, B136/2597 (*BuKa*).
154 See report by German embassy, London, 7 August 1958, *AA*: West I

200/351. See also Maudling to Macmillan, about an earlier meeting with Erhard, 28 July 1958, PREM11/2351, and record of the meeting, 24 July 1958, T234/204.
155 Van Scherpenberg, 24 July 1958, AA:MB 157.
156 Minute by the new Head of the FO's Mutual Aid Department, Gilbert Holliday, 22 August 1958, FO371/134507.
157 See Steel to FO, 9 September 1958, FO371/134507.
158 See Adenauer, *Erinnerungen, 1955–1959*, pp. 424–36. See also de Gaulle, *Memoiren der Hoffnung*, pp. 217–23; Adenauer and Heuss, *Unter vier Augen*, p. 272 and pp. 276–9; M. Couve de Murville, *Außenpolitik 1958–69* (Weltforum: München, 1973), p. 30; and F. Seydoux, *Beiderseits des Rheins* (Societäts-Verlag: Frankfurt, 1975), p. 207.
159 See protocol of the Venice meeting, 18–20 September 1958, B102/10912 (*BMWi*).
160 See draft protocol of the Brussels meeting, 7–8 October 1958, B102/10912 (*BMWi*).
161 See report by German embassy, London, 2 October 1958, AA: West I 200/150.
162 See Ellis-Rees to FO, 26 September 1958, FO371/134509 and T234/710, and UK delegation to OEEC to FO, 7 October 1958, FO371/134509.
163 As reported by Steel to the Foreign Office, 27 October 1958, FO371/134511.
164 See protocol of meeting between Müller-Armack and Maudling, 3 October 1958, CAB130/134. See also report by German embassy, London, 2 October 1958, AA: West I 200/150.
165 Holliday's minute on a letter by Ellis-Rees, 29 September 1958, FO371/134510.
166 See brief for Macmillan's visit, 2 October 1958, FO371/134510.
167 See record of the meetings Adenauer/Macmillan, 8–9 October 1958 (Brentano and van Scherpenberg also present), PREM11/2328.
168 See Adenauer to de Gaulle, 10 October 1958, AA:MB 56 and StBKAH 10.36. See also Seydoux, *Beiderseits des Rheins*, pp. 215–16.
169 Record of the meetings Adenauer/Macmillan, 8–9 October 1958, PREM11/2328.
170 See record of the meetings Adenauer/Macmillan, 8–9 October 1958, PREM11/2328.
171 The following paragraph, including the quotations, is based on the record of conversation between van Scherpenberg and Seydoux, 21 October 1958, AA:MB 157.
172 See van Scherpenberg to Müller-Armack, 17 October 1958, AA: West I 200/150.
173 See Sub-Department E A 5 'Tariff questions' to Meyer-Cording, 17 October 1958, B102/11159 (*BMWi*).
174 See protocol of EEC Council of Ministers' meeting, 23 October 1958, B102/10912 (*BMWi*).
175 See ES (EI) (58) 95, 16 October 1958, FO371/134510.
176 See Steel about conversation between Majoribanks and Müller-Armack, 10 October 1958, T234/710, and note by David Ormsby-Gore (Minister of State, FO), 10 October 1958, FO371/134510.

204 Notes

177 Macmillan to Selwyn Lloyd, 15 October 1958, PREM11/2532.
178 For the evolution of Treasury opinion, see Clarke to Sir Leslie Rowan, 16 October 1958, and Rowan to Chancellor Derick Heathcoat Amory (Thorneycroft had resigned in January 1958 following disagreements about fiscal and monetary policy), 16 October 1958, both T234/378. On the suggestion of renouncing the WEU treaty, Macmillan to Selwyn Lloyd, 26 October 1958, PREM11/2532, and Rowan to Chancellor, 29 October 1958, FO371/134545.
179 Selwyn Lloyd to Macmillan, 31 October 1958, PREM11/2352. For the evolution of Foreign Office thinking, see note by Mutual Aid Department, 30 October 1958, FO371/134545. On WEU, see note by FO, 4 November 1958, CAB130/135.
180 For the former point, see Clarke, to Rowan, 16 October 1958, T234/378, and 54th meeting of Clarke's European Free Trade Area Steering Group, 3 November 1958, CAB130/132. For possible negative consequences on Anglo-American relations, see Rowan to Heathcoat Amory, 16 October 1958, and Chancellor's scribble: 'Yes, I agree' (both T234/378). See also minute by Holliday, 16 October 1958, FO371/134545.
181 See Holliday about meeting with US officials, 31 October 1958, FO371/134513, and Caccia to FO, 8 November 1958 and 13 November 1958, FO371/134512 and FO371/134513, respectively. For the suggestion of reducing tension, see 54th meeting of Clarke's Steering Group, 3 November 1958, CAB130/132, and Holliday to Gore-Booth, 8 November 1958, FO371/134545.
182 Gore-Booth's reply to Caccia's letter of 13 November 1958, dated 14 November 1958, FO371/134513.
183 Summary record of 8th session of Maudling Committee, 24 October 1958, B102/11160 (*BMWi*).
184 For the following, see protocol of meeting of EEC Council of Ministers prior to Maudling Committee meeting, 24 October 1958, B102/10912 (*BMWi*). See also Müller-Armack's reports, 29 October 1958, B136/2597 (*BuKa*), and Müller-Armack to Erhard, 30 October 1958 and 3 November 1958, both B102/11 160 (*BMWi*).
185 Reference to these bilateral talks was only found in report by Department E to Westrick, 29 October 1958, B102/11160 (*BMWi*).
186 Memorandum by Chancellory Sub-Department B 2, sent to Haenlein and Adenauer, 3 November 1958, B136/2597 (*BuKa*).
187 See Brentano to Erhard (copy to Adenauer), 10 November 1958, B136/2597 (*BuKa*).
188 Noting Erhard's decreased influence were Hoyer-Millar (now Permanent Under-Secretary, FO) to Gore-Booth, 7 November 1958, FO371/134512, and Holliday to Coulson, 12 November 1958, FO371/134513. That such hopes were illusionary was stated in a confidential note by the Mutual Aid Department, 30 October 1958. That they would be counterproductive was argued by Horace Rumbold (Deputy Under-Secretary, FO), 16 October 1958 (both FO371/134545).
189 See Macmillan to Adenauer, 25 October 1958, PREM11/2706, and to de Gaulle, 8 November 1958, FO371/134511. Sending the latter was opposed by the Chancellor: see Heathcoat Amory to Prime Minister,

Notes 205

7 November 1958, T172/2138. For Macmillan calling the meeting, see his note, 30 October 1958, CAB128/32.
190 Eccles to Foreign Secretary, 13 November 1958, FO371/134517.
191 See Cabinet Committee (Ministerial) 6th meeting, 31 October 1958, CAB130/123. See also Macmillan's Cabinet memorandum, C (58) 229, 4 November 1958, CAB129/95.
192 See Chancellory Sub-Department B 2 to Adenauer, 17 November 1958, B136/2597 (*BuKa*).
193 Record of meeting between Macmillan, Selwyn Lloyd and Couve de Murville, 6 November 1958, FO371/134513. See also de Gaulle's reply to Macmillan's letter, 15 November 1958, FO371/134514.
194 See Müller-Armack to *AA*, 13 November 1958, and Chancellory Sub-Department B 2 to Adenauer, 17 November 1958 (both B136/2597 [*BuKa*]).
195 Werkmeister to *AA* and *BMWi*, 17 November 1958, B 102/11159 (*BMWi*), reporting that Soustelle belonged to a small new party 'Union de la nouvelle République', which sought to attract not only votes but also financial help from French industrial federations. See also *AA* report to Adenauer, 19 November 1958, *AA*: West I 200/150, and German embassy, Paris, to *AA*, 15 November 1958, *AA*: West I 200/351. Compare Ellis-Rees to FO, 17 November 1958, FO371/134514.
196 Müller-Armack's impression as reported by Chancellory Sub-Department B 2 to Adenauer, 17 November 1958, B136/2597 (*BuKa*).
197 Herwarth to *AA*, 20 November 1958, B102/12121 (*BMWi*). For first British reactions to the breakdown, see Herwarth, 17 November 1958, *AA*: West I 200/351.
198 See Werkmeister to *AA* and *BMWi*, 17 November 1958, B102/11159 (*BMWi*).
199 See Cabinet Committee (Ministerial) 7th meeting, 17 November 1958, CAB130/123.
200 Cabinet Committee (Ministerial) 7th meeting, 17 November 1958, CAB130/123.
201 For the agreement about the futility of a possible attempt to influence Adenauer, see Wright to Hoyer-Millar, 20 November 1958, FO371/134512. For the report by officials, see ES (58) 36, 21 November 1958, CAB134/1837, discussed in ES (58) 14th meeting, 20 November 1958, CAB134/1837.
202 See report by officials, ES (58) 36, CAB134/1837.
203 Makins to Heathcoat Amory, 17 November 1958, T234/204.
204 See reports by Steel about conversations with German officials, 15 November 1958, FO371/134513, and 18 November 1958, FO371/134514.
205 See Herwarth to *AA*, 21 November 1958, *AA*: West I 200/150.
206 See Birrenbach to Brentano, 22 November 1958, *AA:MB* 67.
207 See, for example, leader comment in *The Times*, 18 November 1958, entitled 'France the Wrecker'. See also two letters by the Chairman of the *BDI*, Fritz Berg, to Adenauer, both dated 18 November 1958, B136/2598 (*BuKa*) and B102/12121 (*BMWi*).
208 See Peter Tennant to *BuKa*, 21 November 1958, B136/2597 (*BuKa*).
209 See *AA*'s report to Adenauer, 19 November 1958, *AA*: West I 200/150.
210 See de Gaulle's comments, as recorded by Blankenhorn, 24 November 1958, NL351, Vol. 29b, pp. 7–8.

206 Notes

211 See Blankenhorn's reports on meeting Hallstein, 26 October 1958, NL351, Vol. 91, pp. 124–5.
212 See Sub-Department 202 'Peaceful Use of Atomic Eenergy' to Hartlieb, about an intervention of the US embassy, 6 November 1958, *AA*: West I 200/351.
213 See Carstens to Blankenhorn, 20 November 1958, NL351, Vol. 92b, pp. 61–5.
214 See Blankenhorn's note, 26 November 1958, NL351, Vol. 92a, pp. 243–4. See also the French summary protocol, in: Ministère des Affaires Étrangères (ed.), *Documents Diplomatiques Français*, 1958, Vol. 2 (Imprimerie Nationale: Paris, 1993), pp. 754–63.
215 See Seydoux, *Beiderseits des Rheins*, pp. 218–20, and H.-P. Schwarz, *Adenauer: der Staatsmann: 1952–1967* (DVA: Stuttgart, 1991), pp. 466–7.
216 Agreement at Bad Kreuznach, dated 26 November 1958, B102/10912 (*BMWi*) and *AA*: West I 200/1.
217 See record of the meeting between van Scherpenberg and Couve de Murville, dated 19 November 1958, NL351, Vol. 94, pp. 7–14. Wolfram Kaiser holds that German acquiescence at the abandonment of the FTA and de Gaulle's support over Berlin represented a straight quid pro quo at Bad Kreuznach, see Kaiser, *Using Europe Abusing the Europeans*, p. 97. The fact that security concerns did not feature at this earlier meeting suggests otherwise.
218 See Blankenhorn's note, 26 November 1958, NL351, Vol. 92a, pp. 243–4. De Gaulle, in contrast, recalled that the two sides had explicitly agreed to put an end to the FTA negotiations (see de Gaulle, *Memoiren der Hoffnung*, pp. 218–20), while Adenauer blamed the *BMWi* and Maudling for incompetent handling of the negotiations (see Adenauer and Heuss, *Unter vier Augen*, pp. 287–8).
219 For de Gaulle's success in charming Erhard, see report by HM embassy, Paris, 3 December 1958, FO371/134518. For Müller-Armack's respect for de Gaulle's arguments, see meeting of the special FTA committee of the *Bundesrat*, 29 November 1958, *AA*: West I 200/289.
220 See Meyer-Cording to Erhard, 22 November 1958, B102/11163 (*BMWi*).
221 Ministère des Affaires Étrangères, *Documents Diplomatiques Français*, 1958, p. 754.
222 See summary protocol of the Council of Ministers' meeting, 3/4 December 1958, B102/10912 (*BMWi*).
223 To combine notification of the OEEC about the EEC Council directive on the interim solution with such a commitment would have required a separate motion. However, the final decision about this notification was taken by the meeting of permanent delegates on 4 December, at which such a motion could no longer be introduced. See summary protocol of the Council of Ministers' meeting, 3/4 December 1958, B 102/10912 (*BMWi*).
224 See van Scherpenberg about Erhard's visit to London, 5 December 1958, *AA:MB* 49.
225 See Steel reporting on a conversation with van Scherpenberg, 29 November 1958, PREM11/2352 and FO371/134517. See also record of meeting between Erhard and Maudling, 4 December 1958, PREM11/

2352, British ministerial appreciation of Erhard's arguments, 4 December 1958, CAB130/123, and Maudling's charge that 'the Germans gave in to them [the French]', in his letter to Macmillan, 2 December 1958, PREM11/2352.
226 See note by Board of Trade, 26 November 1958, CAB130/135. See also leader of *Financial Times*, 28 November 1958.
227 See FO to HM embassy, Brussels, 2 December 1958, FO371/134517. How overstated this point in fact was became clear later during Anglo-French bilateral negotiations, revealing that discrimination against British goods amounted to a total of 1 200 000 pounds worth of its exports: see 75th meeting of Clarke's European Free Trade Area Steering Group, 24 February 1959, CAB130/133.
228 Cabinet Committee (Ministerial) 8th meeting, 27 November 1958, CAB130/123.
229 FO submission to Cabinet, 11 December 1958, FO371/134519.
230 See, for example, Blankenhorn to *AA* about threats voiced by Lord Landsdowne (Parliamentary Under-Secretary, FO) at the NATO meeting, 17 December 1958, *AA*: West I 200/150.
231 See Figgures to Coulson, 9 December 1958, FO371/134519. See also 2nd meeting of the new 'Ministerial Committee' (established December 1958), 11 December 1958, CAB130/154.
232 See van Scherpenberg about 'lively conversation' with Selwyn Lloyd, 18 December 1958, *AA:MB* 49. The British Ambassador was also very heavy-handed in his approach, much to the annoyance of the FO: see Steel to FO, 29 November 1958, PREM11/2352 and FO371/134517. See also various comments on the latter.
233 Adenauer to Macmillan, 12 December 1958, *AA*: West I 200/150 and FO371/134519. See also resolution in favour of the FTA, passed unanimously by the *Bundestag*, 9 December 1958, *AA*: West I 200/150.
234 Carstens to Adenauer, 12 December 1958, *AA*: West I 200/150.
235 The parallel to the Commonwealth was pointed out by Spaak in a letter to Duncan Sandys (Minister of Defence), but when passing this on to the Prime Minister the Paymaster-General's Office mounted a feeble defence based on the political value of Commonwealth Preference to the rest of the world, failing to notice that here was another striking parallel to the EEC! See H. S. Lee to Prime Minister, 12 December 1958, FO371/134520.
236 Excerpts from the protocol of OEEC Council meeting, 15 December 1958, in Werkmeister to Erhard, 20 December 1958, B102/12121 (*BMWi*). See also the account of the meeting and the final phases of the negotiations in Couve de Murville, *Außenpolitik 1958–69*, pp. 34–6.
237 See Bretherton's report on the mediation attempt, 16 December 1958, T234/204. See also report on the OEEC meeting, 17 December 1958, FO371/134519.
238 See note by McKean, 18 December 1958, T234/357.
239 Erhard to Adenauer, 17 December 1958, B136/2597 (*BuKa*).
240 See Carstens to Brentano, 19 December 1958, *AA:MB* 49, State Secretary Hans Globke to Adenauer, 18 December 1958, B136/2597 (*BuKa*), and Carstens to Brentano, 22 December 1958, *AA*: West I 200/150.

241 See *AA* to *BMWi*, 31 December 1958, following the interministerial meeting of 30 December 1958, B102/12121 (*BMWi*). See also Haenlein to Adenauer, on a further meeting on 14 January 1959, B136/2598 (*BuKa*).
242 See van Scherpenberg to *BuKa*, 15 January 1959, B136/2598 (*BuKa*).
243 L. Erhard, *Gedanken aus fünf Jahrzehnten, Reden und Schriften*, edited by Karl Hohmann (ECON: Dusseldorf, 1988), p. 569.
244 64th and 68th meeting of Clarke's European Free Trade Area Steering Group, 31 December 1958, and 12 January 1959, respectively (both CAB130/133).
245 For details of the reorganization of the *AA*, see footnote 132 in this chapter.
246 Hartlieb to Carstens, 5 December 1958, *AA*: West I 200/150.

4 'Bridge-Building' or: the Trade War That Never Was

1 For the assessment of the French position, see, for example, UK delegation to OEEC to FO, 8 January 1959, T234/358, and HM embassy, Paris, to Hoyer-Millar, 10 January 1959, FO371/142609. On bilateral negotiations, see Figgures to Ellis-Rees, 9 January 1959, and Figgures to Clarke, 22 January 1959, both T234/358. See also Gore-Booth's report of 24 February 1959, CAB130/133, and FO to HM embassies in OEEC capitals, 3 April 1959, T234/379.
2 See 13th meeting of the Cabinet Committee (Ministerial) 'The Free Trade Area', 9 February 1959, CAB130/123.
3 See Gore-Booth to Caccia, 1 January 1959, Coulson's meeting with US officials, 9 January 1959, Caccia to Treasury, 11 January 1959. See also Steel to FO, 9 January 1959, and – about meeting Brentano – 12 January 1959. All T234/358. See also Steel to Coulson about meeting Erhard, 29 January 1959, Figgures to Clarke about meeting van Scherpenberg, 30 January 1959 (both T234/359), and Steel to FO about meeting Herwarth, 14 February 1959, FO371/145858.
4 Report by officials to Cabinet Committee (Ministerial), 3 March 1959, CAB130/124 and CAB130/156, discussed in 14th meeting, 5 March 1959, CAB130/123.
5 Report by officials to Cabinet Committee (Ministerial), 3 March 1959, CAB130/124.
6 Report by officials to Cabinet Committee (Ministerial), 3 March 1959, CAB130/124.
7 Müller-Armack and van Scherpenberg agreed on this: see their meeting with French representatives, 10 January 1959, *AA*: West I 200/457.
8 See Meyer-Cording to Ophüls, 2 January 1959, B102/121212 (*BMWi*), and Haenlein's report on interministerial meeting, 14 January 1959, B136/2589 (*BuKa*).
9 This suggestion was first made by a study of the *BDI*, sent to Erhard, 2 January 1959, B102/12132 (*BMWi*). Also sent by Commercial Department of HM embassy, Bonn, to FO, 23 February 1959, FO371/142588.

10 See note by Horn, after talks with Müller-Armack, 19 January 1959, B102/12216 (*BMWi*).
11 See Hünke, discussing the findings of the study, 6 March 1959, B102/12230 (*BMWi*).
12 See *BMWi*'s 'post-mortem' of the FTA negotiation, 14 February 1959, B102/12235 (*BMWi*).
13 See *BMWi*'s 'post-mortem', 14 February 1959. In an earlier in-house draft of this paper, British tactics throughout and Eccles's comments after the FTA negotiations were strongly criticized: see comments on Hünke's draft, 5 February 1959, all B102/12235 (*BMWi*).
14 For Müller-Armack's and van Scherpenberg's meeting with EEC Commissioner von der Gröben, see note, 29 January 1959, B102/12230 (*BMWi*).
15 See note, 29 January 1959, B102/12230 (*BMWi*). The AA attempted to enlist Dutch support for the *BMWi*'s ideas: see report by Carstens, 21 February 1959. Van Scherpenberg also tried to persuade the French: see his letter to Wormser, 12 February 1959. Both AA: West I 200/457.
16 See first memorandum of the European Commission, 26 February 1959, B102/12215 (*BMWi*) and AA: West I 200/459. English translation sent by UK delegation to ECSC to Holliday, 25 March 1959, FO371/142590.
17 See protocol of interministerial meeting, 12 March 1959, B102/12215 (*BMWi*), and the resulting instructions for German representatives, 13 March 1959, B102/12132 (*BMWi*). For the *BMWi* resolution, see Council document, 16 March 1959, B102/12230 (*BMWi*). See also Hünke to Meyer-Cording, 17 March 1959, B102/12215 (*BMWi*).
18 See protocol, dated 14 April 1959, B102/10914 (*BMWi*). See also resolution adopted, 16 March 1959, B102/10912 (*BMWi*).
19 For AA approval, see protocol of interministerial meeting, 12 March 1959, B102/12215 (*BMWi*), and Hünke to Meyer-Cording, 16 March 1959, B102/10913 (*BMWi*).
20 See Werkmeister to Erhard and van Scherpenberg, 24 April 1959, B102/12132 (*BMWi*).
21 See Wormser to Müller-Armack, 31 March 1959, B102/12230 (*BMWi*), and report by Harkort, 28 March 1959, AA: West I 200/457.
22 The British government was aware of the German initiative: see report by Steel, 11 March 1959, FO371/142589, and record of meeting between Clarke, Figgures, Gore-Booth, Wright, Ellis-Rees and others, 7 April 1959, T234/362.
23 See, for example, Maudling to Macmillan, 3 March 1959, and draft brief for Macmillan's meeting with Adenauer, 4 March 1959 (both T234/361).
24 Steel's report, 29 January 1959, T234/359. Foreign Secretary Selwyn Lloyd underlined this point in his letter to Macmillan, 4 March 1959, T234/361.
25 See report by officials, 3 March 1959, CAB130/124 and CAB130/156, discussed by ministers, 5 April 1959, CAB130/123.
26 See Herwarth's comments as reported by Steel, 14 February 1959, FO371/145858.
27 For the press campaign, see report by German embassy, London, 25 February 1959, AA: West I 200/344. For the impact of British threats,

see also Hartlieb to Carstens, 6 February 1959, *AA*: West I 200/457, and Brentano to Birrenbach, 10 February 1959, *AA:MB* 67. The former contains an appreciation of a speech by Maudling. The text of Macmillan's speech to the Foreign Press Association on 21 January 1959 is contained in a report by the German embassy, London, 26 February 1959, *AA*: West II 304/104. The British Cabinet merely concluded that German complaints were unfounded: see Cabinet's 22nd meeting, 9 April 1959, CAB128/33.
28 See, for example, Birrenbach to Brentano, 10 February 1959, and the latter's reply, 2 March 1959, both *AA:MB* 67.
29 Note for the record by Hartlieb, 6 February 1959, *AA*: West I 200/349.
30 See Hartlieb's report, 23 February 1959, *AA*: West I 200/349. After the Adenauer/Macmillan meeting, Hartlieb purported to even recognize a coordinated timing of Russian and British actions; see his letter to Carstens, 24 April 1959, *AA*: West I 200/457.
31 See Herwarth's comments as reported by Steel, 14 February 1959, FO371/145858, and Steel to FO, 26 June 1959, PREM11/2706. On Adenauer's reaction to the Moscow visit, see Adenauer and Heuss, *Unter vier Augen*, pp. 290–1, 294–5 and 300.
32 See records of the meeting, 12/13 March 1959, PREM11/2676; see also Carstens's report, 19 March 1959, *AA*: West I 200/457.
33 See Adenauer to the French Prime Minister Michel Debré, 25 March 1959, *AA:MB* 56. See also Steel to FO, quoting Adenauer: 'I have only three enemies, the Communists, the British and my own Foreign Office', 26 June 1959, PREM11/2706.
34 During 1958 and 1959, this policy was also frequently referred to as UNISCAN, UNISCANSA, the 'non-Six', the 'Seven', the 'Outer Seven', or the 'Stockholm Group'.
35 This was explicitly agreed with regard to the German proposals: see meeting between Clarke, Figgures, Gore-Booth, Wright, Ellis-Rees and others, 7 April 1959, T234/362.
36 See Maudling's note to ministers, 18 March 1959, CAB130/124.
37 For a summary of British motives, see Clarke to Gore-Booth, 19 May 1959, T234/362. See also ES (EI) 59 11, 14 May 1959, CAB134/1870.
38 See Cabinet memorandum by Chancellor, 7 May 1959, CAB128/33, and his comments at 17th meeting of Cabinet Committee (Ministerial), 5 May 1959, CAB130/123.
39 Clarke to Gore-Booth, 19 May 1959, T234/362.
40 See 14th meeting of Cabinet Committee (Ministerial), 5 March 1959, CAB130/123. See also Figgures to Clarke, 27 January 1959, T234/359.
41 The main difficulties in the EFTA negotiations concerned the treatment of bacon, canned luncheon meat and fish: see 39th meeting of Cabinet, 7 July 1959, CAB128/33.
42 See Clarke to Rowan and Makins, 10 March 1958, T234/357. Thereafter, the idea reappeared whenever the success of the FTA was in question; see, for example, Figgures to Clarke, 8 May 1958, T234/376, Makins to Chancellor, 4 July 1958 and 16 July 1958, and finally Clarke to Lee, 6 August 1958 (all T234/377). For the evolution of the EFTA plan, see W. Kaiser, 'Challenge to the Community: the Creation, Cri-

sis and Consolidation of the European Free Trade Association, 1958–1972', in: *Journal of European Integration History* (1997/1), pp. 7–33. The origins of the idea date back to the late 1940s: see A. S. Milward, *The Reconstruction of Western Europe 1945–51* (Methuen: London, 1984), pp. 316–19.
43 McKean to Figgures, 12 March 1958, T234/203.
44 See Macmillan's scribble, dated 6 August 1958, on Maudling's memo of 5 August 1958, PREM11/2531.
45 See Maudling's comments at 13th meeting of Cabinet Committee (Ministerial), 9 February 1959, as well as Macmillan's summing up at 14th meeting, 5 March 1959 (both CAB130/123).
46 See FO to Maudling in Oslo, informing him of ministers' decision, 6 March 1959, T234/361.
47 See Selwyn Lloyd to Macmillan, 4 March 1959, T234/361. See also FO submission to Cabinet, 11 December 1958, FO371/134519.
48 McKean to Clarke, 20 February 1959, T234/360.
49 See Gladwyn Jebb to Selwyn Lloyd, 22 May 1959, T234/362. See also Majoribanks to Holliday, 24 June 1959, FO371/142595.
50 See, for example, Macmillan's summing up at 17th meeting of Cabinet Committee (Ministerial), 5 May 1959, CAB130/123. See also ES (EI) (59) 11, 14 May 1959, CAB134/1870. The Germans were a prime target of such reassurances: see reports by Herwarth to *AA*, 2 June 1959 and 19 June 1959, *AA*: West I 200/353 and *AA*:HPA 410/240.
51 See Clarke to Gore-Booth, 19 May 1959, T234/362.
52 See, for example, Steel to FO, reporting on conversation with Müller-Armack, 11 March 1959, FO371/142589. See also report by HM embassy, Bonn, 27 May 1959, FO371/142593.
53 Clarke's comments at meeting with Figgures, Gore-Booth, Wright, Ellis-Rees and others, 7 April 1959, T234/362.
54 For British awareness of the changing views of Erhard, see undated brief for the visit in June of Franz Etzel (now German Finance Minister), FO371/142595.
55 See *BMWi* submission to Chancellor, 9 June 1959, B102/12132 (*BMWi*) and B102/12230 (*BMWi*), sent to *AA*, 16 July 1959, *AA*: West I 200/353.
56 See Harkort to van Scherpenberg, 22 June 1959, *AA*: West I 200/353.
57 See Hartlieb to Carstens, 18 June 1959, describing EFTA as a British 'Kampfinstrument', *AA*: West I 200/353. See also Hartlieb to Carstens, 8 July 1959, *AA*: West I 200/457, and Carstens to van Scherpenberg, 2 June 1959, *AA*: West I 200/353.
58 See protocol of interministerial meeting, 18 June 1959, *AA*: West I 200/353.
59 See Müller-Armack's note, 30 June 1959, B102/126799 (*BMWi*).
60 See comments by Hünke, 22 June 1059, B102/12132 (*BMWi*).
61 See Majoribanks to FO, 3 June 1959, FO371/142593. See also undated brief for Etzel's visit (17 June 1959), FO371/142595. It was only the UK delegation to Brussels, which recognized the 'delight' of Hallstein about the diversion of British energies elsewhere: see UK delegation to ECSC to FO, 13 June 1959, FO371/142593.

62 See Horace Rumbold's note for the record, 15 April 1959, and Gladwyn Jebb to Selwyn Lloyd, 22 May 1959 (both T234/362). Adenauer's favourite candidate for the Chancellorship was in fact Etzel, and his reluctance to back Erhard led to some ill-feeling between the two men. For Adenauer's view on the affair, see his letters to Heinrich Krone (Chairman of the *Christlich Demokratische Union/Christlich Soziale Union* [CDU/CSU] parliamentary party), 20 May 1959, and two letters dated 20 June 1959 (all *StBKAH* 10.40), as well as Adenauer, *Erinnerungen, 1955–1959*, pp. 483–551. The British government was well informed about these developments, see Steel to FO, 26 June 1959, PREM11/2706. On this episode, see also D. Koerfer, *Kampf ums Kanzleramt: Erhard und Adenauer* (DVA: Stuttgart, 1987), and Schwarz, *Adenauer*, pp. 502–26.

63 See German proposal to the Comité Spécial to establish a limited customs union with progressive harmonization of tariffs, in Hünke's minutes to van Scherpenberg, 27 May 1959 and 22 June 1959, B102/12216 (*BMWi*) and B102/12132 (*BMWi*) respectively. See also his proposals for Comité Spécial to consider EEC membership in EFTA, 7 July 1959, B102/12216 (*BMWi*). For examples of bilateral contacts, see Erhard's meeting with the French Finance Minister, Antoine Pinay, as discussed by van Scherpenberg, 15 July 1959, *AA:MB* 157, Erhard's meeting with the Danish Foreign Minister, Jens Otto Krag, as discussed by the Head of *AA* Sub-Department 401 'European Economic Organizations', 26 June 1959, *AA*: West I 200/353, and meeting between Müller-Armack and Maudling, protocol dated 9 September 1959, B102/12132 (*BMWi*), report also in FO371/142595.

64 See, for example, Hünke's report on the first meeting of the Comité Spécial, 29 April 1959, B102/12230 (*BMWi*).

65 See Hünke's report on Comité Spécial, 9 July 1959, B102/12216 (*BMWi*). See also Harkort's report on the Comité, 27 July 1959, *AA*: West I 200/459. The Comité's final report could only record the disagreements of the parties, 23 November 1959, B102/10916 (*BMWi*).

66 Hartlieb to Carstens, 8 July 1959. See also Hartlieb to Carstens, 24 April 1959. Both *AA*: West I 200/457.

67 See Hartlieb to Carstens, 8 July 1959, *AA*: West I 200/457, Carstens to Brentano, 3 August 1959, *AA:MB* 50, and Brentano to Adenauer, 3 September 1959, *AA:MB* 49.

68 See Harkort on meeting with US representative, 20 July 1959, and 25 August 1959, *AA*: West I 200/353.

69 Maudling and others consistently argued that the initiative lay with the Six: see report by *BMWi* Sub-Department E 3, 28 April 1959, B102/12216 (*BMWi*), meeting between Müller-Armack and Maudling, protocol dated 9 September 1959, B102/12132 (*BMWi*), and Etzel's report on meeting Maudling, sent to Carstens, 10 July 1959, *AA*: West I 200/349. See also Müller-Roschach to Carstens, 23 October 1959, *AA*: West I 200/349.

70 See 23rd meeting of ES (EI) Sub-committee, 8 September 1959, CAB134/1869. Erhard had been informed as early as April: see FO to HM embassy, Bonn, 20 April 1959, T234/362.

71 2nd memorandum of the European Commission, 17 September 1959, B102/12215 and B102/12230 (*BMWi*).
72 See Müller-Armack's meeting with van Scherpenberg and Wormser, 16 September 1959, and his meeting with Maudling, protocol dated 9 September 1959 (both B102/12132 [*BMWi*]). This latest attempt originated in discussions between representatives of Benelux and Italy: see report by German embassy, Rome, to *AA*, *AA*: West I 200/353.
73 See interministerial debate, 17 September 1959. Hünke later called it a tactical rather than whole-hearted acceptance: see his appreciation of the 2nd memorandum, 28 September 1959. Both B102/12132 (*BMWi*).
74 The US government had strongly welcomed the Commission's proposals for its emphasis on the global approach: see Ophüls to *AA*, 15 October 1959, *AA*: West I 200/456.
75 See, for example, the assessment of the 2nd memorandum prepared by *BMWi* Department V 'Foreign Trade Policy', 6 October 1959. Hünke then called another internal *BMWi* meeting 'in the interest of the house peace': see his invitation, 4 October 1959. Both B102/12215 (*BMWi*).
76 See internal *BMWi* meeting, 16 October 1959, B102/12132 (*BMWi*).
77 See comments by Harkort and *Bundesbank* representative during an interministerial debate, 17 September 1959, B102/12132 (*BMWi*).
78 See comments by Carstens and others at interministerial meeting, 17 September 1959. Reference to the Cabinet decision is found in the *BMWi* meeting, 16 October 1959. Both B102/12132 (*BMWi*). For the continuation of internal conflict within *BMWi* and *AA*, see Carstens's brief for Adenauer's visit to London, 11 November 1959, *AA:MB* 67.
79 Maudling to Macmillan, 27 November 1959, PREM11/2679.
80 See, in particular, Steel to FO, 3 November 1959, FO371/142597. Macmillan was also informed: see Steel to Macmillan, 16 October 1959, PREM11/2714.
81 Gore-Booth's minute on conversation with Steel, 30 November 1959. For Erhard's claim, see Steel to FO, 1 December 1959. Both FO371/142599.
82 See Selwyn Lloyd's paper EQ (59) 3 'Relations with Europe', 5 November 1959, CAB134/1818. His assessment was based mainly on a report on Adenauer's motives: see Steel to Hoyer-Millar, 3 November 1959, FO371/142597, and on Holliday's draft for the upcoming Western Summit, 22 October 1959, FO371/142596. The need to reassure Adenauer was also advocated by Jackling to Hoyer-Millar, 16 November 1959, FO371/142598.
83 De Zulueta to Macmillan, 21 October 1959, PREM11/2985.
84 See Macmillan's request for such a list, 24 October 1959, PREM11/2714.
85 See record of the meeting, 18 November 1959 and 19 November 1959. See also impressions of Selwyn Lloyd in his letter to Macmillan, 4 December 1959. All PREM11/2714.
86 See summary record of meeting, 29 November 1959, PREM11/2676 and PREM11/3132.
87 See, for example, Caccia to Gore-Booth, 6 October 1959, FO371/142596,

214 Notes

and Gore-Booth's note to ministers, 2 December 1959, CAB130/156.
88 Caccia to FO, 27 November 1959, T234/717.
89 See brief for the visit prepared by the Official Steering Group on European Economic Questions, EQ (59) 10, 29 November 1959, CAB134/1818. See also Makins to Heathcoat Amory, 18 November 1959, FO371/142598, and unsigned Treasury paper for forthcoming Dillon visit, 19 November 1959, T234/717.
90 See record of meeting, 8 December 1959, PREM11/2870.
91 Macmillan to Heathcoat Amory, 10 December 1959, T234/717.
92 Macmillan to Heathcoat Amory, 10 December 1959, T234/717.
93 Note by European Economic Organisation Department, 2 December 1959, FO371/142600. See also Holliday's comments on Clarke's paper on the economic danger of the Common Market, 21 December 1959, FO371/142600
94 See Selwyn Lloyd's paper EQ (59) 3, 5 November 1959, CAB134/1818.
95 See Foreign Office note sent to Macmillan, 27 November 1959, PREM11/2679. The ministerial meeting at Chequers discussed but dismissed both options as too radical: see summary record of meeting, 29 November 1959, PREM11/2676 and PREM11/3132.
96 Rumbold's minute on the note by the European Economic Organisation Department, 4 December 1959, FO371/142600.
97 Note by European Economic Organisation Department, 2 December 1959, FO371/142600.
98 See, for example, Treasury paper EQ (59) 3, 6 November 1959, CAB134/1818, and Board of Trade memorandum, ES (EI) (59) 163, 17 November 1959, CAB134/1874.
99 Clarke's note on EQ (59) 3, 27 November 1959, T234/717, and his undated (December) report for Macmillan on the economic consequences of the Common Market for Britain, FO371/142600.
100 Memoranda by Figures, 1 October 1959, and Clarke, 18 January 1960, both FO371/150154.
101 See Cabinet memorandum by Chancellor, C (59) 188, 14 December 1959, CAB129/99. Discussed and approved at 63rd meeting, 15 December 1959, CAB128/33.
102 See ministerial meeting discussing the Stockholm EFTA conference, 24 November 1959, CAB130/155.
103 See Macmillan to ministers meeting at Chequers, 29 November 1959, PREM11/2676 and PREM11/3132, and Selwyn Lloyd to ministerial meeting, 7 December 1959, T234/717.
104 See record of the meeting between de Gaulle, Eisenhower, Adenauer and Macmillan, 20 December 1959, PREM11/142600.
105 See Cabinet's 1st meeting, 4 January 1960, CAB128/34. See also 1st meeting of Economic Steering Sub-Committee on Closer Association with Europe, 5 January 1960, discussing note by Treasury, ES (EI) (60) 1, 4 January 1960 (both CAB134/1875), and note by Treasury, 6 January 1960, CAB134/157.

5 'Bully the Germans – Buy the French': Towards Britain's First Application

1. For examples of the former view, see Treasury brief for Prime Minister's meeting with de Gaulle, 25 January 1960, PREM11/3132, and Chancellor's summing up of the conference results, C (60) 6, 9 February 1960, CAB129/100. See also Roger Jackling (now Assistant Under-Secretary, FO) to Steel, 22 February 1960, FO371/150267. For the last view, see Gore-Booth to Hoyer-Millar, 19 January 1960, FO371/150151.
2. For the former, see Majoribanks to FO, 22 February 1960, FO371/150267. For Maudling's comments, see his note EQ (60) 12 and his contribution to the 4th meeting of the (Ministerial) European Economic Association Committee (established December 1959 to replace Cabinet Committee [Ministerial] 'The Free Trade Area'), 16 and 18 March 1960 respectively, both CAB134/1819.
3. See Macmillan's summing up of the 4th meeting of the Ministerial Committee, 18 March 1960, CAB134/1819.
4. See, for example, Treasury brief for Macmillan's meeting with de Gaulle, 25 January 1960, PREM11/3132.
5. Note by Board of Trade, EQ (O) (60) 5, 21 March 1960, CAB134/1823, and 1st meeting of the European Economic Question (Official) Committee, which had replaced the European Economic Questions Official Steering Group, 22 March 1960, CAB134/1822. Its conclusions were submitted to the equivalent European Economic Questions (Ministerial) Committee which replaced the European Economic Association Committee in April, and which inherited the code EQ as opposed to EQ (O).
6. Sir Frank Lee during the 24th meeting of the European Economic Questions Steering Group, 4 February 1960, CAB130/155.
7. See the Swiss proposals, 16 February 1960, FO371/150155.
8. See Maudling's report to 4th and last meeting of (Ministerial) European Economic Association Committee, 18 March 1960, CAB134/1819.
9. Macmillan's comment on a Treasury paper on the Trade Committee, 27 March 1960, PREM11/3132.
10. See German embassy, London, to *AA* about Maudling, 7 January 1960, *AA*: West I 200/492, and Birrenbach to Brentano about Selwyn Lloyd, 26 January 1960, *AA:MB* 50.
11. See, for example, German embassy, London, to *AA*, 18 March 1960, *AA:MB* 50.
12. See Carstens's brief for Adenauer's visit to London (postponed due to ill-health), 11 November 1959, *AA:MB* 67.
13. See, for example, Carstens's report on Dillon's talks with Hallstein and Ophüls, 11 December 1959, *AA*: West I 200/354. See also note by van Scherpenberg, 16 December 1959, *AA:BStS* 296, and Harkort to van Scherpenberg, 5 January 1960, *AA*: West I 200/492.
14. See Brentano to Etzel, 16 December 1959, *AA:MB* 50, and Hartlieb to Müller-Roschach, 18 March 1960, *AA*: West I 200/489.
15. See report by Carstens on meeting Maudling, 24 November 1959, *AA*: West I 200/345. See also reports by German embassy, London, 4 and

216 Notes

7 January 1960 (both *AA*: West I 200/492), and Birrenbach to Brentano, reporting on Selwyn Lloyd's speech to Council of Europe, 26 January 1960, *AA:MB* 50.
16 Brentano to Birrenbach, 31 January 1960, *AA:MB* 50.
17 For the 'Special Economic Conference', see minutes, 12/13 January 1960, and Harkort's summary, 15 January 1960, both B102/12204 (*BMWi*).
18 See Sub-Department 401 'European Economic Organizations' to Brentano, 10 February 1960, *AA*: West I 200/492, and Brentano to Etzel, 16 December 1959, *AA:MB* 50. See also note by van Scherpenberg, 16 December 1959, *AA:BStS* 296.
19 For a *BMWi* attempt to be given responsibility for the Trade Committee, see Harkort to van Scherpenberg, 4 February 1960, *AA*: West I 200/492.
20 See records of consultations between the delegations of the Six, 11 and 12 January 1960, both *AA*: West I 200/492, and protocol of Council of Ministers' meeting, 12 January 1960, *AA:BStS* 289. See also van Scherpenberg to *AA*, 14 January 1960, and Head of *AA* Sub-Department 401 'European Economic Organizations' to Adenauer, 16 January 1960, both *AA*: West I 200/492. For US support, see Grewe to *AA*, 30 January 1960, and Sub-Department 401 'European Economic Organizations' to Brentano, 10 February 1960. For internal discussions, see interministerial meeting, 6 February 1960 (all *AA*: West I 200/459).
21 See Hünke's note, 6 February 1960, B102/12204 (*BMWi*).
22 See position paper by Department E, 8 January 1960, B102/12124 (*BMWi*) and Meyer-Cording's assessment of the conference results, 25 January 1960, B102/12204 (*BMWi*).
23 See report by German embassy, London, 3 February 1960, B102/12204 (*BMWi*).
24 See *BMWi* paper on Contact Committee, 5 February 1960, B102/12204 (*BMWi*).
25 See Hünke's note, 6 February 1960, B102/12204 (*BMWi*).
26 See Hünke's note for meeting of Comité Spécial, 7 March 1960, B102/12204 (*BMWi*).
27 For details of the Müller-Armack/van Scherpenberg compromise, see record of conversation, 11 February 1960, *AA:BStS* 296, and summary protocol, 11 February 1960, B102/12204 (*BMWi*).
28 See protocol of first meeting of Trade Committee, 29–30 March 1960, B102/12205 (*BMWi*).
29 For initial British reactions to the Hallstein plan, see German embassy, London, to *AA*, 8 March 1960, *AA*: West I 200/349.
30 The *AA* attempted to prevent Erhard's presence in Paris: see Brentano to Erhard, 19 January 1960, and Müller-Armack's reply, 28 January 1960, both B102/11032 (*BMWi*). See also Sub-Department 401 'European Economic Organizations' to van Scherpenberg, 29 December 1959, *AA:BStS* 296.
31 See Hünke's note, 6 February 1960, B102/12204 (*BMWi*).
32 In order to form such a coalition, the *BMWi* attempted to have internal EEC tariff issues included in the remit of the Contact Committee: see *BMWi* correspondence to *AA*, and the latter's negative reaction, 5 February 1960, *AA*: West I 200/459.

33 See, for example, copy of Erhard's interview with the NDR (*Norddeutscher Rundfunk*), 9 March 1960, *AA*: West I 200/489, and the federal press office's disapproval thereof, 9 March 1960, *AA:BStS* 289. See also Müller-Armack's speech to the economic committee of the *Bundestag*, 17 March 1960, B102/12124 (*BMWi*). For the impact of British threats, see also Seydoux, *Beiderseits des Rheins*, pp. 236–7.
34 On this opposition, see Hartlieb to van Scherpenberg, 1 April 1960, *AA:BStS* 289, and *Bundesrat* Vice-President Kai-Uwe von Hassel to Adenauer, 6 May 1960, B102/12206 (*BMWi*).
35 See, for example, *AA* press office's summary of Erhard's press conference about acceleration of 19 March 1960, which led *Welt am Sonntag* (20 March 1960) to diagnose open conflict within the government, *AA:BStS* 289.
36 A summary of Brentano's 'extraordinarily pessimistic and bitter letter' is contained in Adenauer to Krone, 22 March 1960, *AA:MB* 50.
37 Adenauer to Erhard, 22 March 1960, *AA:BStS* 289.
38 Steel to FO, quoting German press, 31 March 1960, FO371/150269.
39 See Cabinet resolution, 5 April 1960, B102/12205 (*BMWi*).
40 HM embassy, Bonn, to Holliday, 12 April 1960, FO371/150275. See also Steel to FO, 11 April 1960, FO371/150271, and earlier embassy reports, 31 January 1960, FO371/150169, and 31 March 1960, FO371/150273. See also Sir Edward Tomkins (Head of the FO's Western Department) to Rumbold, 31 March 1960, FO371/150269.
41 See conclusions of 1st meeting of Economic Steering Committee, which also strongly criticized the continued use of threats, 31 March 1960, CAB134/1852. See also S. Toschi, 'Washington – London – Paris an Untenable Triangle', in: *Journal of European Integration History* (1995/2), pp. 81–109.
42 Brentano had apparently confirmed this in a conversation with Thorneycroft: see Thorneycroft to Macmillan, 22 April 1960, FO371/150274. For the FO's less optimistic interpretation, see EQ (O) (60) 17, 20 April 1960, CAB134/1823.
43 See Steel to FO, 24 April 1960, and reply, 29 April 1960, both PREM11/3133. For an optimistic assessment following the *Bundestag* debate, see Steel to FO, 5 May 1960, FO371/150279. On industry and ministerial opinion, see Steel to Gore-Booth, 5 May 1960, FO371/150283.
44 See note by officials in EQ (O) submitted to Economic Steering Committee, ES (E) (60) 6, 12 April 1960, discussed and approved, 13 April 1960 (both CAB134/1852).
45 See Tomkins to Rumbold, 31 March 1960, FO371/150269.
46 See Hoyer-Millar to Selwyn Lloyd, advocating a complete rethink of British policy because of 'recent excitement', 5 April 1960, FO371/150270.
47 See *The Times*, 4 April 1960, and Macmillan's positive reply to Selwyn Lloyd's letter, 22 April 1960, FO371/150160.
48 See Macmillan to Selwyn Lloyd, 8 May 1960, FO371/150160.
49 See 4th meeting of EQ (O), 5 May 1960, CAB134/1822.
50 See letters to FO by George Labouchère (HM Ambassador to Brussels) and Sir Ashley Clarke (HM Ambassador to Rome), both 7 May 1960, FO371/150160, and by Gladwyn Jebb (HM Ambassador to Paris) and

218 *Notes*

Sir Paul Mason (HM Ambassador, The Hague), 7 and 9 May 1960, FO371/150161.
51 See H. W. A. Feese-Pennefather (HM Ambassador, Luxembourg) to FO, 7 May 1960, FO371/150160.
52 Steel to FO, 6 May 1960, FO371/150160.
53 EQ (O) 5th meeting, 10 May 1960, CAB134/1822, discussing EQ (O) (60) 30, 9 May 1960, CAB134/1823.
54 For a summary of the ECSC/Euratom episode, see FO minute, 8 June 1960, FO371/150162.
55 See 32nd Cabinet meeting, 20 May 1960, CAB128/34.
56 See FO minute, 8 June 1960, FO371/150162. The text of Profumo's speech to WEU is dated 2 June 1960, FO371/150161.
57 For continental indifference, see record of WEU Council meeting, 16 June 1960, FO371/150162, and record of meeting of FO representatives with Ambassadors of the Six, 22 June 1960, FO371/150163. For American hostility and EFTA concerns, see HM embassy, Washington, to FO, 30 May 1960, FO371/150161, and note of conversation between Macmillan and Norwegian Foreign Minister, Halvard Lange, 7 June 1960, PREM11/3133.
58 See Brentano's comments during WEU Council meeting, 16 June 1960, FO371/150162, and Steel's report on German reaction to Profumo's speech, 8 June 1960 and 23 June 1960, FO371/150285 and FO371/150168 respectively.
59 See 3rd meeting of Economic Steering (Europe) Committee, 13 April 1960, discussing EQ (O), paper, 12 April 1960, respectively, both CAB134/1852.
60 Sir Frank Lee's memorandum, 25 April 1960, PREM11/3133.
61 See 6th meeting of Economic Steering (Europe) Committee, 19 May 1963, CAB134/1852.
62 EQ (60) 7th meeting, 16 May 1960, CAB134/1819.
63 See Steel to FO, 24 April 1960, and FO reply, 29 April 1960, both PREM11/3133, and Steel to Gore-Booth, 5 May 1960, FO371/150283.
64 Macmillan to Foreign Secretary, 24 May 1960, PREM11/2988.
65 32nd meeting of Cabinet, 20 May 1960, CAB128/34.
66 Steel to FO, 24 May 1960, FO371/150284.
67 EQ (60) 8th meeting, 27 May 1960, CAB134/1819.
68 See EQ (60) 29, 1 June 1960, CAB134/1820.
69 See Sir Arnold France (Third Secretary, Treasury) to FO, 30 May 1960, FO371/150360, and the Economic Steering (Europe) Committee's 10th meeting, 1 July 1960, 11th and 12th meeting, both 4 July 1960 (all CAB134/1852). See also its final report, C (60) 107, 6 July 1960, CAB129/102.
70 C (60) 107, 6 July 1960, CAB129/102.
71 For the text of de Gaulle's speech of 31 May 1960, see EQ (O) 60, 10 June 1960, CAB134/1824. De Gaulle's new position was specifically referred to in the answers to Macmillan's list of questions, C (60) 107, 6 July 1960, CAB129/102.
72 C (60) 107, 6 July 1960, CAB129/102.
73 C (60) 107, 6 July 1960, CAB129/102.
74 Steel to FO, 7 July 1960, FO371/150168.

75 41st Cabinet meeting, 13 July 1960, CAB128/34.
76 See Hoyer-Millar to Ormsby-Gore and Gore-Booth, 5 July 1960, FO371/150362.
77 See Gore-Booth's note on his meeting with Harkort, 19 July 1960, FO371/150289, and report by Steel, 5 August 1960, PREM11/3133.
78 See Selwyn Lloyd's memorandum on meeting Herwarth, 19 July 1960, FO371/150288.
79 Steel to FO, 3 August 1960, PREM11/2993.
80 See FO brief for Macmillan's visit to Bonn, 8 August 1960, FO371/150364.
81 Minute by the Head of the FO's European Economic Organisation Department, 18 July 1960, FO371/150363.
82 See, for example, van Scherpenberg to Brentano, 25 March 1960, *AA:BStS* 289. For the evolutionary approach of the Trade Department, see Harkort's report on interministerial discussions, 3 June 1960, *AA*: West I 200/459. For *BMWi* contributions, see the meeting itself, 3 June 1960, B102/12206 (*BMWi*).
83 See memorandum by *BMWi* Sub-Department EA 'Co-ordination of European Trade and Payment Policy', 22 April 1960, B102/12205 (*BMWi*), and Müller-Armack to *AA*, 9 June 1960, B102/12206 (*BMWi*).
84 See report by Herwarth, 7 April 1960, *AA*: West II 300/104, and Etzel to Brentano, 25 April 1960, *AA:MB* 50.
85 See memorandum by Hünke, 18 May 1960, and interministerial debate, 31 May 1960, both B102/12206 (*BMWi*).
86 The *AA* successfully prevented Erhard from giving an interview to ITV: see *AA* to German embassy, London, 22 April 1960, *AA*: West I 200/489. An attempt to prevent Erhard from meeting the Dutch Foreign Minister was unsuccessful: see van Scherpenberg to Brentano, 7 April 1960, *AA:BStS* 289, and Harkort's report on the meeting, 14 April 1960, *AA:MB* 50.
87 See van Scherpenberg to Brentano, 25 April 1960, *AA:BStS* 289.
88 See German embassy, London, to *AA*, 27 April 1960, *AA*: West I 200/349.
89 See Adenauer to Brentano, 25 April 1960, NL239/158.
90 See K. Adenauer, *Erinnerungen, 1959–1963* (DVA: Stuttgart, 1968), pp. 48–51.
91 Adenauer, *Erinnerungen, 1959–1963*, p. 51.
92 See Adenauer to Brentano, 7 June 1960, *AA:MB* 50.
93 For the impact of Debré's statement, see Adenauer, *Erinnerungen, 1959–1963*, p. 59, and Seydoux, *Beiderseits des Rheins*, pp. 243–5.
94 See Adenauer, *Erinnerungen, 1959–1963*, pp. 56–8. Further on the crisis in Franco-German relations, see Couve de Murville, *Außenpolitik 1958–69*, pp. 200–4 and 297–9.
95 For Adenauer's account of the meeting, see Adenauer, *Erinnerungen, 1959–1963*, pp. 59–67.
96 The explanation offered by the press for Adenauer's disenchantment with Hallstein was the latter's ambition to succeed Adenauer as Chancellor: see *The Economist Foreign Report*, late 1960, sent by US embassy, Bonn, to Meyer-Cording, 16 January 1961, B102/12128 (*BMWi*). See above, p. 112, note 62.

97 See, for example, Blankenhorn's note, 5 August 1960, NL351/103.
98 See Brentano to van Scherpenberg, 1 August 1960, *AA:MB* 52. See also Berthold Martin (CDU member of *Bundestag*) to Brentano, 10 August 1960, *AA:MB* 144, and Blankenhorn's note about meeting between Adenauer, Spaak (now General-Secretary of NATO) and General Lauris Norstadt (Commander of Allied Forces in Europe), 9 September 1960, NL351/103.
99 Note by Blankenhorn, 24 September 1960, NL351/103.
100 See Adenauer to de Gaulle, 15 August 1960, drafted by *AA* and informing the French about forthcoming Anglo-German consultations, NL351/103.
101 See records of conversation between Adenauer and Macmillan and between Brentano and Selwyn Lloyd, both 10 August 1960, PREM11/2993.
102 Record of conversation between Adenauer and Macmillan, 10 August 1960, PREM11/2993.
103 See Harkort to Carstens, about a conversation with Majoribanks, 6 August 1960, *AA*: West I 200/486.
104 See van Scherpenberg's comments in record of conversation between Brentano, Lord Home and their officials, 10 August 1960, PREM11/2993.
105 See Brentano to Adenauer, urging an early meeting with the French President, 28 October 1960, NL239/158.
106 See Adenauer, *Erinnerungen, 1959–1963*, pp. 70–6.
107 Record of Macmillan's visit to Bonn, 11 August 1960, PREM11/2993.
108 See Müller-Roschach to Carstens, 21 September 1960, *AA*: West I 200/489.
109 Herwarth to *AA*, 6 August 1960, *AA*: West II 304/182.
110 See, for example, German embassy, Berne, to *AA*, about Heath's speech to EFTA conference, 12 October 1960, *AA:BStS* 296, and Herwarth to *AA*, 10 November 1960, *AA:BStS* 293. See also meeting between van Scherpenberg and Pietro Quaroni (Italian Ambassador to Bonn), 28 November 1960, *AA:MB* 157.
111 See, for example, note by Meyer-Cording about meeting Majoribanks in advance of the Macmillan visit, 4 August 1960, B102/12127 *(BMWi)*.
112 See Hünke's brief for Erhard's meeting with Maudling, 5 September 1960, and his report on first Anglo-German expert meeting, 3 November 1960, both B102/12127 *(BMWi)*.
113 See Müller-Armack's 'Plan for the Creation of a Customs Union', 5 December 1960, B102/12127 *(BMWi)*. For a summary and British appreciation, see EQ (O) (61) 11, 30 January 1961, CAB134/1828.
114 For one such attempt, see Erhard to Adenauer, 28 November 1960, B102/12127 *(BMWi)*.
115 See memorandum by van Scherpenberg about his talks with Wormser, 16 December 1960, *AA:BStS* 296, and Hünke's note on Franco-German talks, 27 January 1961, B102/12128 *(BMWi)*.
116 See *FAZ*, 3 January 1961, and Erhard to Brentano, 10 January 1961, B102/12128 *(BMWi)*.
117 See Gladwyn Jebb to Macmillan, 1 September 1960, and Heath to Lord Home, 4 October 1960 (both PREM11/3131).

118 See Maudling to Macmillan, reporting on his meeting with Erhard, 12 September 1960, PREM11/2966, Macmillan to Selwyn Lloyd, 14 September 1960, PREM11/2993, as well as Deputy Under-Secretary Sir Roderick Barclay (now FO Adviser on European Trade Questions) to Steel, 16 August 1960, and Majoribanks to Barclay, 19 August 1960 (both FO371/150291). See also reports by Barclay and Steel on first Anglo-German meeting, 3 November 1960 and 4 November 1960 (both FO371/150367).

119 See 13th meeting of Economic Steering (Europe) Committee, 25 August 1960, CAB134/1852, discussing papers 18 and 19 'The Long-term Objective: Next Steps after Bonn', 23 August 1960 and 25 August 1960 (both CAB134/1853).

120 Jackling to Lord Home, 28 August 1960, FO371/150364.

121 For a summary of the attitudes of the Six, see memorandum by Josef Jansen (new Head of Department 'West I' after Carstens had been promoted to State Secretary), 26 January 1961, AA: West I 200/486.

122 The French had rejected trilateral talks: see Steel to FO, 22 December 1960, PREM11/3553. See also Steel and Majoribanks reporting on Franco-German talks, 1 February 1961 and 2 March 1961, FO371/158171 and FO371/158264 respectively. See also record of conversation between Sir Frank Lee and Wormser, 28 February 1961, FO371/158172, and FO record of Anglo-French talks, 4 March 1961, CAB134/1829. For an overall assessment of progress in separate British talks with German, French and Italian experts, see Treasury paper ES (E) (61) 1, 7 March 1961, discussed in 1st meeting of Economic Steering (Europe) Committee, chaired by Lee, 9 March 1961, CAB134/1854.

123 See Norman Brook (Cabinet Secretary, Joint Permanent Secretary to Treasury and Head of Home Civil Service) to Macmillan, enclosing the memorandum, 7 February 1961, PREM11/3553.

124 See de Zulueta to Macmillan, 6 February 1961, PREM11/3553.

125 See Jansen's report on the meeting, 15 February 1961, AA:MB 50.

126 See first Steel's report on Adenauer's continued mistrust of de Gaulle, 26 January 1961, FO371/158170. Later, Lord Home to Steel, about his meeting with Herwarth, noting Adenauer/de Gaulle agreement, 22 February 1961, PREM11/3345.

127 Officials had asked for this earlier: see 2nd meeting chaired by Chancellor Selwyn Lloyd, granting the request, EQ (61) 3, 14 March 1961, CAB134/1821.

128 See record of EQ (O) Committee's 3rd meeting, 7 February 1961, CAB134/1828.

129 Record of conversation between Macmillan and de Gaulle, 28 January 1961, PREM11/3322.

130 Sir Frank Lee's record of his conversation with Wormser, 28 February 1961, FO371/158172.

131 Heath to Macmillan, 7 February 1961, PREM11/3553.

132 See Heath to Macmillan, 7 February 1961, PREM11/3553, and record of the Chequers meeting, 14 February 1961, FO371/158172.

133 Macmillan's minute, 7 February 1961, on a note from de Zulueta, 6 February 1961, PREM11/3553.

222 Notes

134 For the exclusion of Maudling, see de Zulueta to Macmillan, 6 February 1961, Cabinet Office to Norman Brook, 13 February 1961, both PREM11/3553.
135 For the text of Heath's speech to the WEU, see Cabinet paper C (61) 29, 3 March 1961, CAB129/104. See also memorandum by Selwyn Lloyd on meeting Erhard, 27 March 1961, PREM11/3361, and record of Macmillan's meetings with de Gaulle, 28/29 January 1961, PREM11/3322, and with Adenauer, 22 February 1961, PREM11/3345.
136 Heath had to justify his speech to Cabinet: see record of 10th meeting, 28 February 1961, CAB128/35. Strong criticism was voiced in the ministerial EQ Committee which decided that public pronouncements had to be co-ordinated: see 1st meeting, 2 March 1961, CAB134/1821.
137 See, for example, Erhard's articles in the *Handelsblatt*, 23/24 December 1960 and 17 January 1961.
138 See Brentano to Erhard, 7 March 1961, and Erhard's reply, 11 March 1961, as well as Brentano to Erhard, 23 March 1961 (all *AA:MB* 67).
139 See memorandum by Department 2, 14 March 1961, AA: West I 200/486. See also van Scherpenberg to Brentano, 25 March 1961, *AA:BStS* 293.
140 It was agreed to try to evade the issue whenever asked: see memorandum by Jansen, 26 January 1961, AA: West I 200/486, as well as Carstens's report on meeting Steel, 28 March 1961, *AA:BStS* 293.
141 See Brentano's comments during the meeting, 22 February 1961, PREM11/3345.
142 Note by Macmillan, marked top secret, 6 April 1961, PREM11/3554. See also talks between Heath, Lee and US representatives, 6 April 1961, PREM11/3554.
143 EQ (61) 4, 26 April 1961, CAB134/1821.
144 22nd meeting of Cabinet, 20 April 1961, CAB128/35.
145 EQ (61) 4, 26 April 1961, CAB134/1821.
146 As recorded in Department 2 memorandum, 18 May 1961, AA: West I 200/486.
147 Adenauer's statement, 21 April 1961, B102/12129 (*BMWi*).
148 See Department 2 memorandum, 18 May 1961, AA: West I 200/486.
149 Brentano to Adenauer, 23 May 1961, *AA:MB* 50 (emphasis in original). See also van Scherpenberg to Brentano, 6 June 1961, *AA:BStS* 289.
150 See summary protocol of the Comité Spécial meeting, 15 May 1961, B102/12130 (*BMWi*).
151 See Meyer-Cording to Müller-Armack about meeting US representatives, 9 May 1961, B102/12130 (*BMWi*).
152 Quoted in report by the German embassy, Stockholm, 9 May 1961, B102/12130 (*BMWi*).
153 See summary protocol of the Comité Spécial meeting, 15 May 1961, B102/12130 (*BMWi*).
154 See Steel to FO, 17 May 1961, PREM11/3555, and Lord Home to Steel, 21 April 1961, PREM11/3554.
155 3rd meeting of the (Ministerial) European Economic Questions Committee, 9 May 1961, CAB134/1821.

156 See 29th and 35th meeting of Cabinet, 30 May 1961 and 22 June 1961, both CAB128/35.
157 See 42nd meeting of Cabinet, 21 July 1961, CAB128/35. The reports themselves are contained in CAB129/105 and CAB129/106.
158 See Watkinson to Prime Minister, 24 April 1961, and Eccles to Prime Minister, 24 April 1961. See also Macmillan's replies, both dated 25 April 1961. All PREM11/3554.
159 44th meeting of Cabinet, 27 July 1961, CAB128/35. For Maudling's efforts, see record of his meeting with Macmillan, 16 May 1961, PREM11/3555, and Maudling to FO, 15 June 1961, FO371/158177.
160 See summary of ambassadorial responses, EQ (61) 20, 9 July 1961, CAB134/1821. The reluctance of the French to contemplate special treatment for Britain had been made abundantly clear in an earlier French note: see Maudling's commentary thereon, 15 June 1961. See also report by HM embassy, Paris, 6 June 1961. Both FO371/158377.
161 See Steel to FO, 5 May 1961, PREM11/3556.
162 De Zulueta to Macmillan, 16 June 1961. For his recommendations regarding the French government, see his note to Macmillan, 18 June 1961. Both marked 'top secret', PREM11/3557.

Conclusion: Intersection or Periphery?

1 On the difficulties, Britain faced with regard to the Blue Streak and Skybolt missile systems, see I. Clark, *Nuclear Diplomacy and the Special Relationship: Britain's Deterrent and America, 1957–1962* (Clarendon Press: Oxford, 1994).
2 According to one estimate, the average annual rate of growth of real GDP in the EEC was more than twice as high as in the United Kingdom in the 1950s – no causal link with integration implied. See Sir Alec Cairncross, 'The Postwar Years 1945–77', in: R. Floud and D. McCloskey (eds), *The Economic History of Britain since 1700*, Vol. 2 (Cambridge University Press: Cambridge, 1981), pp. 370–416 (table 16.1).
3 Moderate positive discrimination and reductions in transaction costs did, however, accord competitive advantages to the members of the customs union. Yet, given that the outer tariff was to be on average below national tariffs charged previously, these circumstances could only be used as an argument for joining, not as a justification for retaliation.
4 Exemplary applications of the notion of 'cognitive dissonance' to political history are contained in B. W. Tuchman, *The March of Folly: From Troy to Vietnam* (Joseph: London, 1984).
5 For an authoritative critique of determinism stipulating this requirement, compare Sir Isaiah Berlin, 'The Concept of Scientific History', in: W. Dray (ed.), *Philosophical Analysis and History* (Harper & Row: New York, 1966), pp. 5–53, particularly 49.
6 Though in view of the Trend report of autumn 1955 (see Chapter 1, footnote 73), this alternative at least formally fulfills Niall Ferguson's 'key methodological constraint . . . that counterfactuals should be those which contemporaries contemplated'. See Ferguson, *Virtual History*, 87.

7 Though Britain would have had to accept some minimum discrimination in order to make the outer tariff and hence the customs union a meaningful concept.
8 Seven years later, France's dependency on the Common Market had increased, so as to significantly reduce the credibility of any threat to leave the Community. See N. P. Ludlow, 'Challenging French Leadership in Europe: Germany, Italy, the Netherlands and the Outbreak of the Empty Chair Crisis of 1965–1966', in: *Contemporary European History* 8, 2 (1999), pp. 231–48, who interprets this episode not merely as a constitutional exigency, but as a deliberate – and ultimately successful – attempt of the German government to challenge French dominance on the issue of agricultural policy and associated budget contributions.
9 See Ludlow, *Dealing with Britain*, pp. 174–9, on the importance of Adenauer's mistrust in preventing a determined German effort to secure British membership in these negotiations.

Bibliography

Archival Sources

Public Record Office/London
BoT (Board of Trade papers)
CAB (Cabinet papers)
FO (Foreign Office papers)
PREM (papers of the Prime Minister's Office)
T (Treasury papers)

Bundesarchiv/Koblenz
B 102 (*Bundesministerium für Wirtschaft*)
B 126 (*Bundesministerium der Finanzen*)
B 136 (*Bundeskanzleramt*)
B 146 (*Bundesministerium für wirtschaftliche Zusammenarbeit*)
NL 239 (private papers of Heinrich von Brentano)
NL 351 (private papers of Herbert Blankenhorn)

Politisches Archiv des Auswärtiges Amt/Bonn
BStS (*Büro Staatssekretär*)
LA (*Länderabteilung*)
PA (*Politische Abteilung*)
MB (*Ministerbüro*)
Sub-Department 200 (of West I)
Sub-Department 304 (of West II)
Sub-Department 410 (of *Handelspolitische Abteilung*)

Stiftung Bundeskanzler-Adenauer-Haus/Rhöndorf
10.36–10.41 (private correspondence)
III 23 (private correspondence)

Printed Sources

Newspapers
The Economist, Financial Times, Frankfurter Allgemeine Zeitung, Handelsblatt, Manchester Guardian, The Times

Government publications
Auswärtiges Amt (ed.), *Die Auswärtige Politik der Bundesrepublik Deutschland* (Verlag Wissenschaft und Politik: Köln, 1972)
Bundesarchiv (ed.), *Aufbruch zur Gemeinschaft, der Deutsche Beitrag zur europäischen Einigung* (Ausstellungskatalog) (Bundesarchiv: Koblenz, 1992)

226 Bibliography

Bundesarchiv (ed.), *Die Kabinettsprotokolle der Bundesregierung*, Vol. 8, 1955 (R. Oldenbourg: München, 1997)
Bundesarchiv (ed.), *Die Kabinettsprotokolle der Bundesregierung*, Vol. 9, 1956 (Oldenbourg: München, 1998)
Bulletin des Presse- und Informationsamtes der Bundesregierung (Bonn, 1955–61)
Bulletin of the Press- and Information Office of the Federal Government, English Version (Bonn, 1955–61)
Deutscher Bundestag (ed.), *Verhandlungen des Deutschen Bundestages*, Drucksache (Bonn, 1955–61)
A European Free Trade Area: United Kingdom Memorandum to the Organisation for European Economic Co-operation, Cmnd. 72 (HMSO: London, 1957)
Hansard Parliamentary Debates, 5th Series, House of Commons, Vols 542–645, 1955–61
Ministère des Affaires Étrangères (ed.), *Documents Diplomatiques Français*, Vols 1955–60 (Imprimerie Nationale: Paris, 1987–96)
Negotiations for a European Free Trade Area: Documents Relating to the Negotiations from July, 1956, to December, 1958, Cmnd. 641 (HMSO: London, 1959)
Negotiations for a European Free Trade Area: Report on the Course of the Negotiations, Cmnd. 648 (HMSO: London, 1959)
Stockholm Draft Plan for a European Free Trade Association, Cmnd. 823 (HMSO: London, 1959)
Treaties Establishing the European Communities (Office for Official Publications of the European Communities: Luxembourg, 1973)
Treaty on European Union, Cm 1934 (HMSO: London, 1992)
The United Kingdom and the European Economic Community, Cmnd. 1565 (HMSO: London, 1961)

Books

Adenauer, K., *Erinnerungen, 1953–1955* (DVA: Stuttgart, 1966)
Adenauer, K., *Erinnerungen, 1955–1959* (DVA: Stuttgart, 1967)
Adenauer, K., *Erinnerungen, 1959–1963* (DVA: Stuttgart, 1968)
Adenauer, K., *Teegespräche 1955–1958*, Rhöndorfer Ausgabe (Siedler: Berlin, 1986)
Adenauer, K., *'Die Demokratie ist für uns eine Weltanschauung': Reden und Gespräche 1946–1967* (Böhlau: Köln, 1998)
Adenauer, K. and Th. Heuss, *Unter vier Augen: Gespräche aus den Gründerjahren 1949–1959* (Siedler: München, 1997)
Aldous, R. and S. Lee (eds), *Harold Macmillan and Britain's World Role* (Macmillan: London, 1996)
Alford, B. W. E., *British Economic Performance* (Macmillan: London, 1988)
Axelrod, R., *The Evolution of Cooperation* (Basic Books: New York, 1984)
Ball, G., *The Past Has Another Pattern* (Norton: New York, 1982)
Baring, A., *Außenpolitik in Adenauers Kanzlerdemokratie: Bonns Beitrag zur europäischen Verteidigungsgemeinschaft* (Oldenbourg: München, 1969)
Baring, A., *Sehr verehrter Herr Bundeskanzler! Heinrich von Brentano im Briefwechsel mit Konrad Adenauer 1949–1964* (Hoffmann und Campe: Hamburg, 1974)
Barker, E., *Britain in a Divided Europe* (Weidenfeld & Nicholson: London, 1971)

Bibliography   227

Barnett, C., *The Audit of War* (Macmillan: London, 1986)
Becker, J. and F. Knipping (eds), *Power in Europe? Great Britain, France, Italy and Germany in a Post-War World, 1945–1950* (Walter de Gruyter: Berlin, 1986)
Beloff, M., *New Dimensions in Foreign Policy: a Study in British Administrative Experience, 1947–1959* (Allen & Unwin: London, 1961)
Beloff, M., *The United States and the Unity of Europe* (Brookings Institution: Washington, D.C., 1963)
Beloff, N., *The General Says No: Britain's Exclusion from Europe* (Penguin: London, 1963)
Benoit, E., *Europe at Sixes and Sevens: The Common Market, the Free Trade Association and the United States* (Columbia University Press: New York, 1961)
Birke, A. M. and K. Kluxen (eds), *Die europäische Herausforderung: England und Deutschland in Europa* (Saur: München, 1987)
Birrenbach, K., *Meine Sondermission: Rückblick auf zwei Jahrzehnte bundesdeutscher Außenpolitik* (ECON: Düsseldorf, 1984)
Blankenhorn, H., *Verständnis und Verständigung. Blätter eines politischen Tagebuches* (Propyläen: Frankfurt, 1980)
Blumenwitz, D., K. Gotto, H. Maier, K. Repgen and H.-P. Schwarz (eds), *Konrad Adenauer und seine Zeit: Politik und Persönlichkeit des ersten Bundeskanzlers*, Vol. 1: *Beiträge von Weg- und Zeitgenossen* (DVA: Stuttgart, 1976)
Bray, C. and R. Morgan (eds), *Partners and Rivals in Western Europe: Britain, France and Germany* (Gower: Aldershot, Hants, 1986)
Brentano, H. von, *Deutschland, Europa und die Welt, Reden zur Deutschen Aussenpolitik* (Siegler: Bonn, 1962)
Brivati, B. and H. Jones (eds), *From Reconstruction to Integration: Britain and Europe since 1945* (Leicester University Press: Leicester, 1993)
Bull, H., *The Anarchical Society: a Study of Order in World Politics* (Macmillan: London, 1977)
Bulmer, S. and W. E. Paterson, *The Federal Republic of Germany and the European Community* (Allen & Unwin: London, 1987)
Cairncross, Sir Alec, *Years of Recovery: British Economic Policy 1945–51* (Methuen: London, 1985)
Calvocoressi, P., *World Politics since 1945*, 6th edn (Longman: London, 1991)
Camps, M., *Britain and the European Community, 1955–1963* (Oxford University Press: London, 1964)
Camps, M., *The Free Trade Area Negotiations*, Occasional Papers Vol. 2 (Political and Economic Planning: London, 1959)
Carlton, D., *Britain and the Suez Crisis* (Blackwell: Oxford, 1988)
Carr, E. H., *What Is History?* (Penguin: London, 1961)
Cerny, Ph., *The Politics of Grandeur: Ideological Aspects of De Gaulle's Foreign Policy* (Cambridge University Press: Cambridge, 1980)
Charlton, M., *The Price of Victory* (BBC: London, 1983)
Clark, I., *Nuclear Diplomacy and the Special Relationship: Britain's Deterrent and America, 1957–1962* (Clarendon Press: Oxford, 1994).
Couve de Murville, M., *Außenpolitik 1958–69* (Weltforum: München, 1973)
Deighton, A. (ed.), *Building Postwar Europe: National Decision-Makers and European Institutions, 1948–1963* (Macmillan: London, 1995)

Dell, E., *The Schuman Plan and the British Abdication of Leadership in Europe* (Oxford University Press: Oxford, 1995)
Denman, R., *Missed Chances: Britain and Europe in the Twentieth Century* (Cassell: London, 1996)
Deutsch, K. W., *The Analysis of International Relations* (Prentice-Hall: Eaglewood Cliffs, New Jersey, 1968)
Di Nolfo, E. (ed.), *Power in Europe?* Vol. 2: *Great Britain, France, Germany and Italy and the Origins of the EEC 1952–1957* (Walter de Gruyter: Berlin, 1992)
Dockrill, S., *Britain's Policy for West German Rearmament, 1950–55* (Cambridge University Press: Cambridge, 1991)
Dougherty, J. E. and R. L. Pfaltzgraff, Jr, *Contending Theories of International Relations: a Comprehensive Survey*, 3rd edn (Harper Collins: New York, 1990)
Eckardt, F. von, *Ein unordentliches Leben* (ECON: Düsseldorf, 1987)
Eden, A., *Full Circle* (Cassell: London, 1960)
Ellwood, D. W., *Rebuilding Europe: Western Europe, America and Postwar Reconstruction* (Longman: London, 1992)
Erhard, L., *Gedanken aus fünf Jahrzehnten, Reden und Schriften*, edited by Karl Hohmann (ECON: Düsseldorf, 1988)
Etzel, F., *Finanzpolitik, Außenwirtschaft und Integration* (Bundesministerium der Finanzen: Bonn, 1960)
Evans, D., *While Britain Slept: the Selling of the Common Market* (Gollancz: London, 1975)
Ferguson, N. (ed.), *Virtual History: Alternatives and Counterfactuals* (Picador: London, 1997)
Fulbrook, M., *Germany 1918–1990: the Divided Nation* (Fontana Press: London, 1991)
Fursdon, E., *The European Defence Community: a History* (Macmillan: London, 1980)
Gasteyger, C., *Europa von der Spaltung zur Einigung* (Europa Union Verlag: Bonn, 1997)
Gaulle, C. de, *Memoiren der Hoffnung: die Wiedergeburt 1958–1962* (Molden: Wien, 1971) pp. 231–3
George, S., *Britain and European Integration since 1945* (Blackwell: Oxford, 1991)
Gilligham, J. (ed.), *Coal, Steel and the Rebirth of Europe, 1945–1955* (Cambridge University Press: Cambridge, 1991)
Gilpin, R., *The Political Economy of International Relations* (Princeton University Press: Princeton, New Jersey, 1987)
Gladwyn, Lord, *De Gaulle's Europe: or, Why the General Says No* (Secker & Warburg: London, 1969)
Gladwyn, Lord, *The European Idea* (Weidenfeld & Nicholson: London, 1966)
Gladwyn, Lord, *The Memoirs of Lord Gladwyn* (Weidenfeld & Nicholson: London, 1972)
Gore-Booth, P., *With Great Truth and Respect* (Constable: London, 1974)
Greenaway, J., S. Smith and J. Street, *Deciding Factors in British Politics: a Case-studies Approach* (Routledge: London, 1992)
Greenwood, S., *Britain and European Cooperation since 1945* (Blackwell: Oxford, 1992)

Grewe, W. G., *Deutsche Aussenpolitik der Nachkriegszeit* (DVA: Stuttgart, 1960)
Grieco, J. M., *Cooperation among Nations: Europe, America, and Non-Tariff Barriers to Trade* (Cornell University Press: Ithaca and London, 1990)
Griffiths, R. T. (ed.), *The Netherlands and the Integration of Europe, 1945– 1957* (NEHA: Amsterdam, 1990)
Griffiths, R. T. and A. S. Milward, *The Beyen Plan and the European Political Community* (European University Institute working papers no. 85/199: Florence, 1985)
Griffiths, R. T. and S. Ward (eds), *Courting the Common Market: the First Attempt to Enlarge the European Community* (Lothian Foundation: London, 1996)
Groeben, H. von der, *The European Community – the Formative Years: the Struggle to Establish the Common Market and the Political Union (1958–66)* (Office for Official Publications of the European Communities: Luxembourg, 1986)
Grosser, A., *Die Bonner Demokratie: Deutschland von draußen gesehen* (Rauch: Düsseldorf, 1960)
Haas, E., *The Obsolence of Regional Integration Theory* (Center for International Studies: Berkeley, CA, 1975)
Haas, E., *The Uniting of Europe: Political, Social and Economic Forces* (Stevens: London, 1958)
Hallstein, W., *Die europäische Gemeinschaft* (ECON: Düsseldorf, 1975)
Hallstein, W., *Europe in the Making* (Norton: New York, 1973)
Halperin, M. H., *Bureaucratic Politics and Foreign Policy* (The Brookings Institution: Washington, D.C., 1974)
Hanrieder, W. F., *Deutschland, Europa, Amerika: die Aussenpolitik der Bundesrepublik Deutschland 1949–1989* (Schöningh: Paderborn, 1991)
Hanrieder, W. F., *West-German Foreign Policy, 1949–1963: International Pressure and Domestic Response* (Stanford University Press: Stanford, 1967)
Heater, D., *The Idea of European Unity* (Leicester University Press: Leicester, 1992)
Hennis, W., *Richtlinienkompetenz und Regierungstechnik* (Mohr: Tübingen, 1964)
Hentschel, V., *Ludwig Erhard: ein Politikerleben* (Olzog: München, 1996)
Herwarth von Bitterfeld, H.-H., *Von Adenauer zu Brandt: Erinnerungen* (Propyläen: Berlin, 1990)
Holsti, K. J., *International Politics: a Framework for Analysis*, 6th edn (Prentice-Hall: Eaglewood Cliffs, New Jersey, 1992)
Horne, A., *Macmillan*, Vol. 1 (Macmillan: London, 1988)
Horne, A., *Macmillan*, Vol. 2 (Macmillan: London, 1989)
Huth, S., 'British-German Relations between 1955 and 1961' (Ph.D. thesis, Cambridge University, 1992)
Iklé, F. C., *How Nations Negotiate* (Harper and Row: New York, 1964)
Jahn, H. E., *An Adenauers Seite: sein Berater erinnert sich* (Langen Müller: München, 1987)
Jansen, J., *Britische Konservative und Europa: Debattenaussagen im Unterhaus zur westeuropäischen Integration, 1945–1972* (Nomos: Baden-Baden, 1978)
Jensen, W., *The Common Market* (G. T. Foulis & Co.: London, 1967)
Kaiser, K., *EWG und Freihandelszone: England und der Kontinent in der europäischen Integration* (Sythoff: Leiden, 1963)

Kaiser, K. and R. Morgan (eds), *Strukturwandlungen der Außenpolitik in Großbritannien und der Bundesrepublik* (Oldenbourg: München, 1970)
Kaiser, K. and J. Roper (eds), *Die stille Allianz: Deutsch-britische Sicherheitskooperation* (Europa Union Verlag: Bonn, 1987)
Kaiser, W., *Grossbritannien und die europäische Wirtschaftsgemeinschaft, 1955–1961* (Akademie: Berlin, 1996)
Kaiser, W., *Using Europe, Abusing the Europeans: Britain and European Integration, 1945–1963* (Macmillan: London, 1996)
Kitzinger, U., *The Challenge of the Common Market*, 4th edn (Blackwell: Oxford, 1962)
Kitzinger, U., *The Politics and Economics of European Integration: Britain, Europe and the United States*, 2nd edn (Frederick A. Praeger: New York, 1963)
Knapp, W., *Unity and Nationalism in Europe since 1945* (Pergamon Press: Oxford, 1969)
Koerfer, D., *Kampf ums Kanzleramt: Erhard und Adenauer* (DVA: Stuttgart, 1987)
Köllner, L. et al. (eds), *Anfänge westdeutscher Sicherheitspolitik, 1945–1956*, Vol. 2 (Oldenbourg: München, 1990).
Kosthorst, D., *Brentano und die deutsche Einheit: die Deutschland- und Ostpolitik des Aussenministers im Kabinett Adenauer 1955–1961* (Droste: Düsseldorf, 1993)
Krone, H., *Tagebücher*, Band 1: *1945–1961* (Droste: Düsseldorf, 1995)
Küsters, H. J., *Die Gründung der europäischen Wirtschaftsgemeinschaft* (Nomos: Baden-Baden, 1982)
Lamb, R., *The Failure of the Eden Government* (Sidgwick and Jackson: London, 1987)
Lamb, R., *The Macmillan Years, 1957–1963: the Emerging Truth* (John Murray: London, 1995)
Lee, S., *An Uneasy Partnership: British–German Relations between 1955 and 1961* (Brockmeyer: Bochum, 1996).
Lieber, R., *British Politics and European Unity* (University of California Press: Berkeley, 1970)
Lindberg, L. N., *The Political Dynamics of European Economic Integration* (Stanford University Press: Stanford, 1963)
Lipgens, W., *Europa-Föderationspläne der Widerstandsbewegung, 1940–1945* (Oldenbourg: München, 1968)
Lipgens, W., *A History of European Integration, 1945–1947*, Vol. 1: *The Formation of the European Unity Movement* (Clarendon Press: Oxford, 1982)
Little, R. and S. Smith (eds), *Belief Systems & International Relations* (Blackwell: Oxford, 1988)
Loth, W. (ed.), *Die Anfänge der europäischen Integration 1945–50* (Europa Union Verlag: Bonn, 1990)
Loth, W., *Der Weg nach Europa: Geschichte der europäischen Integration 1939–1957*, 2nd edn (Vandenhoeck & Ruprecht: Göttingen, 1991)
Loth, W. and R. Picht *De Gaulle, Deutschland und Europa* (Leske & Budrich: Opladen, 1991)
Ludlow, N. P., *Dealing with Britain: the Six and the First UK Application to the EEC* (Cambridge University Press: Cambridge, 1997)
Macmillan, H., *At the End of the Day, 1961–1963* (Macmillan: London, 1973)

Macmillan, H., *Pointing the Way, 1959–1961* (Macmillan: London, 1972)
Macmillan, H., *Riding the Storm, 1956–1959* (Macmillan: London, 1971)
Macmillan, H., *Tides of Fortune, 1945–1961* (Macmillan: London, 1969)
Milward, A. S., *The European Rescue of the Nation State* (Routledge: London, 1992)
Milward, A. S., *The Reconstruction of Western Europe 1945–51* (Methuen: London, 1984)
Milward, A. S. and G. Brennan, *Britain's Place in the World: a Historical Enquiry into Import Controls, 1945–60* (Routledge: London, 1996)
Moon, J., *European Integration in British Politics, 1950–63: a Study of Issue Change* (Gower: Aldershot, Hants., 1985)
Moravesik, A., *National Preference Formation and Interstate Bargaining in the European Community, 1955–86* (Harvard University Press: Cambridge, MA, 1992)
Morgan, R., *Britain and Germany since 1945: Two Societies and Two Foreign Policies* (German Historical Institute: London, 1989)
Morgan, R., *West European Politics since 1945: the Shaping of the European Community* (Batsford: London, 1972)
Müller-Armack, A., *Auf dem Weg nach Europa: Erinnerungen und Ausblicke* (Wunderlich/Poeschel: Tübingen/Stuttgart, 1971)
Müller-Roschach, H., *Die deutsche Europapolitik, 1949–1977* (Europa Union Verlag: Bonn, 1980)
Newhouse, J., *De Gaulle and the Anglo-Saxons* (André Deutsch: London, 1970)
Northedge, F. S., *Descent from Power: British Foreign Policy, 1945–73* (Allen & Unwin: London, 1974)
Nutting, A., *Europe Will Not Wait: a Warning and a Way Out* (Hollis & Carter: London, 1960)
Pfaltzgraff, R. L. Jr, *Britain Faces Europe* (University of Pennsylvania Press: Philadelphia, 1969)
Pinder, J., *Britain and the Common Market* (Cresset Press: London, 1961)
Poppinga, A., *Meine Erinnerungen an Konrad Adenauer* (Lübbe: Bergisch Gladbach, 1986)
Pryce, R. (ed.), *The Dynamics of European Union* (Routledge: London, 1989)
Sanders, D., *Losing an Empire, Finding a Role: British Foreign Policy since 1945* (Macmillan: London, 1990)
Schmid, C., *Erinnerungen* (Scherz: Bern, 1979)
Schwabe, K. (ed.), *Die Anfänge des Schuman-Plan 1950/1* (Nomos: Baden-Baden, 1988)
Schwarz, H.-P., *Adenauer: der Aufstieg: 1876–1952*, 3rd edn (DVA: Stuttgart, 1991)
Schwarz, H.-P., *Adenauer: der Staatsmann: 1952–1967* (DVA: Stuttgart, 1991)
Schwarz, H.-P. (ed.), *Adenauer: Reden 1917–1967. Eine Auswahl* (DVA: Stuttgart, 1975)
Schwarz, H.-P. (ed.), *Adenauer und Frankreich: die deutsch-französische Beziehungen 1958–1969* (Bouvier: Bonn, 1985)
Schwarz, H.-P., *Erbfreundschaft: Adenauer und Frankreich = Amité héréditaire* (Bouvier: Bonn, 1992)
Seydoux, F., *Beiderseits des Rheins* (Societäts-Verlag: Frankfurt, 1975)
Shlaim, A., P. Jones and K. Sainsbury, *British Foreign Secretaries since 1945* (David and Charles: Newton Abbot, 1977)

Silitoe, A., *Britain in Figures: a Handbook of Social Statistics*, 2nd edn (Penguin Books: Harmondsworth, 1973)
Snyder, R. C., H. W. Bruck and S. Burton (eds), *Foreign Policy Decision-Making: an Approach to the Study of International Politics* (The Free Press of Glen Coe: London, 1962)
Steinbruner, J., *The Cybernetic Theory of Decision: New Dimensions of Political Analysis* (Princeton University Press: Princeton, New Jersey, 1974)
Strauß, F. J., *Die Erinnerungen* (Siedler: Berlin, 1989)
Swann, D., *The Economics of the Common Market* (Penguin: Harmondsworth, 1970)
Tuchman, B. W., *The March of Folly: From Troy to Vietnam* (Joseph: London, 1984)
Urwin, D. W., *The Community of Europe: a History of European Integration since 1945* (Longman: London, 1991)
Urwin, D. W., *Western Europe since 1945: a Political History* (Longman: London, 1968)
Varsori, A. (ed.), *Europe 1945–1990s: the End of an Era?* (Macmillan: London, 1995)
Vaughan, R. (ed.), *Post-War Integration in Europe* (documents) (Arnold: London, 1976)
Volle, A., *Großbritannien und der europäische Einigungsprozeß*, Arbeitspapiere zur Internationalen Politik, Vol. 51 (Forschungsinstitut der Deutschen Gesellschaft für Auswärtige Politik e. V. [Vertrieb Europa Union Verlag]: Bonn, 1989)
Wallace, W. (ed.), *The Dynamics of European Integration* (Royal Institute of International Affairs: London, 1990)
Watt, D. C., *Britain Looks to Germany: British Opinion and Policy towards Germany since 1945* (Oswald Wolff: London, 1965)
Weisenfeld, E., *Charles de Gaulle: der Magier im Elysée* (Beck: München, 1990)
Willis, F. R., *France, Germany and the New Europe, 1945–1967* (Stanford University Press: Stanford, 1968)
Winand, P., *Eisenhower, Kennedy and the United States of Europe* (Macmillan: London, 1993)
Wurm, C. (ed.), *Wege nach Europa: Wirtschaft und Außenpolitik Großbritanniens im 20. Jahrhundert* (Brockmeyer: Bochum, 1992)
Wurm, C. (ed.), *Western Europe and Germany: the Beginnings of European Integration 1945–1960* (Berg: Oxford, 1996)
Young, J. W., *Britain and European Unity, 1945–1992* (Macmillan: London, 1993)
Young, J. W., *Britain, France and the Unity of Europe, 1945–51* (Leicester University Press: Leicester, 1984)
Young, J. W. (ed.), *The Foreign Policy of Churchill's Peacetime Administration, 1951–1955* (Leicester University Press: Leicester, 1988)

Articles

Beloff, M., 'Britain, Europe and the Atlantic Community', in: *International Organisation* 17 (1963), pp. 574–91
Berlin, Sir Isaiah, 'The Concept of Scientific History', in: W. Dray (ed.), *Philosophical Analysis and History* (Harper & Row: New York, 1966), pp. 5–53
Brenke, G., 'Europakonzeptionen im Widerstreit: die Freihandelszonenverhandlungen 1956–1958', in: *Vierteljahreshefte für Zeitgeschichte* 42 (1994), pp. 595–633

Brusse, W. A., 'The Failure of European Tariff Plans in GATT (1951–1954)', in: G. Trausch (ed.), *Die Europäische Integration vom Schumanplan bis zu den Verträgen von Rom* (Nomos: Baden-Baden, 1993), pp. 99–114

Bührer, W., 'Die Montanunion – ein Fehlschlag? Deutsche Lehren aus der EGKS und die Gründung der EWG', in: G. Trausch (ed.), *Die europäische Integration vom Schumanplan bis zu den Verträgen von Rom* (Nomos: Baden-Baden, 1993), pp. 75–90

Bullen, R., 'Britain and "Europe" 1950–1957', in: E. Serra (ed.), *The Relaunching of Europe and the Treaties of Rome* (Bruylant: Brussels, 1989), pp. 315–38

Bullen, R., 'The British Government and the Schuman Plan', in: K. Schwabe (ed.), *Die Anfänge des Schuman-Plans, 1950/1* (Nomos: Baden-Baden, 1988), pp. 199–210

Burgess, S. and G. Edwards, 'The Six Plus One: British Policy-Making and the Question of European Economic Integration, 1955', in: *International Affairs* 64 (3) (1988), pp. 393–413

Cairncross, Sir Alec, 'The Postwar Years 1945–77', in: R. Floud and D. McCloskey (eds), *The Economic History of Britain since 1700*, Vol. 2 (Cambridge University Press: Cambridge, 1981), pp. 370–416

Claude, Inis L. Jr, 'Multilateralism: Diplomatic and Otherwise', in: *International Organisation* 12 (1958), pp. 43–52

Deighton, A., 'Missing the Boat: Britain and Europe 1945–61', in: *Contemporary Record* (February 1990), pp. 15–17

Enders, U., 'Integration oder Kooperation? Ludwig Erhard und Franz Etzel im Streit über die Politik der europäischen Zusammenarbeit', in: *Vierteljahreshefte für Zeitgeschichte* 45 (1997), pp. 143–71

Erhard, L., 'Germany's Economic Goals', in: *Foreign Affairs* 36 (1958), pp. 611–17

Fauri, F., 'Italy and the Free Trade Area Negotiations', in: *Journal of European Integration History* (1998/2), pp. 5–21

Griffiths, R. T., 'A Slow One Hundred and Eighty Degree Turn' (Unpublished paper, European University Institute conference: Florence, 17 February–19 February 1994)

Grosser, A., 'France and Germany in the Atlantic Community', in: *International Organisation* 17 (1963), pp. 550–73

Hallstein, W., 'Zollunion und Freihandelszone', in: *Bulletin der europäischen Wirtschaftsgemeinschaft* 1–59 (1959), pp. 5–12

Herwarth, H. v., 'Anglo-German Relations. I: German View', in: *International Affairs* 39 (4) (1963), pp. 511–20

Hesse, J. J. and K. H. Goetz, 'Early Administrative Adjustment to the European Communities, the Case of the Federal Republic of Germany', in: E. V. Heyen (ed.), *Die Anfänge der Verwaltung der europäischen Gemeinschaft* (Nomos: Baden-Baden, 1992), pp. 181–207

Jervis, R., 'The Costs of Quantitative Study of International Relations', in: K. Knorr and J. N. Rosenau (eds), *Contending Approaches to International Politics* (Princeton University Press: Princeton, New Jersey, 1969), pp. 177–217

Kaiser, W., 'The Bomb and Europe: Britain, France and the EEC Entry Negotiations (1961–1963)', in: *Journal of European Integration History* (1995/1), pp. 65–85.

Kaiser, W., 'Selbstisolierung in Europa – die britische Regierung und die Gründung der EWG', in: C. Wurm (ed.), *Wege nach Europa: Wirtschaft*

234 Bibliography

und Außenpolitik Großbritanniens im 20. Jahrhundert (Brockmeyer: Bochum, 1992), pp. 125-53

Kaiser, W., 'To Join, or Not to Join: the "Appeasement" Policy of Britain's First EEC Application', in: B. Brivati and H. Jones (eds), *From Reconstruction to Integration: Britain and Europe since 1945* (Leicester University Press: Leicester, 1993), pp. 144-165.

Kane, L., 'European or Atlantic Community? The Foreign Office and "Europe": 1955-1957', in: *Journal of European Integration History* (1997/2) pp. 83-98.

Keohane, R. O. and J. S. Nye, 'International Independence and Integration', in: F. Greenstein and N. Polsby (eds), *Handbook of Political Science* (Addison Wesley: Andover, MA, 1975), pp. 363-414

Küsters, H. J., 'Adenauers Europapolitik in der Gründungsphase der europäischen Wirtschaftsgemeinschaft', in: *Vierteljahreshefte für Zeitgeschichte* 31 (1983), pp. 616 73

Küsters, H. J., 'The Federal Republic of Germany and the EEC-Treaty', in: E. Serra (ed.), *The Relaunching of Europe and the Treaties of Rome* (Bruylant: Brussels, 1989), pp. 495-506

Küsters, H. J., 'Kanzler in der Krise: Journalistenberichte über Adenauers Hintergrundgespräche zwischen Berlin-Ultimatum und Bundespräsidentenwahl 1959', in: *Vierteljahreshefte für Zeitgeschichte* 36 (1988), pp. 733-68

Küsters, H. J., 'Konrad Adenauer und Willy Brandt in der Berlin-Krise 1958-1963', in: *Vierteljahreshefte für Zeitgeschichte* 40 (1992), pp. 483-542

Küsters, H. J., 'The Origins of the EEC Treaty' in: E. Serra (ed.), *The Relaunching of Europe and the Treaties of Rome* (Bruylant: Brussels, 1989), pp. 211-38

Küsters, H. J., 'Der Streit um Kompetenzen und Konzeptionen deutscher Europapolitik, 1949-1958', in: L. Herbst, W. Bührer and H. Sowade (eds), *Vom Marshallplan zur EWG: die Eingliederung der Bundesrepublik Deutschland in die westliche Welt* (Oldenbourg: München, 1990), pp. 335-70

Larres, K., 'Integrating Europe or Ending the Cold War? Churchill's Post-War Foreign Policy', in: *Journal of European Integration History* (1996/1), pp. 15-49

Lee, S., 'Perception and Reality: Anglo-German Relations during the Berlin Crisis 1958-1959', in: *German History* 13 (1) (1995), pp. 47-69

Lipgens, W., 'EVG und Politische Föderation: Protokolle der Konferenz der Aussenminister der an den Verhandlungen über eine europäische Verteidigungsgemeinschaft beteiligten Länder am 11. Dezember 1951', in: *Vierteljahreshefte für Zeitgeschichte* 32 (1984), pp. 637-88

Loth, W., 'The Process of European Integration: Some General Reflections', in: C. Wurm (ed.), *Western Europe and Germany: the Beginnings of European Integration 1945-1960* (Berg: Oxford, 1996), pp. 208-10

Ludlow, N. P., 'Challenging French Leadership in Europe: Germany, Italy, the Netherlands and the Outbreak of the Empty Chair Crisis of 1965-1966', in: *Contemporary European History* 8, 2 (1999), pp. 231-48

Mauer, V., 'Macmillan und die Berlin-Krise 1958/59', in: *Vierteljahreshefte für Zeitgeschichte* 44 (1996), pp. 229-56

Milward, A. S., 'Der historische Revisionismus zur Einigungsgeschichte Westeuropas; neue historische Erkenntnisse statt überholter Schulweisheiten', in: *Integration* 10, 3 (1987), pp. 100-6

North, R. C., 'Research Pluralism and the International Elephant' in: K. Knorr and J. N. Rosenau (eds), *Contending Approaches to International Politics* (Princeton University Press: Princeton, New Jersey, 1969), pp. 218–42

Riondel, B., 'Itinéraire d'un fédéraliste: Maurice Faure', in: *Journal of European Integration History* (1997/2), pp. 69–82

Schwabe, K., '"Ein Akt konstruktiver Staatskunst" – die USA und die Anfänge des Schuman-Plans', in: Schwabe (ed.), *Die Anfänge des Schuman-Plan, 1950/1* (Nomos: Baden-Baden, 1988), pp. 211–40

Schwabe, K., 'Die Eingliederung der Bundesrepublik in die westliche Welt', in: L. Herbst, W. Bührer and H. Sowade (eds), *Vom Marshallplan zur EWG, die Eingliederung der Bundesrepublik Deutschland in die westliche Welt* (Oldenbourg: München, 1990), pp. 593–612

Schwabe, K., 'Die Vereinigten Staaten und die europäische Integration: Alternativen der amerikanischen Aussenpolitik (1950–55)', in: G. Trausch (ed.), *Die europäische Integration vom Schumanplan bis zu den Verträgen von Rom* (Nomos: Baden-Baden, 1993), pp. 41–54

Steel, Sir Christopher, 'Anglo-German Relations. I: A British View', in: *International Affairs* 39 (4) (1963), pp. 521–3

Thiemeyer, G., 'Supranationalität als Novum in der Geschichte der internationalen Politik der fünfziger Jahre', in: *Journal of European Integration History* (1998/2), pp. 5–21

Toschi, S., 'Washington – London – Paris an Untenable Triangle', in: *Journal of European Integration History* (1995/2), pp. 81–109

Warner, G., 'President de Gaulle's Foreign Policy', in: *World Today* 18 (8) (1962), pp. 320–7

Watt, D. C., 'Deutsch-Britische Beziehungen Heute und Morgen', in: K. Kaiser and R. Morgan (eds), *Strukturwandlungen der Außenpolitik in Großbritannien und der Bundesrepublik* (Oldenbourg: München, 1970), pp. 193–207

Watt, D. C., 'Großbritannien und Europa, 1951–1959, die Jahre Konservativer Regierung', in: *Vierteljahreshefte für Zeitgeschichte* 28 (1980), pp. 389–409

Winham, G. R., 'Negotiation as a Management Process', in: *World Politics* 30 (1977), pp. 87–114

Wright, J., 'The Role of Britain in West German Foreign Policy since 1949', in: *German Politics* 5 (April 1996), pp. 26–42

Wurm, C., 'Britain and European Integration', in: *Contemporary European History* 7, 2 (1998), pp. 249–61

Young, J. W., 'German Rearmament and the European Defence Community', in: Young, *Foreign Policy of Churchill's Peacetime Administration*, pp. 81–107

Young, J. W., '"The Parting of Ways"? Britain, the Messina Conference and the Spaak Committee, June–December 1955', in: M. Dockrill and J. W. Young (eds), *British Foreign Policy, 1945–1956* (Macmillan: London, 1989), pp. 197–220

Young, J. W., 'The Schuman Plan and British Association', in: Young, *Foreign Policy of Churchill's Peacetime Administration*, pp. 109–34

Young, J. W., 'Towards a New View of British Policy and European Unity 1945–1957', in: R. Ahmann, A. M. Birke and M. Howard (eds), *The Quest for Stability: Problems of West European Security 1918–1957* (Oxford University Press: Oxford, 1993), pp. 435–62

Index

Note main entries are in alphabetical order, but subentries are in chronological order.

Adenauer, Konrad, *passim*
  issues guideline to ministers, 39–40
  meets Guy Mollet (November 1956), 56–8
  meets Harold Macmillan in Bonn (May 1957), 71–3
  visit to London cancelled (December 1957), 81
  meets Harold Macmillan in London (April 1958), 87–90
  meets Charles de Gaulle in Colombey-les-deux-Églises (September 1958), 96
  meets Harold Macmillan in Bonn (October 1958), 98–100
  meets Charles de Gaulle (November 1958), *see* Bad Kreuznach meeting
  allegedly troubled by a 'guilt complex' after Bad Kreuznach meeting, 119–20
  meets Harold Macmillan in London (March 1959), 120
  contemplates candidacy for Federal President, 124–5
  meets Harold Macmillan in London (November 1959), 128
  anxious about Summit Conference in Paris (May 1960), 148–9
  meets Antoine Pinay in Bonn (July 1960), 148
  meets Charles de Gaulle in Rambouillet (July 1960), 149
  meets Harold Macmillan in Bonn (August 1960), 149–50
  meets Harold Macmillan in London (February 1961), 135
  meets John F. Kennedy in Washington (April 1961), 156
  reactions to British intention to apply for EEC membership, 156–7
Algerian conflict, *see* Gaulle, Charles de, coming to power
Allchin, Sir G., 178–9
Assemblé Nationale (French National Assembly), 6, 46, 54, 110

Bad Kreuznach meeting, 102–6
  British reactions to Bad Kreuznach meeting, 106–7
Balke, Siegfried, 180
Barclay, Sir Roderick, 193, 221
BDI (*Bund Deutscher Industrie*, Federation of German Industry), 40, 180, 182, 185, 192, 200, 205, 208
Berg, Fritz, 185, 205
Berlin crisis, 104, 120
Bevin, Ernest, 5, 175
Beyen, Johan Willem, 15, 42, 51
Bilateral Anglo-German expert talks (1960–1), 150–3
Birrenbach, Kurt, 103, 120, 205, 210, 215–16
Blankenhorn, Herbert, 12, 104, 178, 205–7, 220
Blücher, Franz, 70, 73, 188–9, 194
Bolton, Sir George, 185
Boothby, Basil, 179–81, 186, 191
Brentano, Heinrich von, *passim*
  visits London (May 1956), 49
  stresses political dimension of the Common Market, 53–4, 57, 62, 68, 78, 125
  reactions to British intention to apply for EEC membership, 156

236

Brentano, Michael von, 12
Bretherton, Russell, 2, 180–1, 184, 186, 193, 195–6, 207
  withdraws from/is dismissed from Spaak Committee, 30
  and the Free Trade Area plan, 45, 51, 76, 90–1
Bridge-building policy, see EFTA (European Free Trade Association)
Bridges, Sir Edward, 27, 181, 184–5
Brook, Norman, 221–2
Butler, Richard Austin 'Rab', 3, 17, 26–32, 36–8, 67, 170, 175, 179, 181, 194
  meets Ludwig Erhard in Istanbul (September 1955), 26

Cabinet reshuffle in advance of British application to join EEC, 151
Caccia, Harold, 47, 88, 128, 184–5, 193, 200, 204, 208, 213–14
Cairncross, Sir Alec, 44
Carli, Guido, see FTA (Free Trade Area) negotiations, Carli Plan
Carstens, Karl, 58, 104, 123–5, 180, 182–3, 188–90, 192–5, 197–201, 207–13, 215, 220–2
Churchill, Winston, 6, 175
  the 'three circles', 3, 5, 162–3, 168
Clarke, Sir Ashley, 217
Clarke, Richard 'Otto', 37, 73, 130, 170, 181, 183–7, 190–1, 193, 195–6, 201, 204, 207–11, 214
  first report of Clarke working group, 44–50
  second report of Clarke working group, 59–60
Collier, Andrew James, 180–1
Comité Special, 119, 125–7
Common Market, see EEC
Commonwealth, 29, 45, 65, 71, 76, 84–5, 87, 89, 91–4, 99, 107
  reaction to FTA, 52–3
  on inclusion of overseas territories in EEC/FTA, 61–3
  preferences, see FTA (Free Trade Area) negotiations

  problems arising from possible British membership in EEC, 144–6, 150–2, 154, 157–8
  reactions to British intention to apply for EEC membership, 157
Cook, Robin, 174
Coulson, John, 22, 91, 178–80, 196, 199, 201, 204, 207–8
Council of Europe, 5, 44, 46
Couve de Murville, Maurice, 93, 97, 100, 102, 108, 202, 205–7
  meets Hilgar van Scherpenberg (November 1958), 104, 111
Crookshank, Harry, 181

Debré, Michel, 210, 219
  describes non-nuclear Germany as a 'satellite state', 148
Denman, Roy, 1
Department E (German Ministry of Economics), establishment, 80–1
Deutsche Bundesbank, 127, 213
Deutscher Bundesrat, 139, 180, 206, 217
Deutscher Bundestag, 49, 81, 103, 120, 139, 141, 182, 189, 196–7, 207, 217, 220
Dillon, Douglas, 129, 137, 214–15

Eccles, David, 101, 195, 205, 223
  speech to OEEC Council meeting (December 1958), 107–8
  opposes Britain's EEC application, 156–9
ECSC (European Coal and Steel Community), 5–6, 15–17
  British government contemplates application, 141–2
EDC (European Defence Community), 6, 16–17
Edden, Alan, 17–21, 26, 28, 59, 178–80, 182–3, 190, 193–8, 200
Eden, Anthony, 3, 6–7, 53, 175, 184
  visits Washington, 43–4
EEC (European Economic Community) negotiations towards: Venice conference (May 1956), 41–2,

EEC – *continued*
  53–4; harmonization of social costs, 54–6; Paris meeting of Foreign Ministers (October 1956), 56–7; inclusion of overseas territories, 61–3
  appoints European Commission, *see* European Commission
  first meeting of the Council of Ministers (1958), 82–3
  Council of Ministers meeting (March 1958), 86–7
  Ockrent Group of Experts, 86, 90–3, 96–7
  Council of Ministers meeting in Venice (September 1958), 96–7
  Council of Ministers meeting in Brussels (October 1958), 96–7
  Council of Ministers meeting (December 1958), 105–6
  Council of Ministers meeting (March 1959), 118–19
  accelleration of timetable, 137–41
  US reactions to accelleration of timetable, 139
  meeting of Heads of Government (February 1961), 153–4
EFTA (European Free Trade Association)
  negotiations towards, 121
  Stockholm Convention, 121
  formulating the British initiative, 121–3
  British doubts about the initiative, 122–3
  German reactions to EFTA, 123–4
  'bridge-building' with EEC, or Six plus Seven, 125–7
  US reactions to possible EEC/EFTA agreement, 125, 127–9
  EFTA ministers meeting in Lisbon (May 1960), 142
Eisenhower, Dwight D., 193, 214
  reaction to FTA plan, 64
  meets Harold Macmillan in Washington (March 1960), 140–1
Ellis-Rees, Sir Hugh, 17–18, 51, 178–9, 183, 186, 190, 192–3, 196–7, 199–201, 203, 205, 208–11
EPC (European Political Community), 7
EPU (European Payments Union), 5
Erhard, Ludwig, *passim*
  disagrees with Hallstein on German approach to Spaak Committee, 19–21, 23–4
  meets Butler in Istanbul (September 1955), 26
  visits London (February 1956), 48
  meets Peter Thorneycroft in Paris (February 1957), 63
  comments on FTA at OEEC Council meeting (February 1957), 65
  comments on FTA at OEEC Council meeting (October 1957), 78–9
  meets Reginald Maudling (March 1958), 84–5
  meets Harold Macmillan in London (April 1958), 89
  reactions to Bad Kreuznach meeting (November 1958), 105–9
  and accelleration of EEC timetable, 139–40, 143
  reactions to British intention to apply for EEC membership, 156–7
Etzel, Franz, 57–8, 77, 140, 188–90, 211–12, 215–16, 219
EURATOM (European Atomic Community), British government considers joining, 141–2
European Commission
  Walter Hallstein is appointed first President, 82–3
  first memorandum on external trade relations of the EEC, 115–19
  second memorandum on external trade relations of the EEC, 125–7

Index 239

Faure, Maurice, 51, 55–6, 80, 90, 194–5, 197
FBI (Federation of British Industry), 52
Feese-Pennefather, H. W. A., 218
Figgures, Frank, 45, 73, 91, 130, 183–6, 193, 195–6, 207–11, 214
France, Sir Arnold, 218
FTA (Free Trade Area) negotiations
  formulating the British initiative, 44–50, 59–60
  Commonwealth reactions, 52–3
  British White Paper, 65
  debate about Commonwealth Preferences, 71, 84–7, 89, 91–4, 99
  exclusion of agriculture, 75–6, 79, 83–4, 89, 99
  establishment of Maudling Committee, 78–9
  formal opening of intergovernmental negotiations, 79
  Maudling Committee meetings, 79–80, 83, 86, 95, 99–102
  French memorandum (March 1958), 84–5
  discussion about definition of origin, 84–7, 91–9, 187
  Carli Plan, 84–7, 93–7
  postponement due to French constitutional crisis, 90–1
  Anglo-German bilateral talks, 91–4
  breakdown of negotiations (November 1958), 101
  discussion about interim agreement, 106–7
  British government threatening retaliation, 106–8
Furler, Hans, 198

Gaitskill, Hugh, 3, 175
GATT (General Agreement of Tariffs and Trade), 14, 16, 45, 80, 88, 126, 131, 146–7
  compatibility of Common Market, 41
  compatibility of Plan G, 50–1, 54
Gaulle, Charles de, *passim*
  coming to power, 90–1
  meets Harold Macmillan in Paris (June 1958), 94–5
  meets Konrad Adenauer in Colombey-les-deux-Églises (September 1958), 96
  meets Konrad Adenauer (November 1958), *see* Bad Kreuznach meeting
  speech on Europe (May 1960), 148
  meets Konrad Adenauer in Rambouillet (July 1960), 149
  meets Harold Macmillan in Rambouillet (January 1961), 154
Globke, Hans, 193, 207
Gocht, Rolf, 57, 189, 194, 197–200
Gore-Booth, Paul, 100, 128, 130, 194–8, 200–1, 204, 208–11, 213–15, 217–19
grand design policy, 71–2, 76
Grewe, Wilhelm, 189, 201, 216
Groeben, Hans von der, 21–4, 35, 54, 178, 180, 188

Haehnlein, Franz, 187–8, 199–201, 204, 208
Hallstein Plan, *see* EEC (European Economic Community), accelleration of timetable
Hallstein, Walter, 14–15, 33–6, 41, 73, 76–7, 81, 87, 103, 108, 139, 146, 149, 178–80, 182–3, 188–9, 192, 197–9, 206, 211, 215–16, 219
  is appointed first Commission President, *see* European Commission
  official statement in Spaak Committee, 19–25
  welcomes EFTA plans, 124
Hancock, Patrick, 196, 198
Hankey, Sir Robin, 193
Hardenberg, Graf von, 196
Hare, John, 157
Harkort, Günther, 188, 200, 202, 209, 211–13, 215–16, 219–20
Hartlieb, Wilhelm, 55, 73–4, 85, 92, 120, 123, 125, 188–9, 192,

Hartlieb – *continued*
  194–5, 197–201, 206, 208,
  210–12, 215, 217
Hassel, Kai-Uwe von, 217
Heath, Edward, 151, 154, 220–2
  tours Commonwealth capitals,
  157
Heath, J. M., 196
Heathcoat Amory, Derick, 107,
  131, 204–5, 214
Herwarth, Hans Heinrich von, 130,
  120, 146, 200, 205, 208–11,
  219–21
Heuss, Theodor, 190
Holliday, Gilbert, 203–4, 209, 211,
  213–14, 217
Home, Lord Alec Douglas, 151,
  154, 220–2
Hood, Lord, 184, 195
Hoyer-Millar, Frederick, 48, 183,
  185, 190–2, 204, 208, 213,
  215, 217, 219
Hünke, Carl, 124, 209, 211–13,
  216, 219–20

Jackling, Roger, 24–6, 36, 180, 194,
  213, 215, 221
Jansen, Josef, 221–2
Jebb, Sir Gladwyn, 52, 187, 192,
  194, 211–12, 217, 220
Johnston, C. H., 183–4

Kennedy, John F., 149, 160
  meets Harold Macmillan in
  Washington (April 1961),
  155–6
  meets Konrad Adenauer in
  Washington (April 1961),
  156
Kiesswetter, Franz, 198–200
Kirk, Peter, 141
Kohl, Helmut, 174
Krag, Jens Otto, 212
Krone, Heinrich, 212, 217
Krushchev, Nikita, 140
  issues Berlin ultimatum, 104

Labouchère, George, 191, 217
Landsdowne, Lord, 207

Lange, Halvard, 218
Lee, Sir Frank, 159, 215, 218,
  221–2
Lee report, 1, 153–4, 170
  proposes 'near identification'
  with the EEC, 142–3
Lee, H. S., 198–9, 201
Lefèvre, Theo, 57, 190
Liebes, Martin, 190
Lloyd, Selwyn, 100–1, 103, 114,
  137, 151, 154, 168, 175,
  199–200, 204–5, 207, 209,
  211–17, 219–22
  proposes British application to
  ECSC and EURATOM, 141
Lübke, Heinrich, 194
Luns, Joseph, 192

Macleod, Iain, 157
Macmillan, Harold, *passim*
  meets Konrad Adenauer in Bonn
  (May 1957), 71–3
  meets Konrad Adenauer in
  London (April 1958), 87–90
  meets Charles de Gaulle in Paris
  (June 1958), 94–5
  meets Konrad Adenauer in Bonn
  (October 1958), 98–100
  visits Moscow (February 1959), 120
  meets Konrad Adenauer in
  London (March 1959), 120
  meets Konrad Adenauer in
  London (November 1959),
  128
  'outburst' in Washington (March
  1960), 140
  meets Dwight D. Eisenhower in
  Washington (March 1960),
  140–1
  contemplates British application
  to ECSC and EURATOM,
  141–2
  initiates policy review on British
  relations to EEC, 144–5
  meets Konrad Adenauer in Bonn
  (August 1960), 149–50
  meets Charles de Gaulle in
  Rambouillet (January 1961),
  154

meets Konrad Adenauer in London (February 1961), 135
meets John F. Kennedy in Washington (April 1961), 155–6
announces Britain's EEC application to the House of Commons, 158
Mahs, Freiherr von, 195
Major, John, 174
Majoribanks, James, 178–9, 197–8, 200, 203, 211, 215, 220–1
Makins, Roger, 183, 191, 196, 201, 205, 210, 214
Martin, Berthold, 220
Mason, Sir Paul, 183, 218
Maudling Committee, see FTA (Free Trade Area) negotiations
Maudling, Reginald, *passim*
appointment as Paymaster-General, 75
visits Bonn (October 1957), 75–7
meets Ludwig Erhard (March 1958), 84–5
argues against early British application, 146
opposes Britain's EEC application, 153–4, 156–8
McKean, Douglas, 193, 195, 207, 211
Meade, James, 45, 49, 184
Menne, Albert, 200
Merkatz, Hans-Joachim von, 180
Messina conference, 13–16
British reactions, 17–19
Meyer-Cording, Ulrich, 94, 140, 202, 203, 206, 208–9, 216, 219–20
Milward, Alan, 4
Mollet, Guy, 56
meets Adenauer (November 1956), 56–8
Monnet, Jean, 13–17, 177
Müller-Armack, Alfred, 15, 35, 61–2, 74, 78–81, 83, 105, 108–9, 118–19, 138, 178, 182, 188–92, 194, 197, 199, 201–6, 208–9, 211–13, 216–17, 219–20, 222
seeks to moderate French demands during FTA negotiations, 86–7, 97, 100

seeks to moderate British demands during FTA negotiations, 89, 91, 99
accepts European Commission's second memorandum, 124–7
suggests partial EEC/EFTA customs union (December 1960), 152, 157
Müller-Roschach, Herbert, 177, 182–3, 188, 201, 212, 215, 220
Munro, Robert, 183, 185
Mutual Aid Committee, 18, 28–31, 43

NATO (North Atlantic Treaty Organisation), 7, 25, 46, 92, 98–9, 101, 116, 148–51, 154
Nichols, Peter, 27, 181
Norstadt, General Lauris, 220
Nutting, Anthony, 174, 184–5

Ockrent, Roger, 86
see also EEC (European Economic Community)
OEEC (Organisation for European Economic Co-operation)
compatibility of Common Market, 41
Council meeting (July 1956), 51
Council meeting (February 1957), 63–6
Council meeting (October 1957), 78–9
Council meeting (August 1958), 95
Council meeting (December 1958), 107–8
'Special Economic Conference' Paris (1960), 127–33
establishes Trade Committee, 132
Ophüls, Carl Friedrich, 21, 178–9, 182, 188, 199, 208, 213, 215
Ormsby-Gore, David, 203, 219

Peyer, Charles de, 179
Pinay, Antoine, 96, 212
meets Konrad Adenauer in Bonn (July 1960), 148
Plan G, see Free Trade Area

242 Index

Profumo, John, 218
  speech to WEU (June 1960), 142

Quaroni, Pietro, 220

Reading, Lord, 182
Rey, Jean, 93, 108, 119, 198, 202
Rodgers, Gerald, 180, 183, 190
Rothschild, Robert, 181
Rowan, Sir Leslie, 184–5, 204, 210
Rumbold, Horace, 130, 204, 212, 214, 217
Rust, Josef, 178, 180

Sandys, Duncan, 207
  tours Commonwealth capitals, 157
Schäfer, Hermann, 180
Schäffer, Fritz, 32, 62, 178, 180–1, 191
  opposes harmonization of social costs and adaptation and investment funds, 24, 33
  visit to London (October 1955), 27–8, 36
Scherpenberg, Hilgar van, 70, 73, 83, 96–9, 106, 119–20, 124, 138, 150, 186, 188–9, 194–5, 198–201, 203, 206–9, 211–13, 215–17, 219–20, 222
  meets Maurice Couve de Murville (November 1958), 104, 111
Schröder, Gerhard, 140
sectoral integration, German debate about, 14–15, 20–2
Seibt, Dankmar, 180
Sergeant, René, 51, 183, 186
Seydoux, François, 98, 203, 206, 217, 219
Six plus Seven, *see* EFTA (European Free Trade Association)
Soustelle, Jacques, 205
  announces end to FTA negotiations, 101–2, 110
Soviet Union, 47, 62, 119, 128, 142, 149
Spaak Committee, 23–9
  French demands for harmonization of social costs, 16, 19–20, 23–4
  debate about British participation in, 18–19
  debate about investment and adaptation funds, 23–4
  discussing tariffs, 24
  British assessment of German position, 24–9
  British telegram to persuade Germany to abandon, 29–33
  British withdrawal from, 30
  German position, *see* Hallstein, Walter
  German reactions to British telegram, 32–3, 43
  expert report, 40–1
Spaak, Paul-Henri, 21, 54, 57, 61, 65, 180–1, 188, 191, 207, 220
Special Economic Conference, *see* OEEC (Organisation for European Economic Co-operation)
Steel, Sir Christopher, 76, 88, 120, 146, 158, 194–8, 200–1, 203, 205–13, 215, 217–19, 221–3
Stockholm Convention, *see* EFTA (European Free Trade Association)
Storch, Anton, 56, 68, 189
Strasbourg tariff scheme, 44–5
Strath, William, 18–19, 27–8, 178–9, 181
Suez Crisis, 58, 60, 162–3, 168
Summit Conference in Paris (May 1960), 140, 142–4, 148–9, 159

Tennant, Peter, 195, 205
Thorneycroft, Peter, 2, 45–6, 50, 53, 58, 63, 65, 67, 71, 75, 151, 181, 184–5, 191–6, 204, 217
  tours Commonwealth capitals, 157
Tomkins, Sir Edward, 217
Trade Committee, *see* OEEC (Organisation for European Economic Co-operation)
Treaty of Rome, *see also* EEC negotiations
  signing of, 66
  ratification of, 71–2, 75, 196

Trend, Burke, 28, 30, 181
  report on the effects of the
    Common Market, 30–1, 36–7
TUC (Trade Union Congress), 63
Turnbull, Frank, 181

U2-incident, 148
United States
  supporting the Common Market,
    41, 43, 103–4

Warner, Sir Christopher, 21,
  179–80
Watkinson, Harold, 157, 223
Weir, Cecil, 178
Welck, Freiherr Wolfgang von, 192

Werkmeister, Karl, 89–90, 93, 186,
  200–2, 205, 207, 209
Westrick, Ludger, 23, 33, 54, 178,
  180, 204
WEU (Western European Union),
  7, 41
  ministerial meeting (June 1960), 142
  plans for political co-operation
    (1961), 153, 155
Wormser, Olivier, 100, 154, 209,
  213, 220–1
Wright, Denis, 183, 185–7, 190,
  194–5, 198, 205, 209–11

Zulueta, Philip de, 128, 158, 195,
  202, 213, 221–3